Teaching Children Dance

Second Edition

Theresa Purcell Cone

Stephen L. Cone

Human Kinetics

Library of Congress Cataloging-in-Publication Data

Cone, Theresa Purcell, 1950-
  Teaching children dance / Theresa Purcell Cone, Stephen L. Cone.-- 2nd ed.
     p. cm.
  Includes bibliographical references.
  ISBN 0-7360-5090-6 (soft cover)
  1. Dance for children--Study and teaching. I. Cone, Stephen Leonard. II. Title.
  GV1799.P87 2004
  792.8'083'4--dc22

                         2004010612

ISBN-10: 0-7360-5090-6
ISBN-13: 978-0-7360-5090-6

The Web addresses cited in this text were current as of August 3, 2004, unless otherwise noted.

Acquisitions Editor: Judy Patterson Wright, PhD
Developmental Editor: Laura Hambly
Assistant Editor: Bethany J. Bentley
Copyeditor: Amie Bell
Proofreader: Darlene Rake
Permission Manager: Dalene Reeder
Graphic Designer: Fred Starbird
Graphic Artist: Tara Welsch
Photo Manager: Kareema McLendon
Cover Designer: Keith Blomberg
Photographer: Photos courtesy of Theresa Purcell Cone and Stephen L. Cone
Art Manager: Kelly Hendren
Illustrators: Mary Yemma Long (6, 7, 8, 20, 25, 28, 49, 50, 52, 57, 141) and Argosy
Printer: United Graphics

Printed in the United States of America   10 9 8 7 6 5 4

Human Kinetics
Web site: www.HumanKinetics.com

United States: Human Kinetics
P.O. Box 5076
Champaign, IL 61825-5076
800-747-4457
e-mail: humank@hkusa.com

Canada: Human Kinetics
475 Devonshire Road, Unit 100
Windsor, ON N8Y 2L5
800-465-7301 (in Canada only)
e-mail: info@hkcanada.com

Europe: Human Kinetics
107 Bradford Road
Stanningley
Leeds LS28 6AT, United Kingdom
+44 (0)113 255 5665
e-mail: hk@hkeurope.com

Australia: Human Kinetics
57A Price Avenue
Lower Mitcham, South Australia 5062
08 8372 0999
e-mail: info@hkaustralia.com

New Zealand: Human Kinetics
Division of Sports Distributors NZ Ltd.
P.O. Box 300 226 Albany
North Shore City, Auckland
0064 9 448 1207
e-mail: info@humankinetics.co.nz

Dedicated to

Our family
Our friends and colleagues
All our students who inspire our creativity and love for dance
and
Those who will carry dance into the future

Contents

Pg. 37 - cute animal dance idea.

v

Preface

It has been 10 years since I wrote the first edition of *Teaching Children Dance,* and during that time I have seen dance education receive increased attention in both arts education and physical education curricula. Ten years ago, national standards in the arts and in physical education were in the initial stages of development; now these standards are widely referenced as a guide for development and revision of curricular content. Dance has begun to take its rightful place in arts and physical education programs by providing a body of content that meets the needs of children who experience and understand the world through the medium of movement. This second edition reflects the renewed attention and commitment by educators toward strengthening dance instruction as an integral component of a comprehensive education.

As a result, several changes are evident that have an impact on the content of the book. First, Steve, my husband, and I are coauthoring the book. We enjoy collaborative writing and believe that the content is stronger because of our discussions and varied perspectives. Blending Steve's university experience in teaching physical education preservice students and my experience as an elementary school physical education and dance teacher provides an appropriate mix for a book suited for a variety of elementary educators and preservice students. Our goal is to offer a framework and practical approach for teaching children's dance for physical educators, arts educators, dance educators, and elementary classroom educators.

In writing this book, we have focused the content primarily on creative dance for children; but, we also acknowledge that dance content includes teaching dance from a cultural, social, and fitness point of view. Several new learning experiences have been added, and the original learning experiences have been edited to reflect insights we have gained as a result of teaching them to many different children and presenting these ideas at workshops. As in the first edition, the learning experiences are written in a dialogue format to paint a picture of how the dance experience may be presented to a class. The text of the learning experiences, however, is revised into smaller segments that outline how the learning experience can be presented over several class sessions. Our hope is that the text is easier to access and thus easier to implement.

Part I provides a framework of content and strategies for program development and implementation. You will find ideas on how to design and present a dance learning experience composed of units and lessons, suggestions for class management, updated assessment content, and strategies for interdisciplinary connections. The revisions emerged from the insights we have gained from teaching dance over the past 10 years. We view teaching as an ongoing learning process characterized by sharing with our students as well as other educators. The first edition captured the best practice of each learning experience at that moment in time; yet, because our everchanging student populations always bring a new perspective to a learning experience, we have woven these new understandings throughout the chapters in part I. New to this edition are questions for reflection at the end of each of the six chapters. The reflective questions are designed to get you to think about how you can blend what you know with what you need to create and present a dance learning experience. Reflection, an important part of teaching, helps us all to question what works, what changes need to be made, and what new ideas can be added. Use the questions to stimulate your thinking in an effort to make each learning experience effective and meaningful.

Part II has also undergone many changes. First, we organized the learning experience into two grade-level categories in response to educators and their need to find dances appropriate to a particular grade level. We have also added assessment suggestions and interdisciplinary connections.

One of our challenges in writing this book was not only to provide the essential dance content appropriate for an elementary-level program but also to offer detailed descriptions of strategies and approaches to help educators feel comfortable with teaching dance. We believe within every child an idea or feeling exists that calls for a creative medium for expression. Through a creative dance experience, children can dis-

cover their ways of understanding and knowing. The teacher becomes the designer, facilitator, guide, encourager, and believer and sets a welcoming environment for learning and creating. Our hope is that, as a result of this book, more children will gain the opportunity to dance and more educators will be willing to expand their curriculum content to include dance. We know you will benefit both professionally and personally from the opportunity to teach dance and offer your students a valuable experience in learning about themselves.

A Framework for Teaching Children's Dance

Part I provides answers to the following questions: What is children's dance? Why should it be taught? How does one design and assess a dance program? Educators and administrators ask these foundational questions frequently when developing a dance program. We hope that in the following six chapters you find the necessary information that will help you to gain an understanding of children's dance and develop the skills needed to enhance or initiate dance as part of a physical education or arts education curriculum. An overview of the content in each chapter is as follows:

Chapter 1: Understanding the Importance of Teaching Children's Dance. This chapter addresses the essential content needed for teaching dance. It provides a description of what is considered children's dance and explains the significance and benefits of a children's dance program.

Chapter 2: Presenting Essential Content for Children's Dance. This chapter offers a description of the essential content of children's dance that includes the body, space, time, effort, and relationships. It explains different forms of children's dance and how they contribute to a comprehensive dance program.

Chapter 3: Designing a Dance Program. In this chapter, the nuts and bolts of program construction and delivery are described. We have included examples for planning a yearlong program and indicated where the learning experiences described in this book can appear in a K–5 program. A new focus for this edition is on making interdisciplinary connections between dance and other subject areas.

Chapter 4: Creating a Dance Education Setting. This chapter includes a discussion on how to tailor a dance program to fit various teaching situations. Teachers are frequently faced with justifying to their students, parents, administrators, and other colleagues why dance should be included as part of the curriculum. To make such justification easier, we have included advocacy strategies for maintaining and developing a program.

Chapter 5: Making Teaching Effective. We believe that the *way* we teach is as important as *what* we teach. In this chapter, we discuss how teaching and learning styles affect the success of a dance experience. Also included are strategies for establishing protocols and rules that lead to a safe and productive learning environment and strategies for student feedback, demonstrations, and observations.

Chapter 6: Assessing Children's Learning in Dance. Assessment, a new initiative in children's dance 10 years ago, has now become a cornerstone of all learning experiences. In this edition, we have added more examples of assessment in dance and provided a suggested assessment at the end of each learning experience.

chapter 1

Understanding the Importance of Teaching Children's Dance

Imagine a class of young children running as fast as they can, waving red streamers over their heads, and then spinning around and slowly descending to the floor with the streamers floating down beside them. Through these dance movements, children might be expressing their interpretations of a fast-burning flame slowly flickering out, or they may be pretending to sprinkle red paint all over a room. Now, imagine yourself as the teacher who designed and presented this dance idea to the class. The children responded with great enthusiasm, and you feel successful in sharing this experience with them. It would be wonderful if every dance experience resulted in this feeling of success.

You may feel a little uncertain, however, about how to design and present a dance experience to your students. Many teachers who want to teach dance may not be sure where to start. Before you considered teaching dance, you may have asked yourself these questions:

- What benefits will my students gain from the opportunity to learn and create dances?
- How do I plan a dance lesson, a dance unit, or a yearlong program of study?

Teaching children dance may be a new area of professional development or an area in which you would like to improve your current knowledge and skills. In either situation, planning and presenting successful dance learning experiences can be a challenge. Teaching dance does not require being an accomplished dancer or knowing everything about every form of dance. Dance instruction does require teachers who are dedicated to delivering quality physical education and dance programs and view dance as essential to a student's education. Even if you agree that dance is integral to physical education or arts education, you may feel unprepared to be an effective teacher. We ask you to consider the knowledge and skills you already have and use them as a foundation as you teach dance, whether you are taking your first steps or reaching for the next level.

As a physical educator, you have chosen your profession because you enjoy physical activity. You may also like to create new possibilities for movement, for example, developing a new game strategy, a new gymnastics floor exercise, or a new way to shoot a basketball. Every day, movement specialists generate ideas for new sport movements when they explore new ways of moving. Those of you who already teach dance also enjoy moving and welcome the challenges of learning and creating new movements.

You can also rely on your past teaching experiences to provide a background for selecting the types of dance activities that are appropriate for your students. Your familiarity with their past learning experiences in dance can help you anticipate their attitude toward and acceptance of future experiences. Your experiences have taught you that all children enjoy creating new ways to move and that they are eager to share their successful accomplishments. You acknowledge that each student needs to learn in a caring and nonthreatening atmosphere and does not want to feel vulnerable. You have already planned and implemented successful movement experiences, and your teaching experiences have taught you to try another approach if a lesson does not go well the first time. This knowledge of children and teaching applies easily to teaching dance. You already have a wealth of teaching strategies that will be helpful for presenting dance; all you need are some ideas and plans.

Everyone has had the opportunity to experience dance either as a participant or a spectator. Think about the times you heard a piece of music and you could not resist the urge to move. Perhaps you have been at a social gathering where everyone is having fun dancing, and you are drawn into the energy of the group and find yourself moving your feet, laughing, and enjoying a moment of friendship and fun. If you think of yourself as a nondancer, then consider changing this perception and instead calling yourself a beginning dancer.

It may be appropriate to tell students that dance is a new experience for you as well as for them. Be confident that when you allow students to become more involved in the learning experience, they will be helpful and full of ideas. Learning to teach dance begins with a willingness to try something new, to take a risk, and to persist so you can improve. Dance instruction will offer challenges—you may encounter reluctant students, require new teaching materials, or need additional professional development. But, why not make your teaching career full and exciting? Be open and willing to accept the challenges of learning something new, just as you ask your students to do every day.

What Is Children's Dance?

Dance is a unique form of moving that holds various meanings for each of us, depending on how and why dance is a part of our lives. Judith Lynne Hanna (1987) spoke of dance as human behavior that is purposeful, intentionally rhythmical, and culturally patterned; involves nonverbal body movement; is beyond ordinary motor activity; and holds inherently aesthetic value. In the elementary-school setting, dance also has many purposes and can exist in a variety of forms. Children enjoy learning folk and ethnic dances, social dances, aerobic dance, square dances, and line dances, as well as composing their own dances through creative dance. No single specific dance form should be taught exclusive of others. We recommend that children have an opportunity to experience different dance forms throughout their education.

Children's dance is a way of knowing that fully integrates all aspects of being human. Kinesthetically, intellectually, socially, and emotionally, children learn about themselves and others through the medium of dance. Ruth Murray (1963), dance educator and writer, notes the following:

> Perhaps the best interpretation [of dance] is one that emphasizes not only body mastery and discipline in movements but even more the use of such movement for expressive and imaginative purposes. Dancing may borrow from and lend to many other kinds of movement activities. It is when the ultimate concern is with the meaning of movement that the term *dancing* is accurately applied. (p. 7-8)

Within the elementary curriculum, dance can be taught as a discrete subject, as a component of the physical education or arts program, or as a component that is integrated with another subject area (e.g., science, language arts). In all of these contexts, regardless of the type of dance that is taught, dance exists simultaneously as an art form and a movement form (see figure 1.1). Dance becomes the means through which children develop, express, and communicate their life experiences. As a result, they gain an aesthetic awareness about how the body and its movements are connected to meaning and intention.

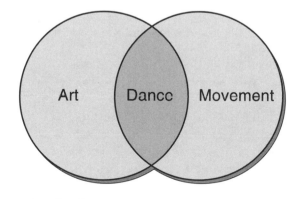

Figure 1.1 Dance, as a discrete subject, is simultaneously a movement and an art form.

When dance is part of the physical education curriculum, it provides children with an expressive way to use movement in addition to fulfilling the functional purposes of games, sport, and gymnastics. Fraleigh (1987) notes, "Dance movement is not functional movement used to accomplish a purposeful task. . . . Dance is movement set apart from life; that is, movement seen for itself, most particularly its aesthetic qualities" (p. 30). Dance is the only form of moving that meets the child's innate need to express thoughts, feelings, understandings, and ideas through movement. All other types of movement in the curriculum are functional—students acquire skills, such as throwing or kicking a ball, to improve their motor skills and ultimately use the skill in a game to perhaps score points (see figure 1.2*a*). In gymnastics, children may learn the principles of balance to perform a handstand efficiently and deliberately (see figure 1.2 *b*). Although similar movements may appear in a dance, they are detached from their functional purpose (e.g., raising the arms high to catch a ball or to get a stretch through the body) and instead become movements that illustrate or express an idea, thought, understanding, or feeling, such as the feeling of reaching toward the sky (see figure 1.3). Both functional and expressive types of movement experiences are necessary for children to develop their full potential.

Children's dance involves more than exploring different ways to make a shape or learning a series of steps to music; it is a way of making meaning that uses the body as the instrument for expression and communication. The child, as a dancer, can be compared to an artist's paintbrush as it moves on the canvas making an idea into a tangible form. Dance movements are like the colors, lines, shapes, and textures a painter uses to express ideas. The dancing space becomes the canvas. Just as every painter might interpret a sunset, a flower, or the feeling of anger differently, children, too, will demonstrate their own unique interpretation of an idea, dance movement, or feeling using the body and its movements as their expressive tools. Dance at the elementary level allows for personal decision making; exploration of new ways to move; and development of new ways of knowing,

Figure 1.2 Functional movement: *(a)* shooting a basket, *(b)* supporting body weight in a handstand.

Figure 1.3 Expressive movement: Children stretch their arms up to express the feeling of reaching toward the sky.

creating, and learning. Learning experiences in dance are based on a set of goals for student achievement. We offer the following set of goals that can guide curriculum development.

Through participating in dance experiences students will accomplish the following:

- Develop the knowledge and skills to use dance for self-expression and communication of ideas, understandings, and feelings.
- Increase their creative, imaginative, cognitive, and perceptive abilities.

- Foster an understanding of the role of dance within cultural and historical contexts.
- Acquire skills in learning to cooperate with, respect, and move with others in a social context.
- Develop an understanding and appreciation for dance as a movement form and as an art form.
- Gain an understanding of the aesthetic elements involved in creating, performing, and responding to dance.
- Recognize how dance relates to other arts and to other subject areas.
- Develop motor skills, coordination, balance, strength, and flexibility and increase fitness knowledge and abilities.

For many children, the elementary school dance program may be their first encounter with dance. Students may bring perceptions and opinions about dance that influence their level of participation. Through offering a variety of dance forms throughout the school year, children will be able to explore and become more comfortable with different ways that movement is used as a basic human means of expression and communication.

Awakening of New Perceptions

Each time children experience dance, whether as dancers, observers, or creators, they gain new perceptions about themselves and their world. Through dance, children learn more about who they are, how they move, what they think, how they feel, and how they relate to others. They also learn that there are multiple ways to express the same idea. For example, as a result of participating in a cloud dance where the children created their own body shapes and movements to express clouds they observed in the sky, the children expanded their insights into how clouds move and observed their classmates' unique interpretations of cloud shapes and movements.

Awakening of new perceptions and understandings is an aesthetic experience. Through manipulating the elements of dance, students make aesthetic choices about what movements to use and the quality of those movements. In the cloud dance, the teacher may suggest the following explorations to help shape students' aesthetic choices: "Find a way to use your arms to create a long cloud shape. What pathway will you use to travel across the room in your cloud shape? Change your speed to show how slow and how fast the clouds move. How can you and another person connect your cloud shapes and move together?" (See figure 1.4.)

All dance movement is the result of a series of qualitative decisions about how the elements of dance will be used to express an idea. The way the dance movement appears, using space, time, force, and the relationship of the dancers to each other, is the result of purposeful decision making. This decision making is applicable to all types of dance. Traditional folk and ethnic dances were designed in a specific way to reflect a particular aspect of a culture. The formations, dance steps, costumes, and music all reflect what a group of people hold as significant representations of their history, traditions, values, and beliefs. Social dances evolve from the needs of people to move together as a community, to share in celebrations, to meet others, and to maintain a connection. Creative dances are also based on individual or group decisions about how to manipulate movement to express an idea or feeling.

Dance in the elementary school curriculum provides students with a variety of dance experiences. These experiences allow them to create their own dance movements and to learn dances created by others. Creating and learning dances help children make meaning of what happens in their lives as well as in the lives of others.

Student-Created Dance

In student-created dance, commonly referred to as creative dance, students generate, vary, and manipulate movement using the elements of dance (the body, space, time, force, flow, and relationships; see chapter 2) through the process of improvisation. Creative movement is the product of improvisation and becomes the first step used to develop movements for a creative dance. Children may select improvised movements and arrange them into a sequence or choreographic structure to form a dance. The teacher or the students may generate the initial idea for the dance. The following are examples of creative dance:

Figure 1.4 Young children holding hands in a circle to demonstrate the shape of a cloud.

⊛ A first-grade class is studying a science unit on bubbles. They form a list of vocabulary words that describe how bubbles move and create dance movements to illustrate the vocabulary words. Next, the students develop a three-word sequence such as *pop, float,* and *burst* to create a dance that reflects the word sequence.

- A second-grade class has collaborated to write several poems. They select a poem they would like to express through dance. The class breaks into three groups, and each group creates a dance to represent the selected poem.

- A fourth-grade class creates a large-group dance sculpture representing straight, twisted, and curved shapes. They focus on how to change from one shape to another using different tempos.

- The kindergarten classes create a dance about the animals and people they recently saw at the circus. They dance about lions jumping through hoops, elephants balancing, tightrope walkers moving forward and backward, acrobats swinging on the trapeze, and clowns juggling bowling pins.

- A fifth-grade class, organized into groups of three, creates dances that use movements from everyday life such as brushing teeth, riding a bicycle, petting a dog, eating a sandwich, or reading a book. The dances focus on exploring range, levels, and rhythms. They perform the dances to different types of music and discuss how the movements changed to fit the music.

- The opening of baseball season hits the front page of the newspaper. A third-grade class creates a dance that reflects the movements that occur in a baseball game. They include movements that reflect running, catching, batting, and pitching.

Dances Created by Others

Traditional folk, ethnic, square, and social dances are the types of dance forms that are created by others, as are dances choreographed by a professional choreographer, the teacher, or another student. These types of dances can be handed down from one generation to the next; they can be recorded on film, videotape, or in a written form; or they can simply exist within the mind and body of the person who composed it. The following are some examples of dances created by others:

- A dance designed by one student or a group of students with designated movements and a repeatable sequence that is taught to other students

- A dance created by the teacher (see figure 1.5)

- A traditional folk dance such as the la raspa, troika, or Virginia reel

- A popular dance from a particular time period such as the twist, electric slide, or Lindy

- A children's social dance such as the hokey pokey, alley cat, or bunny hop

- A square dance such as the Texas star or Oh, Johnny

- Contemporary line dances

- A dance by a professional choreographer

Figure 1.5　Learning dances created by others expands a child's movement vocabulary.

Why Teach Children's Dance?

Dance is an essential element of a high-quality, comprehensive physical education or arts education program. Dance provides the necessary balance in a curriculum that is focused primarily on functional movement. Children need to have the opportunity to develop their abilities to use movement for both functional *and* expressive purposes. They should participate in a full range of experiences to learn the many possibilities for movement. As the *New Jersey Literacy in the Arts Task Force Report* (1989) states,

> Since the dawn of time, dance has been used to express joy and sorrow. In no other activity do human beings, in a very fundamental way, become their own creations. The experience of self-creation is one that must be nurtured in all our children, and it can be achieved most powerfully, perhaps, through the language we call dance. (p. 20)

Dance addresses the needs of children to express and communicate their ideas, to understand and know themselves and their world, and to expand their own movement abilities. Using movement to express ideas is already familiar to children. Along with their language development they use locomotor (traveling) and nonlocomotor (body gestures in place) movements to support and emphasize what they wanted to "say." This natural use of movement for expression and communication becomes a foundation for learning dance. Also, children's life experiences, culture, physical and intellectual abilities, and understanding of themselves influence how they perceive and integrate dance into their lives.

Children Need to Express and Communicate Their Ideas, Feelings, and Understandings

Dance addresses children's need for expression and communication in the following ways:

- Allows children to use their natural creative instincts to make a statement about their world
- Encourages children to reach beyond the conventional response to a movement task and discover new ways to move, feel, perceive, and understand themselves and others in their environment
- Teaches children another avenue of expression and communication in addition to writing, speaking, the visual arts, music, and theater (literacy in all these areas is important to provide options for increasing the quality of interaction with others)
- Develops imagination, creativity, and the ability to make decisions through creating new dance movements
- Provides opportunities for children to share in the experience of creating and learning together
- Increases opportunities for children to create, perform, observe, and discuss movement

Children Need to Know and Understand Themselves and Their World

Dance enables children to gain an understanding of themselves and the world around them as follows:

- Reinforces learning about the basic dance elements of space, time, force, flow, and relationships, which are common to all movement activities in the physical education and arts education curriculum
- Recognizes the contributions of all cultures to the fabric of the American society through learning traditional folk and ethnic dances and creating new dances
- Increases understanding of how dance represents the history, traditions, beliefs, and values of a culture
- Enhances the skills of perception, observation, and concentration

ⓢ Defines and clarifies one's ideas, thoughts, understandings, or feelings

ⓢ Plays a significant role in total education by integrating cognitive, motor, affective, and aesthetic development within each learning experience

ⓢ Increases knowledge about the different ways to move

ⓢ Develops self-concept, self-esteem, and self- and group identity

ⓢ Helps children recognize similarities and differences among people

ⓢ Changes the way children perceive their world

Children Need to Develop Their Own Movement Abilities

Dance helps children develop their movement abilities by accomplishing the following:

ⓢ Expanding their basic vocabulary of motor skills

ⓢ Developing strength, flexibility, cardiorespiratory endurance, and balance

ⓢ Increasing experiences that provide learning about the infinite ways the body is capable of moving

ⓢ Enhancing motor learning through repetition and practice of dance movements

Children who participate in a variety of dance experiences have the opportunity to discover how to use their bodies as instruments of expression and communication. They will find the joy of moving to a rhythm, running across a space and leaping into the air, spinning around and collapsing to the floor, and freezing in a shape. All children have a right to experience the benefits of dancing—it is the responsibility of the teacher to ensure that they have the opportunity.

What Are the Benefits of Children's Dance?

The chapter's opening dance scenario illustrates the joy children experience as they inter-

pret the movement of a red streamer. Although enjoyment and celebration are apparent when children dance, they are also learning infinite ways to use movement to explore an idea or a feeling. The primary goal of dance education is for children to learn how to use movement as a means to explore, express, and communicate an idea, understanding, concept, or feeling, whether a movement is initiated by them or by others. For the teacher, what children are learning can be clearly evident and easily assessed, and yet, for the child, there are intangible benefits that are unique and personal and cannot be measured or seen. Children who view the world primarily through movement rely on what Root-Bernstein and Root-Bernstein (2000) call "kinesthetic thinking," in which the images and feelings that emerge are best understood when a symbolic language, such as dance, is used to translate what they have experienced. Through multiple dance experiences, children benefit in a variety of ways that can affect other experiences in their lives.

Psychomotor Benefits

The dance component in a physical education or arts education curriculum provides a variety of experiences to help children develop and improve motor skills and fitness. All dance learning experiences are characterized by the body moving through space, in time, and with force. Children run, jump, twist, leap, wiggle, crawl, dodge, and roll in many directions, using different tempos with varied amounts of force. They learn to effectively move their whole body or its parts in isolation in a safe and effective manner. Moving from one shape to another or performing a combination of locomotor movements that require body control is developed through exploration and repetition. Children gain strength, improve balance, and increase flexibility and coordination through creating movements or learning movement patterns. Motor skills and abilities developed through dance become the tools that children use for expression and communication.

Dance learning experiences provide children with opportunities to continue development of motor skills and to expand the use of these skills in their lives. Teaching a child to skip, for example, involves the motor pattern of combining a step and a hop and alternating the right and left foot (Buschner 1994). In addition, rhythm, direction, force, position of the body in space, and the relationship of one foot to the other must be considered in skipping. After the basic skip is developed the child can then perform it in a variety of different ways—as part of a folk dance that describes how a group travels or as a way of expressing excitement.

Cognitive Benefits

The cognitive benefits of dance include learning about one's body and how it moves and relates to others and the environment. Children gain information about themselves and their world through active interaction; that is, they learn best through doing. Ultimately, the way children think is influenced by the type of experiences they have in their lives (Eisner 1998). Through dance, children comprehend the concepts of direction, range, pathways, tempo, shape, force, and levels by experiencing many different ways to move.

Dance nurtures cognitive development with each task in a learning experience. For example, when the teacher directs the student, "Using your hand and arm, draw a curved line in the air in front of your body," children need knowledge of body parts, of the concept "curved," of the frontal plane of the body, and of how to make the movement physically. If the child does not demonstrate the anticipated response, knowledge of one of the components of the task may be missing. The teacher will need to take the task apart, investigate what knowledge is missing, and then develop tasks that help children learn the appropriate information. Dance experiences increase a child's knowledge of the body and its infinite movement possibilities. Through dance, children will go beyond developing the basic cognitive abilities of recognition and recall to manipulate factual knowledge to a new level of comprehension (New Jersey Literacy in the Arts Task Force 1989).

Critical thinking is another cognitive ability used in creating, performing, and responding to dance. As children create, perform, or observe dances, they make a judgment, either objective or subjective, about the movement. An objective evaluation is clearly observed and reported in a factual manner. For example, you may ask students to observe their partners holding their bodies in a balanced shape and count how many body parts are touching the floor. Asking questions that require personal reflections, opinions, or analysis as part of the response will elicit subjective evaluations. You may ask students, "What do you think was the theme of the dance?" or "What was the most exciting part of the dance for you?"

Through dance, children gain an understanding of their own aesthetic preferences, as well as the preferences of others. Aesthetic understanding involves how the elements of dance are manipulated into meaningful patterns of body movements that express and communicate an idea or feeling. When children laugh at a dance they may view the movements as amusing in reference to their own life. The ways in which quality, rhythm, and space appeared in the dance may have elicited amusing feelings and thoughts through humorous actions. Thinking, talking, or writing about the characteristics of the dance that caused the watching students to laugh are how children reflect on the experience and gain an understanding of their own aesthetic preferences.

The process of making a dance also involves cognitive development through encouraging the use of imagination to create new ways of expressing ideas and feelings. Children instinctively use imaginative thinking as they play and create. We encourage you to not only attend to correct replication of a particular movement pattern but also to cultivate the powers of innovation through encouraging the use of children's imagination and creativity (Eisner 1998).

Last, assessment of a student's cognitive abilities—recall, comprehension, application, and evaluation—can take the form of a verbal, written, or movement response. For example, after a dance learning experience, students can be asked to verbally describe a sequence of movements used in a folk dance, to draw the shapes used in a partner body sculpture, or to demonstrate a movement from the lesson that used strong energy.

Affective and Social Benefits

Children need to feel successful about the experiences they pursue and accomplish. They also have a need to express their joy, fear, anger, frustration, and excitement and to communicate their understanding about their world. Dance recognizes and fulfills these needs. Through dance, children discover who they are, how they move, where they can move, how it feels to move in different ways, what movements they like to do, and how those movements are different from and similar to others. They learn to make decisions, develop their imaginations, express ideas and feelings, and share with others. The discovery and learning experiences become part of a child's self-concept and self-esteem.

Dancing can make children feel proud of the way they move; however, it can also make them feel vulnerable. Children who are unsure of themselves will say, "I can't do it" or "I don't know how." Children are immediately aware of what they can and cannot do as they begin to move, and they know that others are also aware of how they are moving. Teachers need to recognize children's discomfort and to encourage them gently and with sensitivity to their feelings.

The body and its movements are the medium that reveals how a child feels inside. The way children move through space, use time and force, and relate to others and their environment reveals these feelings. Pioneer modern dancer Martha Graham states, "Movement is the one speech that cannot lie (de Mille 1991, p. 22). Dance provides children with the means to express and communicate what they really feel and know about themselves and their world. For example, children can express feelings of anger by stomping their feet and pounding their hands. These movements can then inspire a dance that explores the expression of anger.

Socially, children enjoy interacting with others through movement. They laugh and talk with each other while sharing an experience that is fun and personally rewarding. Dance in the school environment usually occurs as part of a whole-class experience, with the teacher facilitating the session. Children participate in dances as individuals, as partners, as members of a small group, or as part of the whole class dancing in unison. While dancing in a small group, children assume various leadership roles, learn to share ideas, practice moving together, and develop a group identity. They experience the perspectives of others and see that an idea can be expressed in a multitude of ways.

The teacher plays an important role in ensuring that the dance experience is positive and successful for all children. Each learning experience must be designed to match the appropriate developmental level of the children. Dance learning experiences for 5-year-old children, for example, are very different in content and presentation than experiences designed for 9-year-old children. All children need frequent positive reinforcement from the teacher and from peers. Most children want the teacher to watch them and respond with a positive comment. Young children frequently say things such as, "Watch me," "Watch how I can do it," and "Look at me." They depend upon the teacher for approval, and the positive attention helps motivate them to stay focused on the learning experience. Positive comments followed by a specific description of what the teacher observed reinforces that the child's effort is acceptable and has value. For example, a teacher commenting on a turn may say, "That was wonderful," and then continue, "That turn was very high off the floor, your head stayed up, and you landed with control." The teacher can continue to question the child, "What did you do that helped your landing to be so smooth?" In another example, two children have designed a repetitive movement to reflect the movement of a machine part. The teacher may use the following positive comment to clarify for students what they are doing well and support their collaborative effort: "Your movements are very clear, and both of you can keep the rhythm going at the same time. That's great the way you both work together."

Teachers can make the difference in the attitudes that children develop about dance. Commitment to prepare and present a dance experience that is exciting, relevant, and developmentally appropriate is essential for effective and meaningful teaching. The reasons to teach dance must go beyond meeting the requirements of a curriculum. The teacher should support the benefits of teaching dance, be enthusiastic, be open to new experiences, and be willing to make revisions when a lesson does not seem to be working. Extending what you already know will not only be challenging but also personally and professionally rewarding, and your positive attitude will affect your students' feelings of success.

Learning Outcomes

The content of a dance experience for children reflects the characteristics unique to different age levels. Every child comes to school with a different set of life experiences and needs. A dance curriculum that encourages and celebrates what each individual brings to the learning experience recognizes these differences. The outcomes of a dance program describe what a student should know and be able to do as a result of participating in a kindergarten through fifth grade (K–5) dance program. We offer a set of outcomes as an example of guiding statements for a dance program (Cone and Cone 2003). The outcomes are divided into two levels: kindergarten through second grade and third through fifth grade.

Children in kindergarten through second grade should *know* the following as a result of the dance education program:

- How to describe their movements using the elements of dance. For example, children may describe a shape with the phrase, "I am making a big shape," or describe a level when they are moving on the floor by saying, "I am moving at a low level."
- How to describe the movements of others using the elements of dance. For example, a child may say, "Briana is skipping in a circle," or "Josh is wiggling very fast."
- Recognize that dance is a way to express an idea or a feeling.
- Identify different locomotor and nonlocomotor movements that can be used to create and perform dances.

- Understand that an idea or feeling can be expressed through dance in many different ways.
- Understand that different cultures make and perform dances for different reasons.
- Acknowledge that dance can relate to the other arts or to other school subjects.
- Comprehend that dance is a way to exercise and become strong and flexible and improve balance and coordination.
- Recognize that dance is a way to enjoy moving with others.

Children in kindergarten through second grade should be able *to do* the following as a result of the dance education program:

- Demonstrate different movements that exemplify one or more elements of dance. For example, when children are asked to make a round shape or jump in a forward direction, they respond to the task with the corresponding movement.
- Perform the basic locomotor and nonlocomotor movements.
- Reproduce their own and others' movement, movement patterns, and shapes.
- Cooperate with a partner or small group to create and perform a dance.
- Improvise different movements to express an idea or a feeling.
- Observe the dances of others and respond to the observation by drawing, writing, or talking.
- Perform age-appropriate dances from a variety of cultures and time periods.
- Create a dance using a concept from another subject area (e.g., dance about how the planets revolve around the sun).
- Create a dance using a self-selected idea.
- Demonstrate respect for the dances created and performed by others.
- Demonstrate the ability to move safely to avoid injury to their bodies.

Children in third through fifth grade should *know* the following as a result of the dance education program:

- How to describe their movements by noting several elements of dance. For example, children may describe a shape with the phrase, "I am making a stretched shape that is low to the floor," or "I am running forward using a zigzag pathway."

- How to describe the movements or combinations of movements of others by using several elements of dance. For example, a child may say, "Julio is rising up, slowly and softly," or "Julia turned on one foot, then skipped backward, and froze in a curved shape."

- Recognize dance as an art form that uses the elements of movements as the tools to express and communicate an idea or feeling.

- Gain knowledge of the terminology specific to a form or style of dance.

- Acknowledge that dance is representative of different cultures and different historical and social contexts.

- Understand that dance can be combined with other art forms and other subject areas.

- Comprehend that dance is a means of improving body strength, balance, coordination, and flexibility.

- Understand that dance is a way to cooperate with others to perform or create a dance.

- Understand how to use the elements of dance to vary movements.

- Gain knowledge of choreographic structures.

Children in third through fifth grade should be able *to do* the following as a result of the dance education program:

- Perform combinations of the basic locomotor and nonlocomotor movements using changes in space, time, and force.

- Demonstrate safe technique in movement to avoid body injury.

- Demonstrate respect for dances created and performed by others.

- Observe dances created and performed by others and describe their understanding of the work using dance terminology.

- Create and perform a dance using a self-selected idea.

- Create and perform a dance that relates to another art form or another subject area.

- Accurately reproduce the movements, sequences, rhythmical patterns, energy, and use of space with age-appropriate dances.

- Create a dance using one or more choreographic structures.

- Perform age-appropriate dances from another culture or time period.

- Apply the elements of dance to vary movements.

In 1994, the National Dance Association published the *National Standards for Dance Education* (National Dance Association 1994). These standards describe the basic knowledge and skills necessary for developing an effective dance program. They are intended to focus on the content applicable to any dance program and not dictate methodology or a specific curriculum design. Many states have referred to the national standards as a guide in developing state-level dance standards. We suggest that you obtain a copy of the national dance standards or your state dance or arts education standards to use as a reference in planning the content of your dance program. When dance is included as part of the physical education curriculum, you can also refer to the national standards for physical education (National Association for Sport and Physical Education 2004) as a guide to develop a comprehensive dance program. The intent of these standards is to describe the essential concepts and skills needed to participate in a variety of movement forms, interact with others, and use movement for self-expression, enjoyment, and to maintain a healthy active lifestyle. Also, check with your school district for the physical education or arts education standards that may need to be addressed.

Summary

All children need to express their thoughts, understandings, ideas, and feelings. Dance fulfills this need when presented in developmentally appropriate learning experiences. These experiences should include movement that is natural for children yet teaches new movements that expand their movement vocabulary and develop skills. Dance complements the acquisition of motor skills to perform a function by teaching movement for expression and communication. Participation in dance promotes self-discovery, builds self-esteem, engages children in a positive opportunity to interact socially, and increases cultural understanding.

As an integral component of the physical education or arts education curriculum, dance experiences should offer opportunities for students to create dances, learn dances created by others, observe dance, and respond to dance. Planned outcomes for a dance program guide the teacher to develop learning experiences that address what children should know and be able to do as a result of participating in a dance program. In this way, children's learning is meaningful and relevant. For success in teaching any type of dance, the teacher and student must enter the learning experience together with enthusiasm, a positive attitude, and the willingness to allow the joy of dancing to envelop them.

Questions for Reflection

- What role does dance play in your life? Artistically? Socially? Culturally?
- What perceptions do your students have about dance? What influenced these perceptions?
- In what ways have you introduced dance learning experiences, and how have they had an impact on what students learn?
- How is creative dance different from creative movement? How are they similar?
- What skills and knowledge do you have that can be applied to teaching dance?
- What is your definition of dance?
- Throughout a child's education, they participate in many experiences that contribute to their physical, intellectual, emotional, and social development. What unique contributions does dance make to a child's development?

chapter 2

Presenting Essential Content for Children's Dance

This chapter provides a description of the content for dance within the physical education or arts education curriculum. In both program areas, teaching children to learn to move and to use movement as a way to learn is the primary goal. Including dance as a significant component of the curriculum ensures that children have the opportunity to integrate their capacity to think with their body and to analyze its movements as a means to express and communicate what they know and experience. Through dance, children expand their movement abilities and use critical thinking skills to learn, perform, create, and respond to dance.

The elements of dance—the body and its movements, space, time, force, flow, and relationships—are the foundation for the dance curriculum. All the elements are part of every movement we perform; however, dance manipulates and emphasizes specific elements to express an idea or feeling. Compare, for example, the ingredients of a cake to the elements of dance. Using different ingredients in different quantities will produce many different types of cakes; using different elements of dance in different combinations will produce many different forms of dance. The specific way the elements of dance are combined depends on the meaning of the dance. For example, a dancer can illustrate the wind by running with fast, light, and small steps or with slow, strong, and large steps, producing a different feeling. In a creative dance about the solar system, students may choose dance elements that emphasize slowly turning round shapes or movements that rotate quickly with strong energy. Many social and folk dances have predetermined ways of using the elements of movement. The twist, a popular dance from the 1960s, moves the upper and lower body in a strong, fast, side-to-side twisting movement. As soon as the music for the twist is played, everyone performs a similar twisting movement. However, a dancer can personalize the basic twisting movement by adding other dance elements to vary the level or speed. Many folk dances specifically delineate how the elements of dance are applied to reflect particular cultural values, traditions, or beliefs. Variations to a folk dance may represent a regional style or group preference yet still contain basic characteristics of the traditional form.

In this chapter, we offer our version of the elements of dance based on the work of Rudolf Laban (1976) and other dance educators (Gilbert 1992; Wall and Murray 1989; Zakkai 1997). We have organized the elements of dance into six categories—the body, space, time, force, flow, and relationships (see figure 2.1). Each element is individually defined; however, all the elements typically work in combination in every movement we make.

The Body

In dance, children construct infinite variations of movements to express and communicate ideas, feelings, concepts, perceptions, and meaning. The body and mind act jointly to create, perceive, and perform each movement that emerges in a dance experience. Fraleigh (1987) refers to this mind and body connection as a "minded body," in which dancing requires the whole person to be involved in the dance experience. Through dance, students explore, discover, and gain knowledge of all the infinite possibilities for movement. They increase control over their movements while developing body awareness. Children learn the names of body parts, identify where they are located, and learn the different ways the body parts can move in isolation or as a coordinated whole.

Actions of the Whole Body

When the whole body is in motion, all the parts are involved; however, some body parts may be emphasized more than others. In skipping, the feet and legs are primary to the movement and rhythm, and the arms, head, and torso are also involved. Whole-body actions occur in two ways: as traveling movements, sometimes referred to as *locomotor* movements, and as body gestures, also referred to as *nonlocomotor* movements. Locomotor movements take the body to another location in space. Usually, we think about traveling on the feet as in running, jumping, walking, or leaping, yet other body parts can also be used for traveling (see figure 2.1).

The second category of whole-body action is body gestures or nonlocomotor movements that occur without traveling in space (see figure 2.1). A gesture is a movement usually of the body or limbs that expresses or emphasizes an idea, sentiment, or attitude. *Gesture* is appropriately used here to describe a type of body movement that applies specifically to dance. An isolated body part, or all the body parts, can perform movements such as twisting, shaking, or swinging. For example, a child can shake only one hand or all of the body. Two or more body gestures can be integrated to create a new movement such as swinging the arms side to side as the torso twists. Also, traveling movements and body gestures frequently are combined to form more complex movements that allow for a greater interpretation of an idea, thought, or feeling. A student may run and leap to express the idea of a leaf blowing in the air. When the student adds a swinging arm movement to the leap, she or he further defines the shape of the leaf or the path of the wind as the leaf lifts into the air. Offering locomotor and nonlocomotor movement combinations increases a student's movement vocabulary beyond what they already know while challenging them to create, learn, and practice new ways of moving.

The Body	Space
Actions of the Whole Body (Traveling or Locomotor Movements)	**Personal Space and General Space**
Run, walk, jump, hop, combinations of jumps and hops, skip, leap, slide, crawl, roll, gallop, creep, slither, traveling using combinations of body parts	**Levels** *Low, medium, high*
Actions of Body Parts (Gestures or Nonlocomotor Movements)	**Directions** *Forward, backward, sideways, up, down, diagonal*
Twist, shake, bend, stretch, wiggle, swing, turn, rise, fall, stop, sway, rock, push, pull	**Pathways (Floor and Air)** *Straight, curved, zigzag, spiral, circular, geometric shapes, wavy, combinations of pathways*
Body Shapes (Still and Moving) *Straight, curved, twisted, wide, elongated, angular, symmetrical, asymmetrical*	**Range (Size)** *Small, medium, big*
Time	**Force**
Tempo *Fast, sudden, slow, sustain, accelerate, decelerate*	**Strong** *Heavy, firm, powerful*
Rhythm *Uneven, even, accented*	**Light** *Fine, gentle, soft, delicate*
Flow	**Relationships**
Free *Ongoing, unrestrained, uncontrolled*	**Individual**
	Partner and Group *Contrasting, matching, following, connecting, echoing*
Bound *Stoppable, restrained, controlled*	**Formations** *Scattered, lines, circles, squares*

Figure 2.1 The elements of dance.

Actions of the Body Parts

Body parts are involved in movement in three ways: in isolation, leading a movement, and supporting the weight of the body. Isolated movements occur when one body part is moving and the rest of the body is still. This type of movement, which appears quite simple, is actually difficult for young children. Balance, strength, and concentration are required to keep the body still while a single body part moves. When a body part leads a movement, it will initiate the movement and the rest of the body follows with the same movement. A body part can also lead the rest of the body through space, as in running forward with the arms reaching forward. The third way is when a body part supports body weight. In many folk, ethnic, and social dances, the feet primarily support the body weight. Yet, in some dance forms such as break dancing and creative dance, other body parts such as the hands, head, back, knees, and shoulders can be used to support body weight.

Body Shapes

The body is capable of forming an infinite variety of shapes. Our bodies always take a shape, whether we are moving or in a still position. Most body shapes, used in everyday life, are for functional purposes, such as sitting at a computer or standing in the shower. Certain body shapes send powerful messages, however, such as pointing a finger at someone, slumping in a moment of sorrow, or affectionately hugging a loved one.

Shapes that are created or reproduced in a dance experience are classified into three general categories: straight, curved, and twisted (see figure 2.2). Straight shapes can be formed with the whole body or its parts. By bending the elbows, knees, wrists, fingers, and spine, the body can make an angular shape composed of many smaller straight shapes. The second shape category is curved. In this shape, the body can be rounded through curving the spine forward, backward, or sideward. Also, arms and legs can be individually curved or curved as part of the whole body shape. Other words frequently used to describe a curved shape are *rounded, squiggly, curled, wavy, arched,* or *spiraled.* The third category describes twisted shapes in which the body rotates in two opposing directions at the same time. Most twisted shapes begin at the waist with the legs and hips twisted in one direction and the upper body in the opposite direction. A single body part can form a twisted shape by rotating in an opposing direction to the rest of the body such as twisting an arm away from the torso or both legs twisted around each other.

Two additional shape categories are symmetrical and asymmetrical. Symmetrical shapes in dance are positions in which the left and right sides of the body are in exactly the same shape. Asymmetrical shapes are positions in which the two sides of the body are different.

Shapes can be expressed through stillness, like a stone sculpture or a frozen statue. Shapes are also part of every traveling movement. Some shapes appear naturally as the body travels, and other shapes are intentional. For example, a straight, symmetrical arm shape may be combined with a jump, or a curving shape of the back may be combined with a skip.

Space

We are always moving in space, mainly for functional purposes (e.g., walking forward to turn on a light switch). In dance, one moves in space as the result of a series of choices that express or communicate an idea or a feeling. Changing levels from high to low can demonstrate a wave at the beach. Skipping forward on a curved path may express the wind blowing from side

Figure 2.2   In creative dance, children explore different ways to make straight, twisted, and curved shapes.

to side, or the movement can be a metaphor for expressing happiness. Space for a dancer can be compared to the canvas of an artist. As the dancer moves in different directions, levels, pathways, and ranges, she or he creates a spatial design. In many cultural or social dances, the space is designed in circles or lines to represent a community of people sharing an experience together. When children engage in a creative dance experience, they develop new spatial designs that reflect their meaning of the movement. The element of space is further delineated through its six interrelated components: personal space, general space, levels, directions, pathways, and range.

Personal Space

The term *personal space* describes the space immediately surrounding the body, that is, the space that is always around us everywhere we move and when we are not traveling. Although the size of one's personal space changes with each dance activity, it is generally thought of as an adequate amount of space around the front, back, top, and sides of the body so the student can move without touching another person or object. It is like a bubble around the body. Children can find the limits of their personal space by reaching out with their hands and feet in the immediate space around the body and sensing that they have adequate space for their movement.

General Space

General space refers to all the space outside of personal space that is available for movement; everyone shares this space. In a dance where students are running and leaping, each student leaps in the shared general space, but an individual's leap occurs within the limits of their personal space. Dancers carry their personal space with them as they move in the general space. Whether students are creating their own dances or learning a dance from another person, the general space has a defined boundary. The teacher may designate the boundary by the lines on the floor or cones marking an outside space. In a folk, ethnic, or social dance, the general space is usually determined by the for-

mation required for the dance such as a circle, square, or single line.

Levels

The term *level* in dance implies three different heights—low, medium, and high—in which the body moves and makes shapes. A low level is considered close to or on the ground, that is, the space below the knees. Movements such as crawling, rolling, or stretching on the floor occur at a low level. The medium level is the space midway between high and low or generally between an individual's knees and shoulders. Movements such as walking or running can occur at a medium level. The space above the shoulders is considered as a high level. When students are asked to reach for the sky, raising their arms above the shoulders, or to jump and leap, they are using space at a high level.

Directions

When students dance, their bodies move in six general directions in space:

- Forward, defined as the front of the body leading the movement
- Backward, where the back of the body leads the movement
- Sideways to the right or left, in which the right or left side leads the movement
- Up and down, defined as moving up toward the sky or down toward the ground

The first four basic directions (forward, backward, right, and left) can be combined with the up and down directions in many ways, some of which form a diagonal direction (e.g., forward and to the right). A student can move forward and up as in a leap or forward and down by lowering the body to the ground. The same movement performed in each of the directions will have a different feeling and communicate a different idea. For example, reaching forward and up with the hands and arms can illustrate reaching toward the sun to express how wonderful the warm sun feels after a cold winter season, whereas the same reach in a sideward and down direction can demonstrate reaching to help someone who has fallen.

Pathways

Pathways are the places where the body travels in space. Two types of pathways occur in dance. The first type, floor pathways, are created by traveling movements (such as running in a circle or skipping on a straight line), and the second type, air pathways, are created by body gestures moving in the space around the body (as in drawing a zigzag line in the air with an elbow). If a student stepped in a puddle of water and then ran in a circle, the result would be a pathway of footsteps that describe the shape of where the body traveled. All pathways are composed of straight and curved lines or a combination of both. In dance, the student makes a decision about the pathway for movement or learns a specific pathway that has already been designed for a dance. Examples of air and floor pathways are illustrated in figure 2.3.

Range

Range defines the size of a movement. Another word used interchangeably with range is *extensions*. Descriptions about how large or small, long or short, or wide or narrow the movement are all related to size. The steps to a folk dance may require the students to take large running steps in a circle, whereas in another folk dance the students might perform small turning hops.

Time

The time element in dance refers to the tempo and the rhythm of the movement. Time also refers to the duration of the pauses between movements. Dance is composed not only of movement but also of the stillness between movements. For example, in a dance that explores different ways to jump, the student may hold a still shape for a long time between a repeated series of three quick jumps. The next sections describe tempo and rhythm.

Tempo

Tempo is the pace of a movement, that is, how fast or slow the movement occurs. In the action of clapping hands using a steady beat, the tempo

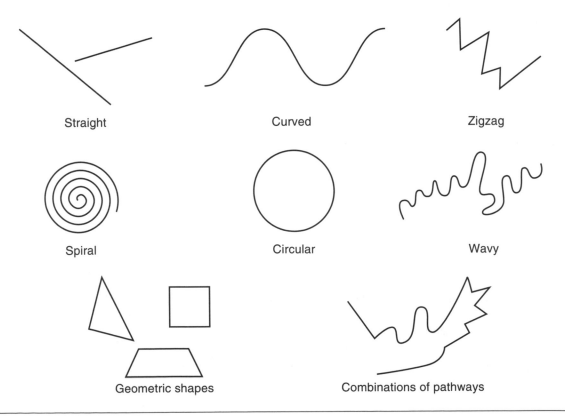

Straight   Curved   Zigzag

Spiral   Circular   Wavy

Geometric shapes   Combinations of pathways

Figure 2.3   Air and floor pathways.

may be fast or slow. Walking can also demonstrate a steady beat—the beat of the steps can be fast or slow, and the number of steps can be short in duration (with only a few steps) or longer in duration (walking for 30 seconds). Tempo can change abruptly from fast to slow or vice versa, and tempo can change gradually through acceleration and deceleration. The increase or decrease in speed can occur over a long duration or very quickly. In the social dance, alley cat, for example, the foot movement pattern accelerates toward the end of the dance to challenge the dancers to repeat the pattern faster and faster. The dance ends with a deceleration of the pattern to the original speed. In a creative dance that interprets a rainstorm, the movement may begin at a slow speed to demonstrate the beginning of a rainfall. The speed of the movement may then accelerate to illustrate a strong rainstorm and end with a deceleration of speed to represent the final raindrop.

Rhythm

Dance movements are organized through rhythm in much the same way that sound in music is organized. Rhythm is the underlying organizational pattern that gives order to music and dance (Fowler 1994). The most basic rhythm is a pulse beat, which occurs at regular intervals. This beat is what we feel in our body when we hear a piece of music. Movement, whether it is the bouncing of the head or tapping of the feet, translates the sound we hear into a kinesthetic and visual response. The pulse or steady beat becomes the foundation for a dance supporting other even or uneven rhythms. Rhythm is also the combination of long and short sounds or slow and quick movements such as a dance using the rhythm, slow-slow-quick-quick-quick. Folk and ethnic dances have definite rhythms inherent to the culture from which the dance originated. These rhythms represent different ways people move in that culture or how they work, play, worship, celebrate, and express their ideas. As students learn different folk and ethnic dances, they will discover that some of the rhythms in the dance movements feel comfortable, whereas other rhythms may be difficult to perform. We all grow up in a culture that has its own rhythm. Learning the rhythms of another culture can be challenging, but it can lead to an understanding of the similarities and differences between and among cultures.

One aspect of rhythm is *accent*. Accent is an emphasis placed on a beat. As the emphasis is repeated in a series of beats, a rhythmic pattern is established of stronger and weaker beats. A regular accent (called the *downbeat*) falls at the beginning of a pattern, whereas a syncopated accent (or *upbeat*) is placed on the weaker beats in the pattern. In dance, an accent becomes evident by a change in the movement or quality of the movement. The accent can be represented through a movement that is stronger, bigger, higher, or faster. An accented dance step may move in a different direction, or the accent may appear as an isolated body part movement. For example, a folk dance may call for a strong stamp on the first beat of a pattern of steps, or a short dance composed of 12 beats may require reaching into the air on the first and fourth beats. Students will notice the accented movement in a dance; it will feel different and perhaps be exciting to express or challenging to coordinate.

In music, repeating patterns of beats are referred to as a *meter* or a rhythmic measure of a certain number of beats (Fowler 1994). Dance also uses these terms to describe a phrase of movements that contains a certain number of beats. In many folk, ethnic, and social dances the pattern of dance movements corresponds to the rhythmical measures in the music. Creative dance uses regular repeating rhythmical patterns as well as rhythmical patterns that are not regularly structured. For example, an 8-beat repeating rhythmic pattern of movement can be R-step, hop, L-step, hop, R-run, L-run, R-step, and L-leap. In another case, a dance may begin with a measure of 4 beats, then follow with a measure of 7 beats, and continue with a measure of 2 beats.

Force

Force is the amount of energy expended in a movement. It can be strong, as exhibited in a punch, or light, as expressed in a floating movement. When we move about in our daily routine, we use force to be efficient and effective. Washing out a crystal glass requires a different force from scrubbing a burned pan. We have learned to use the appropriate amount of muscular energy to complete a task successfully. In dance, too, we learn to use different amounts of force depending on the intention of the movement. Using strong force, with tense, firm muscles, results in a powerful movement that may express the movement of a stalking lion. Using light force, with loose, relaxed muscles, results in soft, gentle movements that can capture the feeling of stepping on a cloud.

In a folk dance, the dancers may perform a pattern that uses several strong foot stamps and then several quick, light kicks. A social dance like the Hokey Pokey may use a strong movement to emphasize placing a body part in or out of the circle followed by a soft turning movement with arms and fingers moving lightly from side to side. Children, in a creative dance unit, can use strong force to illustrate the powerful sound of a thunderstorm or use light force to express a story about a butterfly visiting a garden of flowers.

Flow

Flow refers to how force is controlled or not controlled in a movement. The two words commonly used to describe flow are *free* and *bound*. In free flow, the mover is not completely in control of the energy of the movements and may feel out of control, unrestrained, or unable to stop. This use of force implies taking some risks with balance and experiencing some uncertainty in how space is used. Students may create a dance that has a section where the movement feels out of control and then returns to a sequence of defined dance steps. Bound flow denotes controlling the energy of the movement. The student can stop the movement at any time. For example, in a dance using eight slides to the right and eight slides to the left, the students will need to use bound flow to change effectively from the eighth slide to the right to the first slide to the left. Many dances use bound flow when changing the direction of a movement, pausing in a shape, ending the dance, or dancing with another person.

Relationships

Dance includes different types of relationships. Relationship terms include near, close, far, away, over, under, through, in front, in back, alongside, around, between, inside, outside, above, below, together, and apart. The definition of this element includes three parts: the relationship of a person's body parts to his or her other body parts; the spatial and temporal relationship of individuals organized into partners and groups; and the relationship of one's body to props, equipment, and the dance environment.

Body Parts

As children move their body parts into different relationships, they make different body shapes. A hand may be held over the head or behind the back in a folk dance, or the head is placed close to the knees depicting the curled shape of a caterpillar. Each body part is capable of many different movements that occur in the personal space around the body and in relation to other body parts. When students perform a dance in which they gallop and swing their hands in front and in back of their bodies, they are using body-part relationships. In a creative dance where the students begin as small flower seeds under the earth, their body parts would be close to each other in a small round shape. As the seed begins to sprout, their hands and feet will begin to reach away from their torso to demonstrate the plant growing toward the sun.

Partners and Groups

When students dance with a partner or as a member of a group, they relate to each other in space and time. Partners or groups can move in a spatial relationship to each other such as side by side, facing each other, back to back, one behind the other, or side to back (see figure 2.4). They can also move in a temporal relationship to each other: in unison (moving exactly at the same time) or with a time delay between one person's movement and the other person's movement. The following movement relationship descriptions characterize a variety of different uses of space and time.

Figure 2.4 Partner relationships in space.

- Copy or match: Here students face a leader and perform exactly the same movement at the same time. The right and left sides of the body move in the same way as the leader. *Mirror (group)*

- Mirror: In this relationship, students face partners and perform the same movement as if they are looking in a mirror. When the leader moves the left arm the follower moves the right arm using the same movement. The movements of the follower occur at the same time as the leader's movements.

- Echo: The leader performs a movement and the follower repeats the same movement after a very short time delay between the movements. When a group does a sequence of echo movements, the effect is like falling dominoes.

- Unison: Two individuals or a group all perform the same movement at the same time.

- Shadow: One student is behind another and follows the student, performing the same movement at the same time.

- Call and response: This relationship is similar to having a conversation with words, where one person speaks and the other person responds. One person or a group makes the first movement, considered the "call," and then the other person or group makes a movement, the "response." The movements of the caller and the responder can be the same or different.

- Contrast: Students perform a movement or make a still shape that is opposite to the movement of a partner or another group. A stretched-out movement can be contrasted with a closed and rounded movement, a forward movement can be contrasted with moving backward, or strong movements can be contrasted with light movements. The contrast can also appear in the use of time; for example, one person can be moving rapidly while the other moves slowly.

⊚ Connected: Two or more students move or make a still shape connected by one or more body parts.

⊚ Supported: One or more students hold some or all of the body weight of another student, as in leaning on another person or lifting someone into the air.

⊚ Meeting and parting: This relationship describes how students move toward and away from each other in space.

Spatial Formations

The formation of the dancers in the space reflects the intent of the dance. In traditional folk and social dances, students frequently dance in circles, squares, and line formations. These formations may express the feeling of unity as the dancers move using the same steps to the same rhythm. This type of dance fosters a feeling of acceptance and identity with a group. Other dances use formations that are like the spokes of a wheel, an *X*, or a cross shape. Creative dance also uses these formations in addition to scattered and geometric formations (see figure 2.5). One formation can be used for the entire dance, or the formation can change with different rhythmic patterns or to express different ideas in a dance.

Props, Equipment, and the Dance Environment

The relationship element is used here to describe the spatial relationship of an individual or group to a prop, piece of equipment, or the dance environment. Children relate to a prop by moving it in the personal space surrounding their body, to equipment by moving in the space surrounding the equipment, and to their environment by moving toward or away from the perimeter or center of the room or dance space. Children dancing with a scarf in a creative dance experience, for example, can explore the space in front or in back of the body, over the head, between the legs, or around the waist. In another lesson using a piece of equipment such

as a chair or a cardboard box, the children may explore different ways they can move around, over, or under the equipment. A folk dance may use long colorful ribbons held between the hands of dancers in a circle while other dancers move under and over the ribbons. The dance environment can be used imaginatively and become the sky as students run around the perimeter, or a circle taped in the center of the space can be used as a place to dance inside, outside, around, or to move toward and away.

Dance Forms

This section of the chapter describes the dance forms that are included in a dance curriculum: dances created by the students, defined in this book as creative dance, and dances created by others, such as social, folk, and ethnic dances. A complete and inclusive dance program will provide students with experiences in creative dance, folk or ethnic dances, and social dances. Students will also have an opportunity to learn and create dances as individuals, in partnerships, and as a member of a group.

Creative Dance

In creative dance, children generate their own dances to reflect or interpret an idea, thought, or feeling. Through the process of improvisation, students can manipulate movements using the elements of dance and then select and arrange the movements into a sequence to form a dance. Creating new dance movements is often a challenge to both the student and the teacher. Students must rely on their personal backgrounds to create something new. This process is not always easy for them. Young children may not have an extensive vocabulary of ideas and movements to use. They may look to the teacher to provide examples of movements until they develop a stronger vocabulary. Alternatively, some children have a wealth of movement experiences and are always eager to offer new ideas. The teacher needs to establish a supportive atmosphere that encourages children to be creative and willing to share their ideas. Older children with a richer resource of life experiences may also encounter difficulty

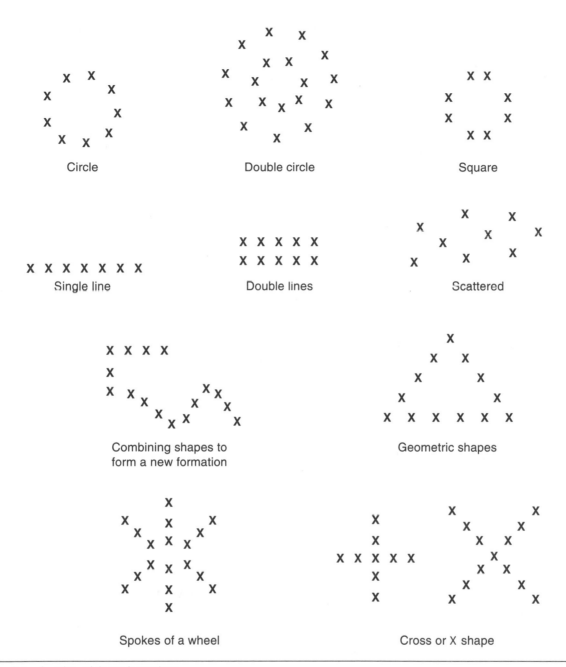

Figure 2.5 A variety of dance formations.

creating new movements. They may feel self-conscious and concerned about what their peers will think. The challenge for the teacher is to design a learning experience that encourages creativity and risk taking. Students need clear tasks that define what is expected yet are open-ended to allow for a creative response.

For students with limited dance experience, a specific task approach is recommended. This approach gives students a clear understanding of what the task requires and still leaves room for personal decision making. For example, in the task, "Find a way to do three consecutive jumps, each one moving in a different direction," a student can choose the shape of the jumps, the direction of each jump, the height of the jumps, and the force of each jump. The task can be more specific if you require that all the jumps be high with strong energy and use a designated rhythm.

The term *personal dancing* refers to the experience of students creating their own dance movements based on a teacher-presented task. The task may be broad, such as "Make up your own way of moving to this slow music," or specific, such as, "Find a way to rise slowly from the floor using a turn." Students make personal decisions about what movements they will use and how they will perform the movement within the guidelines of the task. They use their creativity, point of view, and resources to move in new ways to express a feeling or idea (see figure 2.6).

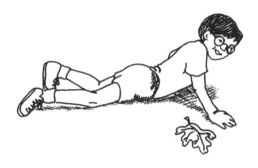

Figure 2.6   A creative dance that reflects the shape of a leaf.

Personal dancing offers students the opportunity to discover what movements they like doing, what movements they may feel comfortable doing, how well they can do a movement, and what movements they would like to perform better. An example of personal dancing in a large-group experience is the floating clouds and rain showers dance (see chapter 7). The dance experience begins with a discussion about the various cloud shapes and how clouds move in the sky. The students might describe cloud shapes as long, wide, puffy, big, or round and cloud movements as slow, floating, fast, or light. Next, each child creates a personal dance in response to the following task: "Think about the words you used to describe the clouds, and make shapes with your body that demonstrate cloud shapes. How many different cloud shapes can you make with your body? Begin moving your body in its cloud shapes around the space. Move your shape forward and backward and turn it as you travel. Keep changing to different shapes as you float in the sky." In this dance experience, each child develops a personal dance even though the whole class responds simultaneously to the same task.

It is not only important to provide the opportunity to create individually but it is also critical to learn to create with others. Children spend most of their time in school interacting with others. They cooperate on science projects, eat lunch together, tutor each other, participate in the school band, and play together at recess. Working together to create a dance, whether with a partner or a group, requires cooperation and active involvement. Not all children are ready for this type of interaction. The teacher needs to keep in mind the motor-skill level of each age, the cognitive level of the students, and their ability to cooperate with others socially. Clearly defined tasks that include assigned roles will help the students to be successful. Young children need to gain some control and understanding of their own bodies before they can interact with other students of their age. They work more easily with a partner than in a group. Older children who are more coordinated and have a broad range of movement experiences are capable of creating partner and small-group dances when they are given a clearly defined task that encourages creating in a cooperative atmosphere. Teachers need to make sure, however, that their students have the social and collaborative skills they will need to successfully create and perform dances. This means that teaching children how to work together is as important as teaching the dance content.

Dances Created by Others

In this type of dance, the student is the performer or learner, not the creator. Students can learn and perform the following types of dances:

- Personal or group dances created by a student or the teacher and taught to others in the class
- Dances created by a professional choreographer
- Social dances such as the twist or waltz that may reflect a particular time period
- Cultural dances that represent a particular country or ethnic population (sometimes referred to as folk dances)

In a large group dance, consider requiring students to have/make contact at some point in their dance.

A description of each type of dance follows.

Dances Created by the Students or the Teacher

Student- and teacher-created dances can be created by an individual or a group and then taught to other individuals or groups. They are new dances created as a result of an idea presented and developed during a learning experience. The student or teacher organizes the movements into a sequence with a definite beginning, middle, and end. The dance is taught in a way that is developmentally appropriate and ensures a positive learning environment. The dances can be recorded in a variety of forms: on videotape, as a written record, or in a series of pictures.

Dances Created by a Professional Choreographer

Students may have the unique opportunity to study dance in their school with a professional choreographer or a dancer, as a guest artist or an artist-in-residence. Complete dances or excerpts of dances from the dancer's or choreographer's repertoire can be taught to the students and adapted to meet the students' developmental level.

Social Dances

This form of dance emphasizes using dance as a means of experiencing the joy of moving with others. Social dances exist within a cultural and historical context and represent one of the ways people share, celebrate, and experience life as a community. They are dances that have become popular and are performed at many social occasions. Examples include the waltz, Lindy, twist, hip-hop dances, cha cha, electric slide, and various partner and group line dances. Students are always ready to teach a new dance that is popular, and they enjoy learning dances from other eras.

Cultural Dances

This dance form focuses on how dance represents events, traditions, and cultural heritage. Through these dances, students learn about what is important to another culture—its traditions, values, beliefs, history, and lifestyles.

The dances are like stories passed down from one generation to another. They hold history and heritage in every movement and formation. Students need to learn more than the sequence of steps; they should be informed about the cultural background of the dance. It is important to teach about the environment and the people from which these dances emerge to promote appreciation and respect for the culture. In this book, American square dance is considered a cultural dance because it reflects how the diversity of cultures in different geographical areas of the United States contributed to the evolution of square dance.

Choosing dances created by others requires thoughtful selection of developmentally appropriate dances. Many cultural dances require dancers to perform movements in unison, in structured formations, or in time to a specific piece of music or rhythm. Young children may not be able to accurately reproduce the movements in the correct rhythm as a large group. As the teacher, you will need to find dances that are suitable for the ability of your students or adapt a dance while maintaining the integrity of the movements and formations. When possible, teach traditional cultural dances as they were originally intended. If you make numerous changes to the steps, gestures, and formations, the characteristics that make it representative of a culture can be compromised, and the authenticity of the dance is lost. As you teach dances from a variety of cultures, be aware that your personal culture will influence your presentation. The best situation is to have someone from the cultural group teach the dance; however, this is not always possible. You can research information on the Internet, in a library, or through other sources for background information, pictures, videos, and artifacts that will make the teaching and learning experience accurate and meaningful.

Summary

Children's dance, as a medium of expression, is manifested through the body and its infinite variations of movement. The elements of dance—the body, space, time, force, flow, and relationships—have an impact on how the movement is designed and performed. Movement in dance has meaning—it expresses an idea or the intention of the performer or creator. When children participate in creative dance, they explore, improvise, and discover new ways to move. They also learn dances created by others—another student, the teacher, a professional choreographer, or dances from a specific historical period or ethnic population. The three forms of children's dance—creative, social, and cultural—make up a comprehensive dance program that provides students opportunities for learning to create, perform, and respond to dance.

Questions for Reflection

- How many ways can you think of to walk using the elements of dance? How would these variations differ for a child in kindergarten and a child in fourth grade?
- How would you develop a series of tasks that use the elements of dance to express the idea of birds in flight or the germination of seeds?
- What are phrases you would use to describe creative dance to your students?
- Teaching dance within a cultural and historical context provides students with an understanding of how the dance movements and formations reflect traditions, values, beliefs, and ways of living. What are some strategies you could use to teach a dance that is new to you and your students?
- Can you think of several instances in which you participated in a cultural dance or a social dance? What did you enjoy about the experience?

1- discuss shape, size, movement, attributes... of birds or seeds

chapter 3

Designing a Dance Program

Teaching dance is both challenging and rewarding. Deciding on the best way to organize and present a learning experience or a unit of study is a constant learning process. In every lesson we teach, we learn something new about the content, the task sequence, and the response from our students. We are constantly evaluating our teaching and making changes for the next session. In this chapter, we offer ideas for developing a yearlong program, specific units of study, and the individual lesson. Your school may already have a dance curriculum to guide your teaching or you may be starting a curriculum. In either situation, planning is essential. Begin by getting to know your students, understand the school's goals, and determine what is critical to the dance program. You will not be able to teach everything in depth, and some content may not be addressed at all. Decisions will need to be made about what to teach and what not to teach. What is important, however, is that children have the opportunity to learn dances, perform dances, create dances, and respond to their dances and the dances of others. These artistic processes form the foundation of any curriculum.

Planning a Yearlong Dance Program

The dance content taught in the span of a school year for each grade level may be determined by the school district's curriculum for dance education. When a predetermined curriculum is not available, the dance educator or physical educator may be responsible for designing and implementing the dance program. Planning a dance program can be an overwhelming task. Knowing what type of dance to teach and how to organize the learning experiences requires combining knowledge of how children learn with knowledge of the dance content. Each learning experience focuses on several objectives that emphasize some or all of the artistic components of dance, that is, learning, performing, creating, and responding. These objectives are met through a sequence of lessons that develop and refine the knowledge and skill children need to express and communicate ideas, thoughts, and feelings through dance. The specific theme for the learning experience, such as traditional West African dance or creating dances about the planets, must be relevant to the students to make their participation personal and meaningful.

Full-time dance educators may teach the same classes for the entire school year, or they may be scheduled to teach different classes that rotate every few weeks. The amount of time available determines the content's amount and depth. In an elementary school where the children attend a dance class once a week for 45 minutes, the teacher may plan five to ten units delivered in four to eight lessons per unit. The units can be different lengths depending on the content and age of the children. We recommend that children have the opportunity to learn about dance from creative, social, and cultural perspectives within the yearlong program.

When dance is part of the physical education program, it may be delivered in one or more units during the school year. This requires the teacher to make some tough decisions about what to teach within the amount of time allotted for dance. Even with a limited amount of time, children need to experience dance as a creative, social, and cultural form of expression. We recommend that dance is taught several times throughout the school year.

One approach to developing a yearlong program is to design one or more units in each of the forms of dance: creative, social, and cultural. An example of a third-grade dance program within the physical education curriculum might be as follows:

- Creative Dance: A unit focused on learning to perform and create different rhythms using different tempos. The unit contains four lessons. In the first lesson, students learn to move body parts and travel using different rhythms selected by the teacher. In the second lesson, children work in pairs to create a dance using the rhythms they learned in the first session. The third session presents the process for creating rhythms using different tempos. During this session, small groups of children work together to create new rhythms and corresponding movements. In the final session, each group shares their rhythm dances and the teacher conducts the assessment.

- Social Dance: A unit focused on learning social dances from the 1950s and 1960s. The unit contains three lessons. In the first lesson, students learn three dances from the 1950s. The second lesson presents three dances from the 1960s. In the third lesson, children, in small groups, choose four dances, practice together, and then videotape themselves for a self-assessment.

- Cultural Dance: A unit focused on learning three dances from Uganda connected to a social studies unit taught by the third-grade teacher. The unit contains four lessons in which a dance artist, hired by the school, teaches the first two sessions. During these sessions, the children learn three traditional dances from different parts of Uganda. In the third session, the physical education teacher sets up three dance stations, one for each dance. The children, organized into three groups, visit each station and practice the dance identified with that station. In the fourth session, the children perform the dances for another third-grade class and write about the learning experience.

A second approach to a yearlong program, applicable for the dance and physical education teacher, is to present units that include all three dance forms. These units are centered on a theme or one or more elements of dance. In this way, students gain a comprehensive understanding of how the theme or elements can be addressed from creative, social, and cultural perspectives (see figure 3.1). For example, a unit based on the outcomes that children demonstrate respect toward others and increase body coordination can include two lessons on learning popular social dances, two lessons on learning dances from a culture not represented in the school, and two lessons on creating dances about friendship. Respect is taught through learning to cooperate and dancing with others, and coordination is increased when children learn and repeat patterns of movement present in all the dance forms taught in the unit.

A third approach is to choose a form of dance as the primary focus and include another form as an extension. The extension provides a more in-depth study and demonstrates how the dance forms are interrelated. For example, in a five-lesson unit focused on social dance, the children learn four line dances in the first three lessons. In the fourth and fifth sessions, creative dance is used as an extension in which the children create their own line dances (Johnson 2002).

Finally, as part of the planning process, consider the following criteria as a checklist to ensure that you have designed a comprehensive, developmentally appropriate, and meaningful dance learning experience:

☐ The annual plan, units, and lessons are aligned with national, state, or local standards.

☐ Each unit and lesson contains clear outcomes and assessments.

☐ The selected content is relevant to the age and interests of the students.

☐ The collection and organization of teaching materials is feasible.

☐ Cultural dance units and lessons are integrated with accurate and relevant information about the culture.

☐ Lesson tasks are designed to follow a sequential progression that builds skills and knowledge.

☐ The dance space is appropriate for student learning and safety.

Planning a Dance Unit

A dance unit of study is a series of dance lessons that focus on a set of instructional outcomes (see chapter 1). The unit outcomes describe what children will know and be able to do as a result of participating in the unit. The individual lessons also have more specific outcomes that can be achieved in a single session, but single-lesson outcomes still relate to the broader unit outcomes. There are many ways to plan and implement a unit; however, what is common to all units is a thoughtful and meaningful design that provides for skill development, social interaction, knowledge attainment, and cultural understanding. For example, if pathways have been selected as the topic for a creative dance unit, the unit outcomes will state that students learn to identify different types of pathways and create ways to move using pathways. The unit is planned to occur in four dance sessions

Theme: Birthdays

Creative	*Social*	*Cultural*
Students create partner dances about making a birthday cake.	Students learn a line dance to the song "Happy Birthday."	Students learn a folk dance performed at a birthday celebration.

Figure 3.1 A theme-based dance unit that incorporates creative, social, and cultural perspectives.

and may be outlined with specific outcomes as follows:

⊛ Session One: Children will explore straight pathways by traveling in different directions on the floor and by drawing with different body parts in the air.

⊛ Session Two: Children will explore curved and circular pathways by traveling on the floor using different tempos and creating curved or circular pathways in the air.

⊛ Session Three: Children will explore zigzag pathways using different levels by traveling on the floor and creating zigzag pathways in the air.

⊛ Session Four: Children will collaborate with a partner to create a dance using two different types of pathways that demonstrates a change in direction, tempo, or level.

Using the elements of dance as a topical theme for a creative dance unit is a good way to begin. Numerous other interesting topics can be selected (see table 3.1) depending on the age and interests of the students.

When planning a unit, decide what content is going to be taught, what students will be expected to learn, and how to assess their learning and then plan each lesson. Grant Wiggins (1998) refers to this process as a backward-design planning process. He suggests that teachers identify the desired results, determine what evidence demonstrates learning, and then design the activities. For example, planning a dance unit

Table 3.1 Topical Themes for Creative Dance

Theme	Topics
Literature	Poems, novels, picture storybooks, folk tales, stories, and poems written by students
Holidays	National holidays, cultural holidays, religious holidays
Special events	Birthdays, graduation
Machines	Car wash, homework machine, computer
Day-to-day activities	Getting ready for school, family dinners, playing games
Media	Films, television programs
School activities	Eating in the lunchroom, recess, walking in the halls
Feelings	Sadness, fear, joy, anger, excitement
Seasons	Fall leaves, snow and ice, spring flowers, summer fun at the beach
Friendship	Name dances, partner dances, moving in unison
Circus	Horses, tightrope walkers, acrobats, clowns, lions
Animals	Bears, dogs, birds, fish, monkeys
Weather	Tornadoes, clouds, wind, rain, lightning, sunny day
Action words	Wiggle, burst, float, punch, press, melt
Sports	Basketball, soccer, tennis, swimming, football
Environments	Mountains, water forms, desert, rainforest
Social issues	Rejection, acceptance, fighting, discrimination
Historical events	Baseball World Series, inauguration of a governor, war
Life experiences	Losing a tooth, welcoming a new student into the class
Current events	Front pages of the newspaper, sports news, popular culture news
Dance maps	Designing pathways and movements
Other subjects	Science, social studies, math, language arts, music, visual art, theater

for first-grade students focused on pathways would begin with identifying the objective: Students will learn to identify different types of pathways and be able to create movements that travel on pathways. Next, the type of assessment is determined. A teacher observation checklist can be used to note how students move on different pathways, or students may draw pathways presented by the teacher or pathways they created. Additionally, students can write the names of the movements or draw pictures of themselves moving on the pathway. Another assessment strategy asks children to verbally describe or demonstrate their pathway to the teacher or their classmates.

The next step in unit design is to delineate how the content will be presented. How many sessions are needed or how many sessions are available? Next, an outline or a detailed description for each session is developed. Remember to include sufficient time for children to fully engage in the process of creating, learning, performing, or responding to the dance content. Student performances and assessment of their work can occur at any point in the unit; however, these activities are sometimes used as a closure activity. Before the unit starts, collect or order music, props, equipment, costumes, or other needed materials. At the beginning of the unit, communicate your expectations to the students, and be clear about what they will be learning. Your planning should reflect a thoughtful sequence of learning experiences that facilitates meaningful and successful student learning.

Finally, after you have presented a dance unit, take time to reflect on the teaching experience. Reflective teaching (Brookfield 1995) is a critical analysis of student responses, the framework of the unit, and what the teaching experience was like for the teacher. What parts were most frustrating, satisfying, unexpected, or challenging? The insights gained from reflection will help to refine your teaching practice and offer you an opportunity to reflect on your own attitudes, beliefs, assumptions, behaviors, and perceptions. Ongoing self-observation and self-evaluation helps you to make changes and deepen the rationale for content selection, design, and teaching techniques.

Planning the Dance Lessons

Once the content, instructional objectives, and assessment of the dance unit have been identified, the lessons and tasks that will occur in each dance lesson can be designed. A similar planning process is appropriate for teaching creative dance, social dance, or cultural dances. Each dance lesson includes four main sections: Introduction, Development, Culminating Dance, and Closure Activity. These sections are discussed next. The dance lesson also emphasizes one or more specific objectives that relate to the broader objectives of the unit. Generally, lessons may be completed comfortably in one session; however, you should not feel the need to complete it based on a specific time period. If appropriate, use a second session, or even a third, to complete the lesson, giving students a chance to fully explore the concept.

Introduction

The introduction serves as a transitional period for children between the activities they have just experienced, perhaps a math lesson or lunch, and the dance experience. The teacher's enthusiasm is critical to motivating students and piquing their interest. Graham (2001) offers several approaches to these first moments of class. One option is to provide an instant activity where students, once in the room, are immediately engaged in practicing skills, viewing instructions, or obtaining materials to be used in the lesson. This teaching technique allows time for a transition as well as time for children to talk informally with the teacher. Another way to begin a lesson is with a brief verbal introduction, which Graham refers to as "set induction." He explains, "Set induction has the advantage of helping [children] to understand why they will be doing certain activities or tasks during a lesson" (p. 57). After you tell students what they will be doing, the class can complete a warm-up. Set induction creates an atmosphere that motivates and prepares children to participate fully.

In the introduction, the teacher tells the students what they are going to learn, why the topic or theme was chosen, and how it relates to them. One way to begin is by asking the students what they know about the topic or theme. As a result, the teacher gains insights into the students' understanding and experience regarding the topic or theme. Another part of the introduction can include a review of skills and concepts taught in a previous lesson or a question about what students remember. In this way, students develop an understanding about how lessons are related to one another as part of a planned sequence.

The introduction for teaching a folk or ethnic dance should include background information on the origin of the dance and its relationship to the culture or ethnic group. The information presented can be supported with a video, pictures, maps, costumes, artifacts, books, newspapers, music, artwork, crafts, food, the language, religion, or other materials that provide a context for the dance. Connect the values, traditions, lifestyle, environment, and history of the culture to the movements, music, and formations of the dance. Avoid stereotyping a culture or making biased or pejorative comments, and present accurate information based on reliable resources.

The beginning of a social dance lesson can emphasize concepts of respect, cooperation, leadership, kindness, or being helpful to others. Children can talk about their understanding of what these words mean to them and how they can demonstrate these concepts through dance. This type of introduction sets the expectation for the learning objective and places the enjoyment of socializing through dance in a broader context. When possible, include historical information about the social dances and discuss the types of social gatherings where they occur.

A creative dance lesson can be introduced to children in many ways. The teacher can begin with a story, a photo, a prop, or perhaps a news event. Children are always curious when they come to class and usually ask, "What are we going to do today?" The first response sets the tone for the day. Be enthusiastic. For example, to introduce the spaghetti dance (see chapter 7), the teacher might say, "Today we are going to dance about straight and curved shapes. I chose these two shapes because they are everywhere in our world. Let's begin to find these shapes by looking at our clothes." As the students are looking at their clothes and pointing to shapes, the teacher can quickly assess if they can identify shapes. A prop can be added or straight and curved shapes drawn on the chalkboard to further illustrate the shapes.

After the verbal introduction, a body warm-up follows. The content of the warm-up is directly related to the type of movements presented in the dance experience. It is also a physical introduction to the movements used in the experience and prepares the body for safe and active participation. The warm-up is not a separate isolated activity from the rest of the tasks in the learning experience; rather, it is the first moving task in the sequence of tasks to be presented. The movements in the warm-up are similar to the movements used in the development section and the culminating dance. If the students will be running, leaping, twisting, and bending during the learning experience, the warm-up should include movements that prepare the body for those actions. Movements in the warm-up should be whole-body actions that include locomotor and nonlocomotor movements.

A cultural dance warm-up may include moving to the music used in the dance or performing specific movements from the dance. Students can move body parts in isolation such as moving the head from side to side, the shoulders up and down, and the hips in a circle; bouncing through the knees lightly; reaching the arms up and out to the side; stepping in place with the feet; and twisting the torso from side to side. Social dance warm-ups can follow a similar format to that of the cultural dance. To emphasize the social aspect, students can do the warm-ups in partners or small groups and then change to another warm-up group. A creative dance warm-up can include a short aerobic section; isolated body part movements; and bending, stretching, and twisting movements. If the lesson is on pathways, the teacher can incorporate the words and types of pathways into the warm-up. In the spaghetti dance (see chapter 7), for example, the warm-up may include instructions related to shape making such as, "Walk around the room and look for straight and curved shapes. Where can you find them? Look high and low. When you find a shape, imitate the shape with your body. Find another shape and another." Here, the students are using walking as the whole-body movement and making shapes with their body. To summarize, through the introduction, the topic is presented, understanding is assessed, relevancy is established, and the students are prepared physically to participate.

Development

During the development section, students experience new ways to move, whether through patterned movements from an ethnic or social dance or a series of movements they have created. The teacher presents a sequence of tasks that leads the students to learn and create movements relevant to the objectives of the lesson. Students explore, improvise, and create movements that express and communicate ideas, thoughts, and feelings. If the focus of the lesson is on an element of dance such as contrasting fast and slow tempos, students can explore a variety of movements using the different tempos. The tasks can be specific, for example, "Find a way to walk eight steps forward using a fast tempo, then walk eight steps backward as slowly as you can," or more open-ended, for example, "How can you change levels, alternating between a fast and a slow tempo?" This task may evolve into a dance or a selected sequence of movements that represent an idea or a feeling. When the lesson focuses on a topic or theme, such as a circus, a sport, a poem, or celebrating a birthday, the students explore movements that interpret the actions, events, or feelings relevant to the topic or theme. Here, the elements of dance are applied as tools to develop the type and quality of movements. For example, in a dance about animals in the zoo, each child can choose an animal. The teacher would ask the following questions related to the elements of dance (EOD) to guide students as they create their movements (see figure 2.1):

⊚ What kind of different movements does your animal make? Does the animal walk, run, jump, gallop, swing, twist, stretch, slither, wiggle, shake, or kick? (EOD: the body)

⊚ How does your animal move its arms, head, shoulders, back, legs, and feet? (EOD: the body)

⊚ What size steps would the animal take? Are its steps big or small? (EOD: space, range)

⊚ In what different directions can your animal move? Can it move forward, backward, and sideward? (EOD: space, direction)

⊚ Can you find a partner and mirror his or her animal movements and then switch roles? (EOD: relationships)

⊚ Does your animal move slow or fast? Can your animal begin moving slowly and increase its speed? (EOD: time, tempo)

⊚ Is your animal very tall, or is it very small and close to the ground? Does it change levels? (EOD: space, level)

⊚ Can you create three still shapes that show different actions your animal does? (EOD: body shape)

⊚ Are your animal's movements light or strong? (EOD: force)

⊚ Does your animal run around wildly, or does it move with a lot of control? (EOD: flow)

⊚ How does your animal use small and big movements? (EOD: space, range)

⊚ Will your animal move smoothly and slowly or sharply and quickly? (EOD: force and time)

⊚ What kind of pathways does your animal use—straight, curved, or zigzag? (EOD: space, pathway)

By exploring the topic through the elements of dance, students will broaden their movement vocabulary. The next step would involve creating a dance about animals. The dance may follow a short story designed by the teacher, or the students may suggest an idea for the animal dance. The students would then choose movements they have explored in the dance. For example, in this teacher-designed dance, the animals begin by sleeping in a shape low to the floor; then they slowly wake up and move in general space to meet other animals. They play follow-the-leader with a partner, and, finally, return to where they started and fall asleep again. Although the students follow the sequence of the teacher's story, they are choosing the type and quality of the movements their animal makes.

The development section is an important component of the learning and creative process and relates directly to the culminating dance or final product and objective of the unit or lesson. This section is the journey children take as they create, learn, practice, and refine new movements. Hawkins (1988) tells us that "This core of the learning period should foster new understandings and growth. The content may be new material or new developments of previous experiences. Activity should be designed with a clear relationship to the focus of the lesson" (p. 128). Knowing the desired result, whether it is a specific line dance, a creative dance about force, or the words of a poem expressed through a dance, is a key element to planning meaningful tasks. In some creative dance experiences, the exact form and sequence of the culminating dance may be unknown until after the children explore and improvise movements; however, a general framework or outline of the final outcome should be planned. Here, Wiggins' (1998) "backward design" concept of unit planning described earlier can also be applied to each lesson.

The sequence of tasks in the development section is presented in what Mosston (1972) refers to as "guided discovery." The tasks are designed and sequenced to prepare and lead the students to create and learn movements that are evident in the culminating dance. One approach to developing an appropriate sequence of tasks is to analyze how the elements of dance are used in the culminating dance. The following questions guide the analysis of the culminating dance:

- What movements of the whole body and its parts are used in the dance?
- How are levels, pathways, range, and direction used?
- What is the speed and rhythm? Are there accents in the movements? Will the movements accelerate or decelerate? Is there a pause in the movements? Will everyone be

moving on the same beat? Is there a contrast in speed? Do the rhythms change?

- What type of force is used? When are the movements strong or light? Do they change force?
- Is the flow of the movements free or bound? Does the flow change?
- How will the students be organized—as individuals, partners, or small groups? Will they follow each other, connect, support, or mirror? What formations will they use? Will the relationships and formations change during the dance?

Chapter 7 includes a description of the culminating dance for the spaghetti dance lesson, which focuses on making straight and curved shapes and movements with the body. From reading the description, the teacher can anticipate the sequence of movements, changes in quality, and the formations used in the dance. During the development section, the presentation of the tasks uses the guided discovery strategy to lead students to experience and create the types of movements that are included in the culminating dance. In the culminating spaghetti dance, children begin in a straight shape and travel on a straight pathway to a pot of water. During the development section, children explore making straight shapes with their bodies and find different ways to travel on a straight pathway. Through the exploration process, the teacher guides the children to specifically experience movements that are used in the culminating spaghetti dance.

A similar analysis for task construction can be applied to a folk, ethnic, or social dance, where the teacher has prepared the culminating dance. The following example demonstrates the first two tasks presented while teaching the Russian troika dance during the development section of the lesson.

- Task One: "Each person will take 4 running steps forward and stop. Now try it again, beginning on the right foot, and take the 4 running steps moving diagonally to the right." This task teaches the first four steps of the culminating dance. The elements of movement to be emphasized are running, direction, and moving in a specific rhythm and tempo.

◈ Task Two: "I will organize you into groups of three. Join hands and practice the 4 steps diagonally right, then left, and then take 8 steps forward." In this task, the students are learning to move in unison connected by their hands. These 16 steps make up the first section of the culminating dance of the troika. The elements of dance highlighted are running, a connected relationship, tempo, rhythm, and direction.

Each task prepares the students for the way they will move in the culminating dance and emphasizes one or more elements of dance.

Culminating Dance

The culminating dance brings together the tasks experienced in the development section. In this part of the learning experience, structure is given to the movements that were created and learned. Students select, organize, and perform movements either individually, in small groups, or as one large group. The dances may follow a choreographic structure such as canon, narrative, ABA, AB, collage, rondo, and theme and variation (Blom and Chaplin 1986). Keep in mind that it may be appropriate for young children to participate in large-group culminating dances until they are ready to work more independently to create their own dances. Large-group dances are also appropriate for older students with little dance experience, as they often feel more comfortable if everyone is doing the same dance at the same time. The large-group creative culminating dance is similar to everyone performing a folk, ethnic, or social dance as a group.

Culminating dances usually have a recognizable beginning, middle, and end. The dance may be a narrative form, telling a story, or express a range of feelings. It may be a sequence of movements that show how a round shape can change size, move at different tempos, or travel in the different pathways. The dance can begin and end in a formation such as a circle, a line, or scattered around the perimeter of the space. In the middle section, students may maintain a formation or change to one or more different formations. In addition to formation changes, the rhythm, movements, force, flow, and relationships of the dancers can change. Another approach for creating the culminating dance may be a spontaneous performance of movements experienced during the development section. For some young children, the act of spontaneously creating dance movements is their dance. They do not make a definitive distinction between the process of creating and the final dance (Cone 2002). In a spontaneous culminating dance, there is no set choreographic structure; instead, the dance is more organic in nature, where the dance is created moment to moment while the children are dancing. The dance may end when the children decide they are tired, or they may keep dancing until the teacher tells them the class session is over.

As the teacher, you may want to create your own new culminating dance for a creative dance unit instead of using a previously created dance like the spaghetti dance. In this situation, you would outline your vision of the dance through a written description or through drawings and notes. You may envision a dance about fall leaves and develop a dance that expresses the action and qualities of the leaves as they fall from the tree and blow around the field. Then, analyze the anticipated movements, changes of quality, and use of space, and plan a series of tasks for the development section that will guide students toward this culminating dance.

Consider the following questions when developing your own culminating dance:

◈ What do you want students to learn as a result of learning this dance?

◈ What is the image, theme, story, piece of literature, idea, or feeling that will be expressed in the dance?

◈ What is the sequence of movements in the culminating dance?

◈ What specific elements of dance can be emphasized to support the movements of the dance?

◈ What formations will be used? Lines? Circles? Scattered?

◈ How will the dance begin?

⊚ Where and how will the students move in the middle of the dance?

⊚ How will the dance end?

To create the spaghetti dance, we began with the idea that we wanted students to learn how to make straight and curved shapes with their bodies and to travel on straight and curved pathways. Making different shapes and finding different ways to travel would be suitable for exploring the concept; however, we believed children would understand the concept better if we created a story about what happened to a box of spaghetti. We knew the image of spaghetti was familiar to the students, and they would find humor and interest in dancing the imagined event of the spaghetti as it cooks. The culminating dance expresses the events of the story. In this dance, the students travel as straight pieces of spaghetti on a straight pathway from an imaginary box to a pot of water and then jump in. They change from straight to curved shapes as they cook and move around in the pot among the other pieces of spaghetti. A giant bubble appears and pushes the spaghetti out of the pot. The spaghetti runs and leaps in a curved shape as it flies around the kitchen and becomes stuck in a curved shape on the wall. Finally, the curvy cooked spaghetti slowly moves off the wall, walks in a curved pathway, steps onto the dinner plate, and ends lying down on the plate in a curved shape. The students experience a change of levels while cooking, flying around the kitchen, and falling onto the dinner plate; a change of tempo; a change of shape; and a change in relationship, moving close together and far apart. The entire class dances the sequence at the same time yet use their own unique ideas about how to express straight and curved shapes and pathways.

Closure Activity

A closure activity is appropriate at the end of each lesson as well as the end of the unit (Graham 2001). The activity may be a performance of culminating dances, a review of all the dances learned during the unit, a written response or drawing of the experience, or a discussion focused on the learning experience. This activity brings a conclusion to the lesson or unit and is one way the teacher can assess students' learning and check for understanding. Children should have a moment to reflect and recall what they experienced during the lesson or unit and think about what knowledge and skills they acquired. The nature of the ending can vary, but provide time for a meaningful closure. Remember that how you end is as important as how you begin (Joyce 1973).

Interdisciplinary Connections

Many different terms are used to describe an integrated learning experience, such as *interdisciplinary, connected, correlated, cross-curricular,* or *multidisciplinary.* These terms imply that two or more subject areas are linked together to create a learning experience that fosters enhanced learning in each subject (Cone, Werner, Cone, and Woods 1998). Integrated learning acknowledges the integrity and uniqueness of each subject area yet recognizes the interrelationships of one subject to another. Students need to have discipline-specific learning experiences as well as learning experiences that demonstrate the relationship among the disciplines (Jacobs 1989). Jacobs states, "The curriculum becomes more relevant when there are connections between subjects rather than strict isolation" (1989, p. 5). Learning experiences are less fragmented and foster a range of perspectives. Knowledge and skills in one subject area are viewed as applicable to learning in another subject area and promoting creative and divergent thinking.

Dance integrates easily with other content areas. It offers children who are kinesthetic learners (Gardner 1983) the opportunity to use movement as a means to understand and communicate their life experiences using their own unique perspectives. For all children, the body and its movements are a means to attaining and expressing knowledge and skills. The body, Lazaroff (2001) notes, can be referred to as a "potential curricular resource that can enrich and amplify learning in a variety of subjects" (p. 27). Educators who believe that dance is an essential mode of learning not only address the goals of a dance education program but also provide students with the knowledge and skills applicable to all aspects of their lives.

Although dance has a discrete body of knowledge, the topics children dance about are frequently related to other subject areas. In a dance about spring flowers, for example, information about how flowers grow is essential when creating a dance that interprets the growing process. Cultural dances represent aspects of how people live, what they value, their traditions, history, and beliefs. These are also concepts taught in the social studies curriculum. Dance is embedded in many cultures for a variety of reasons, and thus integrating dance and social studies becomes a viable teaching strategy for each discipline. In many classrooms, the teacher selects a common theme such as community, change, patterns, conflict and resolution, or

respect. The theme is explored through different subject areas, creating learning from multiple perspectives. In this thematic approach, dance plays a role in adding a kinesthetic, creative, and aesthetic dimension to learning. Children can express their understanding of a particular theme through learning or creating dances that represent different aspects of the theme (see figure 3.2).

Many of the learning experiences in chapters 7 and 8 are applicable for integration. Suggestions for interdisciplinary connections are included at the end of each learning experience. For additional ideas about integrating dance with other subject areas, we encourage you to review the work of Benzwie (1987), Cone (2000), Cone et al. (1998), Donnelly (2002), Gilbert (1977), Kane (1998), Rovegno (2003), and Stinson (1988). These educators offer many wonderful and practical ideas for integration in their books and

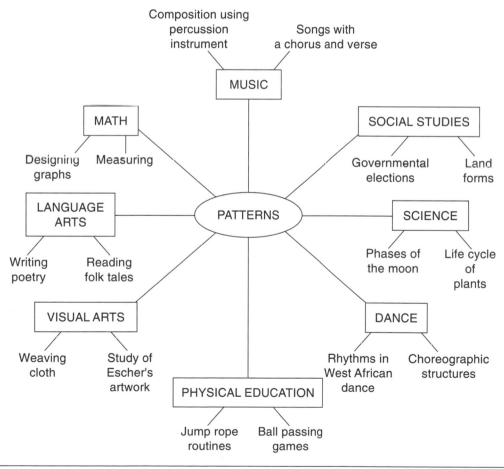

Figure 3.2 Children learn about patterns in different subject areas.

articles. Here are some other suggested strategies that can lead to developing opportunities for interdisciplinary connections:

- Visit the classrooms of your students to see what they are learning with other teachers.
- Talk with the classroom teacher, school librarian, music and art specialist, and find a way to connect what you are teaching in dance with what they are teaching in their classrooms.
- Ask teachers to place a note in your mailbox about upcoming units of study.
- Invite teachers into your class to see your program in action.
- Attend grade-level meetings, or set up a monthly meeting to share ideas.
- Review curriculum guides for information about the content of different subject areas. This information is helpful when planning to integrate concepts and skills from another subject with dance.

The process of integrating content from different subject areas requires an examination of the discrete skills and concepts of each subject area and, specifically, the content you are interested in for an interdisciplinary learning experience.

We suggest considering three models of interdisciplinary teaching that function on a continuum from simple to complex. These models are connected, shared, and partnership (Cone et al. 1998). The models are designed to clarify your intent and objectives and make the learning experience meaningful to the students as well as the teacher (see figure 3.3). In the connected model, the skills, topics, and concepts of the dance curriculum are the primary focus of the learning experience, and the content from another subject area is used to enhance, extend, or supplement the learning experience. For example, you are teaching European folk dances, and you show the students a map to indicate where the countries are located and share pictures of people in traditional dress performing the dance as a means to connect to social studies. The shared model integrates

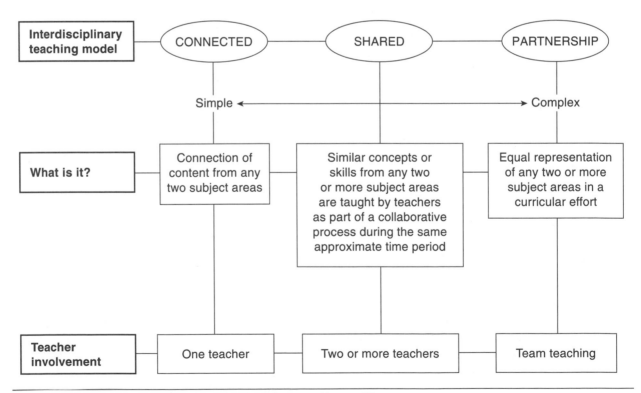

Figure 3.3 A comparison of three selected interdisciplinary teaching models.

Adapted, by permission, from T.P. Cone, P. Werner, S.L. Cone, and A.M. Woods, 1998, *Interdisciplinary teaching through physical education* (Champaign, IL: Human Kinetics), 11.

two or more subjects through presenting similar skills, topics, or concepts that are part of the content of the integrated subjects. In this model, the dance or physical education teacher would coordinate with other subject area teachers to look for common areas that can be taught at the same time. A dance lesson might be shared with a math lesson on fractions. In dance, the students are learning about quarter, half, three-quarter, and full turns, and in the math class children are introduced to the concept of fractions. The third model, partnership, is an equal representation of two or more subject areas taught simultaneously. The line between the subject areas is completely blurred and the learning activities fuse content seamlessly. For example, the dance, visual arts, and music teachers collaborate to teach a partnership unit focused on hip-hop culture. All three teachers teach the unit as a united team. They use their expertise in their respective subject areas to create common objectives and assessments. During the experience, students may learn and create music, dance, and visual arts and discuss other cultural artifacts associated with the topic. This model requires considerable planning and a willingness to view content from a new and different perspective.

As educators, we seek to make connections between what children experience in their lives and the content of dance. Teaching from an interdisciplinary perspective offers an opportunity to deliver knowledge and skills holistically to help children transfer what they learn in one subject area to another. Interdisciplinary learning experiences recognize and promote multiple ways of knowing a concept or skill and enlarge our view about what we can experience in our world. Eisner (1998) believes that what students learn is shaped by the experiences presented to them in their education. Teachers are responsible for providing learning experiences that challenge conventional methods of learning and to embark on a journey with their students to discover and explore the world through a myriad of paths.

Summary

A successful dance learning experience is the result of planning an appropriate sequence of tasks that leads students to learn how movements can express and communicate an idea, a tradition, or a feeling. The teacher will choose an idea for the learning experience that is relevant to the students, has meaning in their lives, and at the same time emphasizes the elements of dance as the foundation of dance.

Each learning experience can make a significant difference in the way children view dance and its importance to them in their world. The learning experience must be well crafted to develop an idea that takes students through a logical and well-planned sequence. This process begins with a verbal and physical introduction to the idea; provides time to explore, learn, or create movements related to the idea; and ends with composing or performing a completed dance. The culminating dance belongs to the students as they become fully engaged and find personal meaning in the movements.

Dance should play a vital role in the school's curriculum. It can be taught as a single learning experience that occurs frequently throughout the school year or as several units that focus on a particular theme. Both creative dance and dances created by others need to be included in the dance program each year at the primary and intermediate levels. Providing students with the opportunity to create, learn, observe, perform, and respond to dances offers them a comprehensive program that includes all dimensions of dance as an art and movement form.

Questions for Reflection

๑ Where do you obtain your ideas for a dance unit of study? Are they prescribed in the curriculum, or do you design your own units within a framework of school objectives?

๑ What parts of a unit are easy to plan? Why? What challenges do you encounter when planning a dance unit? How do you resolve the challenge?

๑ How would you prioritize what content in dance you will teach for a yearlong plan?

๑ The components of a lesson described in this chapter are one way to organize and develop the content. What ideas can you add to the lesson design?

๑ What do you see as the significance of teaching an interdisciplinary unit that integrates dance with another subject area?

chapter 4

Creating a Dance Education Setting

Teaching would be much easier if we could teach in what we consider an ideal environment. Then, our planning and implementation would easily fall into place. The fact is that your teaching situation most likely does not have everything you need and you adapt your ideas to make student learning meaningful, safe, and effective. We all share some similarities . . . and some definite differences! These differences include class size, frequency, and length of the class period; the facilities; equipment and materials; the community; and a broad range of ages, abilities, and special needs within the same class of children (Newnam 2002). In 1995, the National Dance Association, in collaboration with the Consortium of National Arts Education Associations, published the *Opportunity-to-Learn Standards for Dance Education* (National Dance Association 1995). These standards describe the physical and educational conditions necessary to enable students to learn and achieve in dance. Topical areas addressed in the standards include curriculum, scheduling, materials, equipment, facilities, and staffing. As guidelines for developing a dance program, the Opportunity-to-Learn standards present criteria to provide an environment that facilitates effective teaching and learning. This chapter suggests strategies for planning and delivering dance content in various teaching situations to best meet the needs of the children and heighten their enjoyment of learning.

Class Size

Although it is recommended that "physical education or dance classes contain the same number of children as the classrooms (e.g., 25 children per class)" (Council on Physical Education for Children 1992), some schools and districts schedule two or three classes at the same time. This means the physical education or dance teacher may teach 60 or more children during one session. Although this makes teaching a challenge, teachers can find ways to deliver the content to provide children with positive learning experiences. For example, the use of stations or learning centers is an efficient way to organize large groups of children (Graham 2001). Each station can contain written directions, pictures, or diagrams about how to perform a specific movement of a line dance or traditional cultural dance. After visiting each station, the students can put all the steps together in the correct sequence. Another set of stations can focus on tasks that explore a different element of dance. A station about the element of time might include the following tasks: Can you find a way to walk in a circle as fast as you can?" "How about walking in a circle as slow as you can?" or "Begin walking in the circle slowly and accelerate to running and then decelerate to walking."

Safety is an important consideration when many children are moving at one time. The children can keep themselves safe from bumping into other children or objects in the space by being aware of their personal space (the space immediately surrounding their bodies, see chapter 2). This concept needs to be taught and reinforced in each dance lesson. Another way to organize a large class is to place the children into lines. Keep the number of children in the line to a minimum to reduce waiting time and increase activity. Creating a balance between allowing for movement that is fully expressive and ensuring that children can move without injury requires careful planning and a willingness to make the appropriate modifications to the lesson.

Teaching a large group will be more effective when the teacher's voice is amplified so the students can hear the directions. Also, a microphone will be helpful for children to use for asking and answering questions. In this way, the entire class can hear without the teacher's needing to repeat the comments. To list important information needed for the lesson, consider using posters, a chalkboard, an overhead projector, a slide projector, or a liquid crystal display (LCD) projector. These tools will help the children see the information, and they will assist the teacher in delivering directions and valuable knowledge to the class.

Equipment and Teaching Materials

The addition of equipment and materials such as music, props, and costumes enriches the dance learning experience. These items can be used as the stimulus for creating dances or as the accompaniment to a dance. Music and dance are frequently partnered in a learning experience. The voice, percussion instruments, and recorded music support the rhythm of the movement and set an environment for dancing. Props help illustrate the meaning of the movement, exaggerate the movement, and create a visual component that complements the dance. Most props are light, handheld objects that the student manipulates while moving through space. Sometimes larger objects are used for the student to dance around, over, or under; these larger objects help establish an environment for dancing. Costumes are also a wonderful addition to a dance. Children enjoy dressing up as a character, an animal, a tree, a monster, or any other idea from their imaginations. Every dance program should have access to a variety of teaching materials. Videotapes, CDs, books, photos, and posters can be the catalysts for new dance ideas, present critical information, and support the dance concepts that are emphasized in the learning experience.

Music

Most dance experiences use music to accompany the movement, whether it's the voice, percussion instruments, or live or recorded music. Music can stimulate ideas for dance, support the tempo and rhythm, provide a mood or atmosphere, or provide structure to a dance. The voice is one instrument that we always have with us. It can generate sounds and words that express the different qualities of a movement. Even the way the voice is used when giving directions can make a difference in how students respond. To illustrate this point, think of how these action words can be expressed differently to elicit a specific way to move. You can say "splat" in a loud, fast, and sharp voice; "press" in a loud and sustained voice; and "fall" in a voice that begins at a high pitch and ends at a low pitch.

Students' voices can also be used to sing songs as accompaniment for dances. Consider using a familiar song, such as "Row, Row, Row Your Boat," as the accompaniment for a dance based on a round or canon. Students can create movements for each section of the song and then, in small groups, sing and perform the movements to create a dance round. Another possibility is to make up a song that describes a movement sequence. For example, in a dance about planting a garden, the teacher and students sing, "Seed, seed, cover up with dirt, and jump, jump." On the words, "seed, seed," the children pretend to place a seed in the ground. Next, on each syllable of the phrase "cover up with dirt," the students use their feet to stamp quickly while pretending to bury the seeds. A big jump on each word "jump" completes the phrase. This phrase is repeated several times with the students singing and moving simultaneously. You can also vocalize rhythms by making a variety of different sounds with the voice. In a dance about a machine, for example, students can create sounds with their body or voice to accompany the machine movements. Words, poems, and reading a story out loud can all involve the voice as accompaniment.

Develop a collection of percussion instruments to provide an available resource to accompany dance. Most percussion instruments can be carried easily while teaching or dancing. When planning a dance experience, consider what movements could be supported by the strong, percussive beat of a drum; the light, sustained sound of the triangle; or the quick, vibratory sounds of the maracas. Also, consider making instruments to create interesting and unusual sounds (see table 4.1). You don't have to be an accomplished musician to use instruments in dance. Take time to become familiar with the instruments, and explore different ways to play them by hitting, rubbing, or shaking them with your hands. Ask the school's music teacher to help you learn to play a few basic rhythms. Investigate the possibility of borrowing instruments, or look for them in music stores, toy stores, museum shops, yard sales, and school catalogs.

Table 4.1 Percussion Instruments

Traditional instruments	Homemade instruments
Drums, different sizes	Pot lids
Triangle	Spoons
Maracas	Glasses filled with water at different levels
Gong	Garbage cans
Chimes	Cans
Rain stick	Round oatmeal boxes
Bells	Wooden spoons
Sticks	Garbage can lids
Woodblock	Rocks
Guiro	Plastic buckets
Cymbals	Containers filled with beans
Xylophone	Paper bags

Finding the appropriate recorded music for a dance experience is always a challenge. There is such a variety of music that it is hard to know where to begin to look. One option is to purchase music that is prepackaged with ideas for dance lessons. These types of recordings can be a way to begin to develop a personal library of music. Another option is to set some time aside to listen to music and then record selections that could be used for dance. Label the selections with ideas for future use, and then try the music with the students. Include in your collection music that

- has a definite even beat;
- offers different tempos for slow and sustained or fast and percussive movements;
- has different rhythms for skipping, running, or jumping;
- produces various moods, such as feeling peaceful, anxious, or powerful;
- evokes images and feelings (e.g., "sounds like music for strange creatures landing on the earth");
- represents different cultures; and
- denotes a specific time period.

Be sure to include a variety of music that represents a wide range of styles and cultures. Students may prefer music that is popular and familiar to them; however, use the dance experience to present many different types of music to broaden the students' exposure to and knowledge of music. Your list can include classical, jazz, pop, rap, reggae, hip-hop, new age, rock, gospel, opera, a variety of vocal music, movie soundtracks, sounds of nature, children's songs, and traditional and contemporary ethnic music. Different types of dances can be paired with different types of music. African music can be used in a dance about a rainstorm, for example, or ragtime music can be used to accompany a dance about baseball. Traditional folk dances usually require a specific piece of music as accompaniment and can help to make the experience more authentic. The music teacher can be a valuable resource for selecting different types of music and can offer assistance with identifying rhythms and musical structures.

Once you have chosen your music, be sure to become thoroughly familiar with the selection. Play the music in the space where the dance experience will occur to make sure the volume is appropriate and the audio equipment functions properly. Always acknowledge the composer, the name of the musical piece, and the performer when introducing music into the dance session.

Having the proper audio equipment can make a significant difference in the quality of music used in the learning experience. Purchasing state-of-the-art equipment is not always possible; however, a cassette tape or CD player may be available in the school. When you have the opportunity to purchase new equipment, consider the following wish list:

- A tape/CD player with a remote control and speakers that will project into the space. The remote control adds the needed flexibility to position yourself easily for effective teaching.
- A portable microphone and speaker. A wireless lavaliere microphone can allow you to teach in any part of the space and move with the students. You also have the ability to speak over the music to provide directions.
- Blank tape cassettes and CDs for creating music selections.
- Cleaning kits for the cassette tape and CD players to keep the equipment in good shape for effective use.
- Storage cases for tapes and compact discs. Proper storage will eliminate damage.

Props

Dance learning experiences frequently require equipment or handheld props to accompany the dance. Children may manipulate streamers, hoops, elastic strips, balloons, wands, ropes, and pieces of material or scarves as they dance. Or, they may use equipment such as chairs, mats, tires, or tables to move around, over, under, on, or between. Ideally, and when appropriate, each child should have her or his own prop. When there aren't enough of the same prop available for each child, children can share or trade props. For example, in a lesson on making different shapes, one group uses an elastic-stretch rope, the next group uses wands, while another group makes shapes with long pieces of yarn. When choosing equipment or props, consider the child's developmental abilities to handle the equipment or prop safely. Can the child move the prop easily? If the prop falls out of the child's hand, is there a potential for injury? Do children have adequate space in which to move around with the prop?

Props are used to initiate, extend, or accompany movement. Folk and ethnic dance may use scarves, sticks, ropes, flowers, or baskets as part of the movements or to express a character or cultural artifact. In a learning experience focused on creating straight and curved lines, children can lay ropes on the floor in straight and curved lines and then match their body to the rope shape. Streamers or ribbons held in the hand can be imaginary brushes with which to paint letters in the air, and scarves can be flames, leaves, or flower petals (see figure 4.1). Partners and small groups can share a prop and discover different ways to move together. Hoops can be held as an imaginary doorway into outer space or to connect students as rays of the sun. Curtains or long pieces of material are easy for a small group of children to use as a floating cloud, a swirling river, or the wind of a tornado. Most schools have a parachute that can be turned into a giant monster when a group holds one side of the parachute and

runs in the space with the parachute floating in the air. There is no end to the imaginative ways props can be part of a dance experience. When you ask the question "What else could it be?" about any prop, children will enthusiastically offer many new ideas.

You can also use props to illustrate a concept or element of dance. Children often need a concrete object to help them visualize the words and concepts presented in the learning experience. For example, the concept of roundness can be illustrated by showing a ball or a globe, the concept of increasing and decreasing size is best illustrated by inflating and deflating a balloon, or the feeling of strong and light force can become vivid when you wring a towel or float a piece of tissue paper. Using props to create an environment for a dance magically transforms the space and stimulates ideas for creating movements. Imagine a room filled with red and orange streamers scattered on the floor. The children immediately pretend they are dancing on the sun as they run and leap over the streamers. You can also use hoops to move in and out of as if they were different worlds, such as the fast world, shaking world, or frozen-shape world. Ropes tied to volleyball poles can form a web for a spider dance, chairs arranged in lines could depict a dance about traveling on a train or bus, and taped lines on the floor can be used for pathways. An environment created by props encourages students to use their imagination and helps to make an abstract idea real. Here are some additional ideas for creative props:

- Purchase or make pom-poms. Using a paper-towel tube, cover it with contact paper, cut 8-inch strips of plastic, and staple 8 to 10 strips together on one end of the tube.
- Large sheets of plastic cut into different shapes. Plastic tablecloths work well.
- Sheer curtains, sheets, and other pieces of material.
- Stuffed animals or dolls.
- A shiny tree garland.
- Juggling scarves.
- Stretchable plastic bands or pieces of elastic.

Figure 4.1 Children dancing with streamers to express the movements of a flame.

- Long pieces of ribbon.
- Beanbags.
- Deck rings. Streamers can be attached.
- Paper bags.
- Rolls of toilet paper.
- Beach balls.
- Umbrellas.
- Lummi sticks (twelve-inch wood sticks) and wands.

Costumes

Children, especially young children, welcome the opportunity to create and wear costumes while dancing. Costumes can be as simple as a scarf tied around a wrist, a piece of material draped over a shoulder, or streamers taped to a shirt. Adding a costume to a dance can help define a character, a mood, a time period, a culture, or an animal. Aluminum foil can be wrapped around the arms or molded into a headpiece as a costume in a dance about lightning bolts. Monster costumes can be made of large plastic garbage bags with a hole cut out of the bottom for the head and the sides cut into long strips. When designing costumes, consider ease of movement and safety. Make sure the costume is fastened securely and that headpieces allow the child to see and breathe.

Facilities

Although some teachers have adequate indoor and outdoor space, others are less fortunate. In fact, some teachers have no indoor space whatsoever. In some schools, dance may be taught in the children's classroom, outside on the blacktop, in the lunchroom, on a stage, in the foyer of the school, or on an outside grassy area. Following are some ideas and suggestions for how the content in this book can be adapted for limited indoor or outdoor space.

Dance learning experiences can be taught successfully both outdoors and indoors. Teaching dance outdoors can be inspiring, especially when using the outdoor environment as a theme for the learning experience (see figure 4.2). The challenge is to find a way to accompany the dance with music. We suggest using a battery-operated tape/CD player or running a long extension cord. Percussion instruments work well outdoors because they are portable and can be handheld; however, some of the sounds may not carry well in a large open space. Test your voice and musical accompaniment in the outdoor space before you begin to teach to see what adjustments may be needed. To keep students focused and safe in an outdoor area, you need to set spatial boundaries for the dance. We find that cones or ropes laid on the ground are useful as markers to define the space. Be

Figure 4.2 After observing the wind blowing the leaves, children create strong, stretched movements to express the feeling of being blown around by the wind.

sure the outdoor space is free from objects that children can slip on such as loose gravel, glass, or oily spots.

Most gymnasiums are well suited for indoor dance. However, a classroom or hallway is sometimes the assigned space for the dance session. These situations are not ideal. Define the boundaries of the space clearly, and check for objects that may cause injury. Not all floor surfaces are suitable for dancing, and adaptations will be necessary. Excessive jumping on concrete, turning on carpet, or moving on a waxed tile floor can lead to injury for you and the students. You are always responsible for the safe participation of your students. Be aware of the limitations of the environment, and plan lessons that are meaningful, appropriate for the available space, and safe for actively moving children.

Whether teaching inside or outside, use a wall or portable easel to display dance concepts, photos, student work, articles, or drawings. An available chalkboard in the space will allow you to display the lesson plan, list vocabulary words, or draw pathways and diagrams of formations. Storage space is essential for audio and video equipment, instruments, props, and other instructional materials. Also, students learn best when the facilities have good lighting, ventilation, and access to drinking fountains and bathrooms.

Class Frequency and Length

Schools differ in the number of days per week that the children attend physical education or dance classes and the length of those classes. As one might expect, children who have physical education or dance every day for 30 minutes will learn more content and enjoy more of the physical benefits of regular exercise than will children with less contact time. Realistically, the goals that can be achieved in the dance program are determined by the total amount of time children participate in dance during the school year. When planning, keep in mind school vacations, class trips, assembly programs, and special events that affect the regular school schedule. One approach is to obtain an annual school schedule and note how many sessions are available and the time frame for each marking period. Then plan units that fit into the available time.

Dance, as part of the physical education curriculum, can be presented in several units of concentrated experiences or in single-class sessions several times throughout the school year. Sometimes, a single learning experience can be completed in a 30-minute session; and, at other times, it may be necessary to continue in additional sessions. Students may need more time to learn and practice a dance or to complete the process of creating a dance. When a learning experience is continued over several sessions, students will need time to review what happened in the previous session. This connection between the sessions is important for a meaningful experience to occur. Consider that a quality experience may be more important than staying on a set schedule. Having children feel a sense of accomplishment in the learning experience will lead to increased understanding of the value of the dance experience. This understanding builds positive attitudes toward dance in the physical education and dance curriculums.

Community Characteristics

The characteristics of the community in which you teach are important elements to consider when planning and delivering a dance program. A community includes not only the city or town but also the school community. Every town, city, and regional area has its own culture, traditions, history, and ways in which the community functions. The values and beliefs of a community have a direct impact on the children who grow up in the community. As a teacher, you should know the community in which you teach. Learn about how and what the community celebrates, where your students live, what types of recreational activities are available, what religious institutions are located in the community, and what languages are spoken. Become familiar with what it is like to live in the area. Teachers

• Be sure this info. is presented at the time the contract is made.

must be sensitive to the communities in which they are teaching, especially if the customs and traditions of a community are not part of the teacher's background. Sensitivity implies understanding the socioeconomic and ethnic composition of the community as well as what the community values in education. Each community has a vision for its children, and this vision is reflected in the schools' goals. You need to be aware of these goals and ensure that your dance program is in alignment.

As a means of expression and communication, dance helps students understand the unique composition of their community and how it relates to other communities around the world. A specific ethnic population in the community may request that students have the opportunity to learn dances from their ethnic heritage (see figure 4.3). Reach out to the community as a resource if you are not sure how to teach these dances. Parents are usually willing to share their ethnic customs and dances with the class. Religious values of the community are another consideration. Dancing and specific topics for dance that focus on celebration are not part of every religion. You may need to eliminate or change certain dances so children do not feel they must compromise their own beliefs in class. Look to parents and other community members as a resource for cultural and social information that will help you understand what is appropriate and make your dance experiences meaningful to the students.

Figure 4.3 Folk dances can offer students the opportunity to learn about their own or others' ethnic heritage.

School Policies

Every school has policies and procedures for dealing with a variety of situations. This means the school has planned how to address unexpected situations or has carefully anticipated what emergencies could occur and planned accordingly. As a responsible teacher, you must know the school policies and protocols and be prepared to act when necessary. This information may be available in a school handbook or provided by the administration. All schools have requirements to practice fire drills, school lockdowns, and evacuations. Review the procedures and discuss with your students the appropriate behaviors needed to comply with an emergency event.

Be aware, in addition, of what to do if a child is injured in your class. The initial response to an injury requires a careful but speedy assessment followed by safe and appropriate action to help the child. Seeking the advice of the school nurse about injury policies before someone gets hurt is essential. The nurse should also inform you about children with life-threatening allergies or other medical conditions you need to know to ensure a safe learning environment. (See chapter 5, Helping All Children Learn, for ideas on adapting learning experiences for children with disabilities.)

Program Advocacy

You may already be teaching in a school where dance is considered an integral part of the curriculum, or you may be asked to initiate a dance program. Both situations call on you to use your knowledge about dance to communicate the benefits of offering a dance component to the physical education or arts education curriculum. Your efforts to maintain or start a dance program require you to become an advocate for dance. Serving as an advocate means that you must become the voice of support for dance in the school curriculum.

Advocacy is a planned approach to making your views count in the decision-making process. It is communication with a purpose (Alperstein and Weyl 1992). You must always be ready to clearly and concisely express the importance of dance in a child's education. Dance can be a vulnerable area of the curriculum because in many schools it is not considered part of the core curriculum and is often subject to budget cuts; thus, opportunities for children to participate in dance experiences are often minimal. Here are some tips to help you in your advocacy role. To be an effective advocate you need to be

- well-informed about the benefits of dance for children;
- willing to solve problems and collaborate with others;
- open to listening to other perspectives;
- prepared when speaking to an individual or a group;
- sincere, optimistic, and passionate about your goals; and
- ready to seize opportunities to discuss dance with your colleagues, school administrators, and parents.

Advocacy in dance can be proactive or reactive. In the proactive situation, advocacy efforts are ongoing throughout the school year. Listed next are ideas for ongoing advocacy efforts:

- Submit an article, written by you or your students, about the dance program to the school newspaper or the local newspaper.
- Contact a newspaper photographer or reporter to cover a dance class or performance featuring your students.
- Collaborate with another teacher in the school to integrate dance with a different subject area.
- Publicize dance events in the weekly or monthly school calendar.
- Invite parents or your administrator to observe a dance class.
- Prepare a fact sheet about the dance program for distribution to parents on "Back to School" night.
- Present an in-service workshop on dance education to faculty members in your school or district.

- Send letters of invitation, with complementary tickets, to board of education members, school administrators, and community leaders for the school's dance performances.
- Organize a special event such as a "family dance night" to promote dance as a social activity.
- Invite community members or parents with expertise in a specific dance form to share their knowledge and skills with your students.
- Attend a conference, workshop, or convention on dance education to keep updated on current issues, research, and practices.
- Inform parents, administrators, and colleagues of your program goals, and include the skills and knowledge that students gain as a result of participating in the dance program.
- Emphasize to your students what they are learning. Clearly articulate your goals, clarify your assessment strategies, and keep your students actively involved in learning during the class.
- Create a bulletin board to highlight what students are learning in the dance class; include pictures, student drawings, or essays.

If you find yourself in a reactive situation, one where there is the possibility of reduction to or elimination of the dance program, you will want to develop a plan of action. Begin planning by asking yourself the following questions:

- What do I see as the outcome? What do I want to occur?
- Why should this issue be addressed?
- What message about dance do I want to communicate?
- Who is the target audience or whom do I need to influence?
- What strategies can I use to reach my target audience?
- Who can help me deliver the message?

The best way to advocate is to effectively deliver a solid program founded on standards and goals. A good program will be relevant to the students, have clear objectives, present information in multiple ways, and contain a form of assessment. Students can be very influential in what they say to their teachers, the school administrator, and their parents about their dance learning experiences. Consider their voices as a means of advocating for the dance program. When they experience a sense of accomplishment and success, they will know how meaningful dance can be to their lives and be willing to share their excitement with others.

Summary

Numerous factors impact the teaching and learning environment. We may find ourselves teaching a small group of children on a carpeted floor in the classroom or teaching 50 children in one part of a large gymnasium while another class meets in a different section of the gym. The best strategy for making the most of a less than ideal situation is to focus on your goals for the learning experience and the children you are teaching. The facilities, equipment, schedule, and class size certainly influence your planning and implementation; however, teaching is a learning experience, and the challenges we face open new possibilities for a creative teaching opportunity. There are different ways to teach dance regardless of the environment. Your responsibility is to be realistic in what you can achieve, considering the educational parameters of your environment, and to continually seek effective teaching methods. Students and colleagues can be valuable resources for ideas to help you deliver your program. Ask them to help you find alternative solutions. This collaborative effort can lead to increased support for dance, especially when students are asked to contribute their ideas. Last, dance is an invaluable learning experience for children. As a teacher of dance, you are responsible for advocating for your program and ensuring that children have the opportunity to discover the relevance of dance in their lives.

Questions for Reflection

- ✎ Think about a time when you needed to make a last-minute change in your teaching facility or schedule. How did you handle it? What worked best? What could you have done differently?
- ✎ How would your teaching strategies change with the size of the class?
- ✎ What do you see as a benefit of using props or equipment in a dance lesson?
- ✎ Think about different spaces in which you might teach dance. How would you adapt a lesson to work in several different spaces?
- ✎ What do you know about the community in which you teach? How is the community where you live similar and different?
- ✎ How should you prepare yourself for dealing with an emergency at school? What are your plans?
- ✎ What do you think your students would tell their parents about their dance learning experiences? What would you like your students to say?
- ✎ What are some steps you might take to be an effective advocate for dance in education?

chapter 5

Making Teaching Effective

Effective teaching begins with planning a learning experience based on knowledge of child growth and development, the ways in which children learn, the content in the dance program, and lesson development and implementation. The goal is to provide a meaningful learning experience that integrates the needs of children with the content of the dance program. This chapter offers strategies to make the dance experience positive for both the student and the teacher.

Using Different Teaching Styles

Choosing the best teaching style to present a task depends on the task objective. Think about the best way to present the task to promote effective student learning. It may be appropriate to use several different teaching styles within a single learning experience to address the task and students' individual learning styles.

In a warm-up that requires students to mirror the teacher's movements, teaching by imitation or command style (Mosston 1972) may be the best choice. In this style, the students observe and duplicate movement. They make few decisions about how the movements are performed. This method is applicable to teaching folk dances, social dances, and other dances that contain prescribed steps and formations.

Teachers can utilize a problem-solving teaching style when asking the students to create or rearrange dance movements. Graham (2001) describes this style as divergent problem solving, in which there are many different ways to solve the problem. This style is the preferred methodology in teaching creative dance (Stinson 1998). Students make decisions about how to move within the limits of the task. Exploration and improvisation are frequently associated with problem solving. Exploration is a thoughtful response to a task in which the student finds different answers. In the task, "Find different ways to move on your hands and feet," for example, students think about a way to accomplish the task, try the movement out, then think of another way, try that idea, and continue to think about and perform different answers to the task. Improvisation is a spontaneous response to a task, evoking an immediate physical action. In the task, "Move in a way that expresses the word *splatter*," the student immediately responds by moving his or her body with the first idea that comes to mind.

When using the problem-solving teaching style, keep an open mind. Even if you can anticipate some of the responses, you may be surprised when the children try out something new and unexpected. You can elicit a variety of responses from students by repeatedly asking them to find another way to accomplish the movement task. When you first present the task, students will move in ways that are familiar to them, but as you continue to ask for different responses they will begin to explore and create new alternatives. This is when creative thinking occurs.

Presenting a task with a specific solution and allowing the students to discover the solution for themselves is called convergent problem solving (Graham 2001) or guided discovery (Mosston 1972). This teaching style leads the students to a specific solution through a sequence of planned questions. The teacher knows the solution beforehand and chooses this method to provide students with a more in-depth understanding of how to arrive at the solution. For example, the following sequence of questions leads students to discover how to achieve a balanced position with another person when exercising countertension: "Stand facing your partner with your toes touching and gripping each other's hands at the wrists. Now, slowly begin to lean away from each other until your arms are straight. Can you both stay balanced on your feet? How are you using your energy in the pull? Repeat the same balance with one partner pulling more than the other. What happened? When you felt yourself falling off balance, how did you change the energy of the pull to maintain a balanced position? You are now experiencing countertension. What do you think makes it work?"

When students understand the concept and principles of using countertension, switch to a problem-solving task that requires them to demonstrate their understanding through application. For example, direct the class as follows: "Find another way to balance with your partner using countertension. What other body parts can you pull with instead of your hands? Create a countertension balance that uses four people." Students can share their solutions to the problem with others, and use the imitation teaching style themselves to present their solutions to other groups for duplication.

Helping All Children Learn

Every child is unique. Although we may welcome this diversity in learning, it also poses a challenge for us as teachers. Dance and physical education classes include children with a range of abilities; and, for some children, movement is one of the best ways for them to express ideas and feelings. These children are familiar with using movement as a means to communicate and respond eagerly to the sounds and rhythms of music. Not all children, however, respond to movement as comfortably or as easily. Effective planning therefore begins with learning about the physical, cognitive, emotional, and social needs of the students. This knowledge helps to differentiate instruction through providing variations in content, process, and product to meet the individual needs of each child (Tomlinson 1999). Observe students in their classes, and talk with their teachers to identify their strengths and learning styles as well as what teaching strategies seem to be the most effective. Also, talk with the students to learn about their interests and needs. How do they

~ The disabled child.

feel about dancing, and what kind of dance would they enjoy? Most importantly, be flexible and willing to adapt your learning experiences to ensure success for all students in the class (see figure 5.1). Kaufmann (2002) notes, "All students deserve new opportunities to express their thoughts and feelings kinesthetically in a safe and supportive environment" (p.16). Teaching students with a broad range of abilities and learning styles presents challenges that can result in gaining new insights about teaching dance.

Some children may need to experience short, focused activities that have specific expectations. Perhaps, attending a dance class for only a part of a lesson may be appropriate. Children with visual or auditory needs may require specific cues for stopping and starting a movement. Be succinct with your directions, and repeat them when needed. Allow time for the information to be fully understood, and be patient, flexible, and supportive. Praise accomplishments frequently when a child learns a new movement, remains focused on the task, or cooperates with others. Also, be aware of when tasks become frustrating for students and intervene to help them.

You can assist children with disabilities by using techniques such as "teaching by invitation," in which the teacher offers several tasks, thus allowing children to decide which task best fits their abilities (Graham 2001). Another technique suggested by Graham is called "intratask variation." Here, the teacher observes how the child is responding to a task and makes the appropriate modifications to help the child be more successful. Modifications may include breaking the task into smaller pieces or finding another way to explain or demonstrate the task. In other instances, it may be necessary to try multiple adaptations to successfully address the needs of students while always respecting the integrity of the child and keeping the experience positive. Avoid using the term *handicapped* and instead use *disability*. Also, when referring to a child with a disability, respect the child as an individual not solely defined by his or her disability by using the word *child* first before describing the disability (National Assembly of State Arts Agencies and the National Endowment for the Arts 1994). For example, use the phrases *a child who is blind* instead of *a blind child* or *a child with epilepsy* instead of *an epileptic*. In her article on designing adaptations for teaching dance to students with disabilities, Kaufmann (2002) suggests practical tips for including students who use wheelchairs and walkers, students with visual and hearing impairments, students with emotional needs, and students with limited mobility. A positive dance experience for all children begins with the teacher. Acknowledge, encourage, and respect children's differences. See the possibilities instead of the limitations.

Figure 5.1 Students bring their own background of movement experience and creative potential to the dance learning experience. The teacher offers knowledge of the elements of movement and the process for learning about dance.

Motivating Learners

All teachers have students who may be reluctant to try a new activity—particularly dance. The thought of presenting a dance learning experience that may not be received with enthusiasm by all students can deter a teacher from attempting to teach dance. However, there are students in each class who do enjoy participating in a dance experience and welcome the opportunity to do so. These students need to be considered as well. Engage students in the learning experience through establishing a sense of connectedness with the content (Anderson 2002). Ensure that students feel that their insights and contributions are valued and the content is relevant to their lives. When planning, Anderson suggests that teachers are sensitive to their students' conceptions of the subject matter. He advises, "View subject matter through the eyes, hearts, and minds of learning, to be aware of the emotions, perceptions, imaginings, and translations students make of instructional inputs" (2002, p. 36).

One approach to addressing student reluctance is to acknowledge the feelings of students who say, "Why do we have to dance? I don't like dancing. Dance is not for me. I can't dance." The teacher can respond, "I hear what you are saying. I understand that dance is not your favorite activity. I know that dancing makes you feel very uncomfortable," or "I know that you may feel that you are not very good at dancing, but all the movements in today's lesson are movements you already know how to do." Then ask the students to try the dance, and set time aside at the end of the session for them to talk more about their feelings. Students may find all or part of the experience enjoyable, but some will continue to feel reluctant and may not change their minds for the entire school year.

Here are some other strategies for addressing the concerns of the reluctant student:

- Be generous with honest praise for all students during the dance experience. The praise can help alleviate some of the "I can't" feelings.

- Take time at the end of each session to talk about the experience. Discuss with students what parts of the lesson were uncomfortable, what worked well, what could be changed for the next time, and what could be added to make the experience more challenging. This type of questioning allows the students who enjoyed the experience, as well as the reluctant students, to voice their opinions.

- Talk with students individually about their feelings outside of the session, either in a formal conference or casually as you meet them in the hallway. In this way, you can show that you are sincerely interested in their feelings and that you want to help them feel comfortable with learning dance.

- Teach by invitation (Graham 2001). This strategy allows students to make choices. You could say, for example, "You can choose to add percussion instruments to accompany your dance or create the dance without any accompaniment."

- Set a positive atmosphere in the beginning of the learning experience as you would with any area of the curriculum. Children do not want to be viewed as foolish or incompetent in front of their peers. You can tell children that you are trying this lesson for the first time, and you would like their feedback at the end of the session. Then, ask them what parts of the learning experience were the most interesting. What did they learn today about dance? What changes would they suggest for the next session? We stress that students respect the individual differences among their peers. We all bring strengths to the experience and we can all learn something new about ourselves and how we move. What is challenging to one student may not be as challenging to another. These differences must be acknowledged in a positive, accepting atmosphere that helps alleviate the feeling of vulnerability.

- Students seem more reluctant to participate in dance than in other curricular areas. However, when you exhibit sincere enthusiasm as you introduce the learning experience, choose content that is relevant to the students, and ensure a positive atmosphere, your students will begin to understand and value dance as an important part of their experiences.

Frequently, teachers who anticipate reluctance when they use the word *dance* will begin the session by instead saying, "We are going to create some new movements today," or "This lesson is about moving to a rhythm in the music." They purposely avoid using the word *dance* because some children will immediately turn off from the learning experience because of their preconceptions about dance. Using other phrases or words as a substitute for *dance* in the beginning of a lesson may encourage children to participate. We strongly recommend that at some point, either at the end of the lesson or at the end of the unit, you explain that what the children were doing is called dance. When their experiences have been positive they will link a new meaning to the word *dance*. Children must know that they are dancing and that the learning and feelings of success and joy they experience are a result of a dance experience.

Establishing Protocols and Rules

Most teachers have a series of established protocols and rules they use with their classes. Protocols are usually teacher-designed ways of operating during the class that facilitate efficient class management and allow maximum time for active participation (Graham 2001). These include ways to enter and exit the class, obtain and return equipment, stop an activity, and react to fire drills and other emergency situations. Rules establish guidelines for responsible behaviors that foster learning (Brady, Forton, Porter, and Wood 2003). Often, children can suggest rules that address respect, good listening, sharing, and cooperation, as is described later. Dance learning experiences follow similar protocols and rules used in other education experiences.

One important protocol to establish is the stop signal. Clarify your meaning of stop. Explain to students the specific behaviors you expect—the voice is quiet, the body is still,

everyone is looking at the teacher, props are placed on the floor, a shape is held still, or hands that are connected are let go. The signal can be the teacher saying "stop" or "freeze," or it can be another specified signal. For example, when using recorded music you might say, "When the music stops I want you to stop." When using percussion instruments you could tell students, "I am going to play a skipping rhythm on the drum. When I hit the drum loudly, like this, stop." Or you might say, "This movement will not be accompanied by music. Stop when you hear me tap the triangle three times, like this, one, two, and three." You can also incorporate a way to stop in the movement task, for example, "Run, leap, turn, and freeze in a stretched shape," or "As you are running in the space, begin to run slower and slower until you come to a complete stop."

Another protocol that supports effective teaching is to establish a way to begin and end the dance session. To begin class, some teachers have students sit in a circle and take attendance by asking each student to respond with a movement or a clap of their hands. One attendance strategy that allows the teacher to get to know more about their students is to choose a category, such as colors, foods, animals, or sports, and when the teacher calls a child's name the child responds with an answer that fits the category. At the end of the class, students can convene to talk about what they learned or to hear about what will happen in the next session. In Graham's (2001) book, *Teaching Children Physical Education*, he offers specific strategies for establishing and maintaining effective class management protocols. He suggests that teachers design a plan, communicate it to the students, and monitor student reactions. Children need parameters to help them focus on learning, being safe, and respecting others.

Creating rules begins with awareness for the teacher and the student about the goals for learning. Ask students what they hope to learn and what they want to learn. Their comments become the foundation for developing rules that help them reach their goals. The task now is to solicit from the students their ideas for rules. During class, children can offer verbal suggestions, write or draw about rules, or work in small groups on a rule list. Encourage students to frame rules in the positive instead of beginning each rule with "Don't" or "No" (Brady et al. 2003). Consolidate the lists, and make the rules global and concise (see figure 5.2). Once the rules are developed, it is time to bring them to life. Practice the rules with students by having them experience what the rules look like and sound like in action. You can ask, "What does respect look like when you are listening to someone talk?" or "What would you say if you are sharing a prop?" Role play with students about the different situations that occur in the dance session. Here, students can connect the rules to actual situations. These moments of practice model for students the acceptable way to behave and further their understanding of the rules. Consequences for choosing to not follow rules or protocols should be logical, maintain the integrity of the children, and offer an opportunity to learn from the situation. Provide children with problem-solving techniques for settling disputes and the language to express their feelings in an appropriate manner. There is no question that it takes time to establish rules, practice rules, and discuss consequences; however, establishing classroom protocols is a worthy investment that will set a positive environment for effective teaching and learning.

Rules for Dance Learning

Be kind, helpful, and caring.
Respect others and school materials.
Always try your best.
Listen to each other.

Figure 5.2   Sample list of rules.

Making the Classroom Safe

In dance and physical education classes, children are always moving and the potential for injury is greater than in a classroom where children are more sedentary. Establish a safe environment by communicating the safety protocols and rules to the students and then reinforce appropriate behavior during the session. Before you teach, review the lesson and anticipate where an emphasis on safe behaviors will be needed. For example, when asking children to huddle closely together in a group, you can anticipate that some children may push or fall and injure themselves or another child. Before the huddle, explain to the children that they need to move into the huddle slowly, then remain still, and then move apart slowly. When children are traveling in the room, they need adequate space to dance freely without bumping into others. Not all children have fully developed agility and perceptional skills to make quick changes of direction and weight shifts to avoid collisions. As a result, the teacher will need to organize students for safe movement. First, reinforce understanding of the concepts of personal space (the space immediately around the body whether stationary or traveling) and general space (all other available space). Developing an awareness of appropriate personal space takes practice. Many children tend to be too close to others, the walls, and objects. It may be helpful to remind students, "Look in front of your body, to the sides of your body, and in back of you to see if you have enough space to move without bumping into another person." Also, identify safety lines on the floor that border the dance space and instruct students to stay within the lines to protect them from hitting a wall, furniture, or other obstacles.

When students are making quick traveling movements such as running or leaping, have all students move in the same direction in the space. They can be organized into lines of three or four and take turns, or they can move in a large circular path around the space, not necessarily in a single circle. With very large groups, taking turns for fast movement may be the best choice to keep the environment safe. A balance is necessary between the time students spend moving and the time they are waiting for a turn to maintain active participation in a safe space.

Personal safety also needs to be stressed to enable children to perform dance movements without injuring themselves. Joyce (1984) suggests teaching children appropriate techniques to help them express themselves and avoid injury. Teach children to land softly through their feet when coming down from hops, jumps, and leaps. The toes should touch the floor first, followed by the ball and then heel of the foot, and the knees should be bent on the landing to absorb the force. When children lower themselves to the floor, they need to use their hands to help control the body weight and avoid dropping directly onto their knees. Require children to be cautious when bending or moving backward, switching weight from one body part to another, or turning and stopping quickly. As the teacher, you are responsible for the children's safety. Anticipate potential problems, teach safe ways to move, and attend to injuries immediately. Always begin each session with a proper warm-up and end the session with appropriate cool-down movements.

Presenting Demonstrations

In many learning experiences, movement patterns or sequences require a demonstration by either the teacher or the students. When demonstrating a specific movement or dance step for a large group, the teacher has several choices. Facing the students with the front of the body allows the demonstrator to see all the students. The choice of facing the students requires either the teacher or students to reverse the right and left orientation of the movement, similar to looking in a mirror. Having the teacher's back to the students allows the students to match the movement identically, but it is difficult for the teacher to see if the students are following correctly. Another possibility for demonstrating is to stand beside a student. This works well when demonstrating to an individual. The student can match the movement, and the demonstrator can see the student at the same time. This approach is helpful when teaching specific dance steps that are difficult for students to learn easily.

The teacher can also demonstrate from the center of a large group where the students face the center of the circle. In this situation, the students will follow the movement in a general way rather than matching it exactly. For example, the teacher may say, "I am going to move very slowly. I want you to follow my movements and stop when I stop."

Be sure all students can see the demonstration. The demonstrator can repeat the movement in different places in the room or change the position of the students (Graham 2001). Those in back of the space can move to the front or those in the center can switch with students on the periphery of the group. When teaching a large class, it may be possible to teach from a raised platform or stage to allow the students to view the demonstration easily.

Besides the appropriate location, how you present the demonstration requires consideration. Sometimes, showing the whole dance or complete sequence of movements gives students the big picture, and they can see how the individual movements are part of the whole. Then steps or short phrases of movement can be broken down and taught. You may need to first demonstrate the movement slowly so that students can follow, and then demonstrate using the appropriate tempo and quality of movement. Finally, accompany the demonstration with verbal focus or cues to help direct children's attention to the movement (Graham 2001).

Providing Feedback

Frequent positive and constructive comments to children will maintain motivation and reinforce learning (Graham 2001). Because dance can be an area of the curriculum where students may feel more self-conscious and vulnerable, it is important to acknowledge accomplishments, no matter how small, and also to make corrections when necessary. Both types of comments, acknowledgment and correction, should be specific and descriptive. Acknowledge students' work by saying something like, "That's great. I see you have used your back and arms to make a round shape"; "You are using great control to lower your body carefully to the floor"; or "Everyone learned the steps very quickly. Your concentration and coordination are improving." When using corrective comments, acknowledge the positive aspects of the movement first, and then add a comment to help the child improve performance. Say, for example, "You are moving in the right rhythm, but you need to think ahead about which side you move to first," or "I see that you are moving at a low level. Now can you use only your hands and feet for traveling?" Always look for something positive to say to children. They value your comments, and use them to reassure themselves of their progress.

To be effective, the children must be able to hear the positive feedback. Children tend to use their voices and can be noisy when moving. To ensure that children hear your comments, move close to them. Sometimes, however, it is appropriate to comment from across the room. Making sure that children hear your positive feedback is valuable and can help them feel good about their movements. It is also helpful to say the child's name first before commenting. Doing so will gain their attention so they are ready to hear the comment. An example might be, "Tim, I see you are using a jump in three different directions to show your popping movement—that's great!"

Children also want the opportunity to talk about their experiences. Students need to be quiet when the teacher or a child is speaking to allow everyone to hear the comment the first time. When a child answers a question or makes a comment, the teacher should refrain from rephrasing the comment every time. Doing so can send a message to children that their comments are not valued and the teacher can say it better. Some children do not speak loud enough to be heard in a big space. It may take extra time to gather the class closer and make sure they can hear the child speaking, yet you must respect the integrity of the child as the speaker. In dance, value is not only placed on the students' abilities to create and learn movement but also on what they think and say about movement.

Engaging Students in Performances

In a dance class, the purpose of performance is to share dance movement that has been created or learned with other students or the teacher.

Not all student work needs to be performed; however, there are times when student performance is appropriate. Performance provides the opportunity to communicate the intent of the dance to others. When students perform a folk dance, for example, they are communicating an event or custom of a particular culture. A dance about clouds may communicate the different shapes of clouds and how they move across the sky. These performance opportunities can occur at various times throughout the learning experience. Often the teacher will ask one or more students to perform a particular sequence of movements. This pinpointing (Graham 2001) method of performance is valuable when the teacher needs to illustrate accuracy and quality in movement or demonstrate a variety of solutions to a problem-solving task. At other times, the performance will occur near the end of a learning experience to demonstrate the culminating dance that was learned or created.

Generally, the teacher will ask all the students to perform the dance movement at the same time. This is a comfortable approach for students who are hesitant about performing. Many students are afraid to make a mistake in front of others or to show their work in fear that their work will not be well accepted, yet they are willing to perform as part of the whole class. Asking students to perform solo when they are not ready or have not readily volunteered places them in an uncomfortable situation. Do not expect children to perform solo unless they request to do so. Also, if a child refuses to perform, even after your encouraging words, do not demand that he or she does so. Your insistence will only intensify the child's resistance. Respect his or her decision and find a time to talk with the child outside of class to discuss the child's feelings. Together, you and the child can explore other ways the child can share what he or she has learned.

Designing a variety of performance circumstances will allow students to communicate their dances to others, provide students with an opportunity to observe others dancing, and give the teacher an opportunity to observe how the students complete the tasks. The following are examples of performance opportunities:

- A student readily volunteers to perform for the whole class.
- A student shares a movement or sequence of movements with a small group of three or four other students. Each student in the group is encouraged to take a turn.
- Students paired together as partners perform for another set of partners.
- An individual student shares a movement idea or completed dance with one other student.
- Two or three small groups perform at the same time for the whole class.
- Half the class performs at one time while the other half observes, and then they switch roles.
- One small group performs for another small group, and then the groups switch roles.
- Individual students or small groups perform for the teacher at a time other than during class.
- Students perform for the teacher or other students at a performance station.

For reasons that are understandable, children cannot and should not sit and observe or wait for extended periods of time for their turn to perform. Keep the performance time short.

When the students are ready to perform, the teacher should make one or two specific comments that focus the students' attention on how they will perform the dance. Offer comments such as these: "Think about what you want to express in this dance, and make each movement speak clearly"; "Be sure to feel the strong energy in your movement, especially when you jump into the air"; "Take your time in the turn and fall to the floor, thinking of lightly and slowly melting"; or "Listen carefully to the change in the music as the cue to change the dance formation." Request that students begin and end their performance with their bodies still. This stillness defines the beginning and end of a specific movement or a whole dance, both for the dancer and the observers. Remind students who are observing to applaud or comment in a respectful manner after the performance. A great way to show support for the performer is to have the observers applaud before as well as after the performance. Starting a performance on such a positive note promotes self-esteem and encourages students who are reluctant to be more enthusiastic about performing.

Observing Dance   *Older dancers*

Observing dance, whether it is a professional company or student class work, is a valuable component of the dance program. Frequently, dance observation is overlooked because the emphasis of the lesson is experiential; that is, the children are actively involved in physically learning or creating dances. Observing can give children an appreciation for dance as a means of nonverbal communication and expression. It is a valuable means of learning about dance if the teacher prepares the students beforehand. A general statement such as, "Tell me what you liked about the dance after the performance," can precede the observation. Additionally, the teacher can state more specific expectations by telling the students what to look for in the dance such as, "Pay attention to how the dancers use light and strong energy in their locomotor movements." This verbal focus (Graham 2001) makes observation more meaningful and increases comprehension of the dance.

Other suggestions to direct student observation include asking the students to look for the following:

- The different ways the dancers use straight and curved pathways
- Movements where dancers go off the floor and into the air
- How the dance steps match the beat of the music
- How the dances are similar to each other
- If the dance tells a story
- Movements and shapes that remind you of clouds (in a dance about clouds)
- How the dance begins and ends
- Different feelings expressed by the dancers
- Answers to student-created questions for the observation

Following the observation, a discussion in which students can express their thoughts and perceptions and hear a variety of other viewpoints is appropriate. Guide the class discussion by asking questions such as these:

- What movements did you see? Describe how the dancers were moving.
- How did the spatial formations change throughout the dance?
- How did the dancers use gestures to convey a character?
- What ideas or feelings might the dancers have been trying to express?
- What does this dance mean to you personally?
- What other possible meanings might the dance have?
- What did you see in the dance?
- What part of the dance was the most exciting and why?
- Describe the different ways the dancers related to each other.
- Was there a message in the dance?
- Can you suggest another way to end the dance?
- What part of the dance would you like to dance yourself?
- What do you think about the music used for the dance?
- How did the costumes, props, or setting affect the dance?
- How did the dance relate to the title of the dance?

- What do you feel about what you saw?
- What was original or imaginative about the dance?
- What did the dance tell you about the time period it is from?
- What did the dance tell you about the people and their environment?

Children can respond to their observations through drawing pictures (see figure 5.3), writing in a journal (see figure 5.4), writing a review, composing a poem, or demonstrating their response through movement or talking. In a large class, it is not always possible to have the time to listen to everyone's response to a question. A strategy we have found helpful for sharing verbal responses requires that students are organized into pairs or small groups and take turns sharing their comments with each other. Encourage children to use the movement vocabulary from the elements of dance in their comments. In this way, they will be able

Figure 5.3 Drawings depict children's responses to an observation.

	May 20, 2004
○	I thought the dance assembly was very entertaining and informing about dance all over the world. The three dancers showed the movements and told us where it originated from. I liked the Brazilian dancers the best. It was fast and colorful. I wonder how the dancers remembered all the movements and dance so well together. I wasn't always interested in dancing, but now I am because of the cool moves.

Figure 5.4 Journal writing about a dance observation.

to extend and clarify their comments beyond stating simply, "I liked the dance," or "It was interesting." Probe for in-depth comments by asking students what they liked about the dance or what, specifically, did they find interesting. Asking a follow-up question to a comment engages children's critical thinking skills and helps them gain an understanding of what they observed.

Summary

From the moment children step into the space to their last step out the door, the dance experience should be engaging, relevant, and enjoyable. The teacher knows the needs of the children and plans a unit and lessons that invite them to experience dance in a variety of ways. Children are recognized for their individual perspectives, learning styles, and abilities to learn and create dance movements. As the teacher, you have established protocols and rules that help children learn and grow in a safe, kind, and orderly place. Here, children feel their way of learning is respected and are willing to take risks as they collaborate with others to create, perform, and observe dances.

Questions for Reflection

- What is "effective" teaching in dance? What would it look like and sound like in your classroom?

- We can all agree that children learn in different ways. What are some of the strategies that you have used to help children be successful?

- What supportive phrases can you share with students as feedback to their dancing? Create a list of 10 or more comments.

- What strategies can you use to include students in constructing rules for effective learning?

- What suggested strategies for reluctant learners did you find appropriate for your situation? What other strategies in other content areas have you used to help students feel comfortable and motivated to learn?

- Students enjoy learning new activities, yet they also need the security of a routine. What protocols do you already use with your classes that are applicable to teaching dance?

- What do you remember most about your experiences in viewing dances? What about the performers, the costumes, music, stage sets, or props did you find most interesting? What do you look for when you are observing a dance?

- The safety of children is of utmost importance in teaching. Do you have procedures to follow in case of an emergency such as fire, bomb threat, injury, or breach of security? What precautions do you take to ensure the children's safety during the lesson?

chapter 6

Assessing Children's Learning in Dance

Assessment, as a significant part of a comprehensive dance curriculum, can be conducted in a variety of ways. Most important, the type of assessment selected must be directly related to the objectives of the learning experience. Wiggins (1998) contends that the primary goal of assessment is to educate students and improve learning, not merely audit it. As an essential component of the teaching and learning process, assessment is embedded throughout the dance curriculum. Those who teach dance are continually seeking the best ways to assess student learning. They look at how creativity, performance, group cooperation, personal growth, and change in attitude and values can be assessed feasibly in a valid and reliable manner. Many assessments used in dance are designed by the teacher and focus specifically on learning that occurs in a particular unit or lesson. These types of teacher-constructed assessments reflect a student's level of skill accomplishment, the student's understanding of the content, or how the student feels about what he or she has learned. The assessment can be ongoing, meaning that it happens throughout the learning experience, allowing the teacher and student to make improvements in learning (Woods 1997). Assessment can also occur at the conclusion of the learning experience, focusing on achievement accumulated through multiple experiences.

In either type of assessment, whether ongoing or at the conclusion of study, it is important to consider ways to assess learning in the psychomotor, cognitive, and affective domains.

The psychomotor domain involves the student's ability to perform individual dance movements, phrases of movement, and complete dances. This domain requires the students to exercise their coordination, balance, flexibility, cardiorespiratory endurance, and strength. Cognitive assessment determines what knowledge children learned about the content of the unit or lessons. Knowledge can be revealed when a student responds to a task with movement as well as by talking or writing about what they understand. The affective domain involves feelings, reactions, attitudes, social interactions, and self-concept. Assessment of the affective domain should not be limited to assessment of participation, effort, and attitudes. Worrell, Evans-Fletcher, and Kovar (2002) note, "Teachers might consider including other elements such as personal responsibility, cooperation, compassion, self-expression, positive interaction with other students, respect for differences, and being a good team member" (p. 31).

In dance, children learn, perform, create, and observe dances, and thus different types of assessments are needed. Assessment of how a student performs a dance movement or a completed dance or how a student creates a dance is usually a part of most dance lessons and units. Assessment may also take the form of a written test using multiple-choice questions or questions requiring short phrases or paragraphs. Other written assessments can include journal writing in response to their own dancing or the dancing of others, constructed books containing descriptions and drawings of dances, or lists of vocabulary words used in the dance lesson.

Knowledge: Identification and recall of previously learned material.
What are three square dance movements?

Who can demonstrate skipping forward?

Comprehension: Organization and understanding of facts and ideas.
Describe the benefits of participating in a social dance.

Can you demonstrate three different shapes?

Application: Use of facts, rules, or principles.
Draw three formations that you created for your dance.

Create a new line dance using the steps you have learned.

Analysis: Separation of a whole into its component parts.
How is Samir's dance different from Kristen's?

Show a strong movement from your dance.

Synthesis: Combination of ideas to form a new whole.
Create a dance using one movement from each person's dance.

After observing the videotaped dance, suggest a different way to begin and end the dance.

Evaluation: Development of opinions or judgments.
What do you think the dance was about?

What part of your dance did you like best? Why?

Figure 6.1   Sample questions reflecting Bloom's Taxonomy.

Students can also respond orally to questions, lead a discussion, interview a peer, deliver a presentation on dance, or complete a project. Relying on a single type of assessment will not fit all situations and limits the information that a teacher collects about student learning. It is not enough to simply measure a student's ability to recall memorized facts or perform an isolated movement; instead, assessment of what students know and are able to do should include a balance of lower- and higher-order thinking skills, as represented in Bloom's Taxonomy (Bloom, Englehart, Furst, Hill, and Krathwohl 1956) (see figure 6.1).

Assessing dance presents a challenge because of its ephemeral nature. Dance is a live art form that occurs in a time and space that cannot be exactly replicated. As a form of human movement and art, the dance is embodied in the dancer, and as experience affects the dancer so is the dance affected. This is why conducting a single view of assessment captures only one moment, whereas a variety of assessments can provide a more comprehensive picture of what a child knows, understands, and is able to do. Videotaping children dancing may be considered one way to address this concern; however, although videotape can be a useful tool for assessment, it does have its limitations. Dance on videotape is taken through the eye of the videographer and, as a result, may provide a limited view of the dance.

Subjectivity is another issue in dance assessment. One's background, values, and aesthetic preferences play into the interpretation of what the assessor views. Teachers, alone or in collaboration with students, need to define the criteria for the assessment rubric. The criteria become the description of what is considered an appropriate response, and the rubric delineates the range of possible responses. Rubrics can be holistic containing several criteria (see figure 6.2) or analytic where there is a rubric for each criterion (Wiggins 1998). A rubric for five elements of choreography developed by Rovegno and Bandhauer (2000) demonstrates a clear example of how an analytic rubric can be used to make assessment less subjective. For each of the five choreographic elements—originality, transitions, expressing an idea, focus and clarity, and contrasts and aesthetic highlights—the authors included a different range of performance levels accompanied by a description of what the teacher would observe at each level. When rubrics are used to guide self- and peer assessment, students become increasingly aware of how to assess their work and set goals for improvement. It is okay to make changes in the assessment during the unit because as you teach you will also learn more about how students respond to the content.

Assessment in dance should address students' knowledge and skills as creators, performers, and responders to dance. In this chapter, we address dance assessment from four views: teacher assessment of the overall effectiveness of the program, teacher assessment of individual student learning, peer assessment, and student self-assessment.

Criteria for Dance Performance

Everyone stayed in rhythm, the students enjoyed performing the dance, the students remembered the dance steps, the dance movements were clear, and the students kept going even if there was a mistake.

Awesome	Everyone in the group did everything well.
Very Good	Two or three people made a mistake.
OK	A lot of people in the group made a lot of mistakes, or the group gave up.

Figure 6.2 Holistic rubric created by students.

Assessment of Teaching Effectiveness

Effective teaching is the result of creative thinking, planning, dynamic delivery, and reflection on the teaching and learning experience. What worked and why and what can be changed for the next session? These are questions that influence a recurrent cycle of planning, presenting, and reflecting. As an ongoing part of teaching, the experience shared by the teacher and the students is evaluated based on a set of professional and personal standards. The primary focus is on how the experience affected student learning.

- What was the goal of the lesson or unit of lessons?
- What were students expected to learn?
- How did the design of the learning experience contribute to meeting those objectives?
- Did students learn what was intended?
- How do I know what they learned?

Other reflective questions speak to the overall dance program and the benefits for the students.

- What impact does the dance program have on motor development?
- What knowledge was gained of how the elements of movement are used to create and learn dances?
- Have students increased their understanding of how dance expresses and communicates an idea?
- Have students gained an understanding of culture through the medium of dance?

The answers to these questions provide teachers with valuable information to use in evaluating their preparation and presentation of a specific learning experience or the total dance program.

Assessment of teaching is an ongoing process. Teachers look at the way the students respond to each task and adjust the tasks during the learning experience to ensure student achievement of the planned objectives. Questions to consider are as follows:

- How many of the students are focused during the learning experience?
- Do they respond to the task immediately, or is additional information needed?
- Can they perform the task physically? Is additional practice time needed?
- When is the appropriate time to change to the next task?
- Should some of the tasks be reordered?

During and after the unit and lessons, the teacher reflects on the lesson design and how it was presented to the students.

- What parts are working and why?
- What changes are needed? For example, when teaching students a lesson about finding different ways to make round shapes, the teacher can observe how many different ways the students make round shapes.
- Are the students using their whole body and its parts to make a round shape?
- What elements of dance are they using as they make round shapes?
- Are they using different levels and various sizes?

After the lesson the teacher can reflect on what tasks elicited the appropriate response or how the sequence of tasks fostered learning.

One approach to use when evaluating either a single learning experience or a unit is to develop a list of questions that provides a focus for assessment. Each question relates to an objective with a specific reference to motor, cognitive, and affective development. For example, when teaching a folk dance, the objectives can be for students to learn the sequence of steps, understand the cultural background of the dance, and dance with enthusiasm and in cooperation with others. Questions for assessment of the learning experience could include the following:

- How many of the students can perform the steps in the dance?
- How many of the students could remember a sequence of steps and perform them without teacher cues?

- Are the students able to change direction smoothly?
- Can they maintain the spatial formation of the dance?
- Can they describe what the steps represent about the culture in which the dance was designed?
- Are they dancing with a sense of joy in the experience?
- Are the students able to relate positively to their partners and the group as a whole?

You can also include the following suggested list of general questions that are appropriate to the overall experience:

- What tasks need to be repeated in subsequent experiences?
- Which objectives did the majority of children meet?
- What skills do I need to reteach (Holt/Hale 1988)?

At the end of each learning experience, it is helpful to record a few notes about each class, review the written plans, and add or delete tasks for the next learning experience. In addition, review what was successful about the way you taught the lesson. Ask yourself, "Was it the way I demonstrated a movement, how I used my voice, where I placed myself in the space, my addition of a picture or diagram, or my energy and enthusiasm for the topic?"

Assessment of teaching effectiveness is a form of teacher self-assessment. The reflective process of thinking about how the unit and lessons were planned and taught and how the students experienced learning challenges teachers to reconsider prior assumptions, attitudes, beliefs, behaviors, and perceptions and to be open to change. As a result of self-assessment, we are more informed about our teaching and can develop a rationale for better practice (Brookfield 1995; McCollum 2002). We can look at our work objectively and know with some confidence why we believe what we believe and why we do what we do.

Teacher Assessment of Students

The second type of assessment is teacher assessment of student learning. Here, the teacher monitors a student's progress during a single learning experience or over a period of time. Assessing students' learning in dance requires a feasible approach that provides teachers with the information they need when they see many children in a limited amount of time. Tools and formats for collecting information of students' learning can include teacher observations recorded on checklists (see figure 6.3), written

Class: Mrs. G's

Dance: Line dance pattern

+ = Child is able to demonstrate

x = Child is unable to demonstrate

	Correct movements	On the beat	Changes direction
Sharia	+	+	+
Donovan	+	X	+
Robert	+	+	+
Zui	X	X	+

Figure 6.3 Teacher checklist for a single evaluation.

notes, comments made on an audiotape or other electronic form, and videotapes of a session. Teachers can also collect information through tests, quizzes, journal writing, drawings, verbal responses (see figure 6.4), and portfolios.

Teacher assessment of students' performance begins with a discussion of the criteria and the rubric. Show students examples of good and not-so-good work and identify the characteristics of each. McTighe (1997) suggests, "If we expect students to do excellent work, they need to know what excellent work looks like" (p. 9). Articulate the gradations in the rubric, such as beginning, improving, and excelling, so students can set levels of achievement for themselves. For example, in a lesson in which students are creating a dance about geometric shapes and pathways, explain what you are looking for specifically as they perform their final dance—"I want to see you begin your dance in a geometric shape, then travel on a geometric pathway, and end in a different geometric shape. Make sure your dance contains at least one change in tempo and one change in levels. A dance with all these parts and clear shapes and pathways will be graded as excellent, a dance missing one of these parts will be graded as satisfactory, and a dance with two or more missing parts will be

graded as needs more time to improve." After watching each student's performance, record that child's grade.

Another student assessment format is to use a form that notes the rubric and criteria and write the student's name in the rubric category (see figure 6.5). Space is also available for writing specific comments. In addition to the performance of the dance, you can assess students' understanding of how their body represents a geometric shape, for example, by asking them to draw their body or the shape they used in the dance (see figure 6.6). Older students may write about their choreographic process for the dance (see figure 6.7). It is important to be aware that for some children the ability to communicate their understanding through drawing and writing may be limited by their ability to use those mediums of expression. Again, it is important to assess students' knowledge and experience in a variety of ways.

Peer Assessment

Peer assessment provides students with an opportunity to respond to the dancing of their classmates in a one-to-one relationship or as part of a small group. In this form of assessment, students can observe their classmates performing a dance and share what they observed, review a drawing or written comments, interview a student about his or her process to create a dance (see figure 6.8), or respond to a peer teaching or tutoring situation (Townsend and Mohr 2002). When students develop the assessment criteria and rubric they take ownership of their learning and set their level of achievement. We have used this type of assessment in a square dance unit for fourth- and fifth-grade students. During the square dance unit, students learned four dances and chose one for their final assessment. Before the assessment, the class constructed the criteria and rubric. This activity helped the students set a goal for their group's practice and performance. Small groups of students assessed one another. The students developed the criteria for the final performance. They chose a holistic rubric (see figure 6.2). Students observed one another and then checked the level of performance they felt

Figure 6.4   Student responding to the teacher's question.

Type of Dance: Folk Dance

Level of performance	Evidence of student behavior	Student	Teacher comments
Basic	Cannot accurately reproduce all movements Loses rhythm Has steps but not arm or head movement Body parts not coordinated Moves out of formation Not focused during the dance Loses control	*Sue*	*Needs to stay focused on the lesson, demonstrated difficulty staying on rhythm.*
Proficient	Accurately reproduces all movements Loses rhythm, but can regain Remembers the dance sequence Stays focused on dance Moves out of formation, but can regain Loses coordination on a movement Loses control on a movement	*Steve* *Mary*	*Remembered the sequence of the dance and recalled the names of the steps.* *Stayed focused on lesson, demonstrated initial difficulty with coordination on the slide step; successful after continued practice.*
Advanced	Performs all movements accurately in sequence and rhythm Includes movement details and arm and head movements Demonstrates good balance and strength Stays focused Stays in formation the entire dance Coordinates movements with others	*Mark*	*Was very helpful to other students and took time to show them slides to the right and left and how to count the steps in rhythm to the music.*

Figure 6.5 Recording sheet for a folk dance performance with rubric and criteria.

Figure 6.6 Student drawing of a geometric shape.

the group achieved. They also added a written statement of justification for their score.

Peer assessment of a creative dance can include both objective and subjective observations and responses. For example, one student chose to create a dance inspired by water evaporation and cloud formation, and another chose to dance about an erupting volcano. After spending a session creating and practicing the dances, students worked in pairs to assess each other's dance. The teacher created two questions to focus the response to the observation: (1) Name three movements you saw the students do in their dance (objective), and (2) What part of the dance was most exciting and why (subjective)? The students wrote down their answers and discussed their comments with

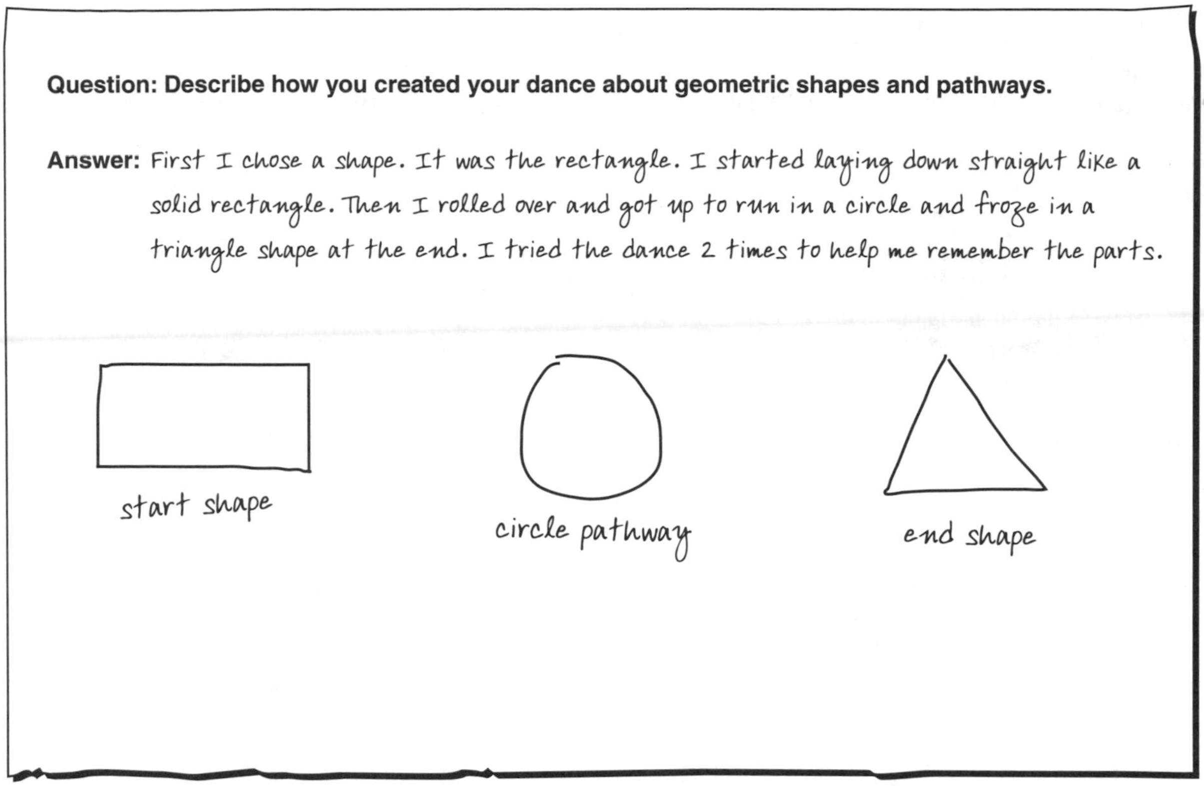

Question: Describe how you created your dance about geometric shapes and pathways.

Answer: First I chose a shape. It was the rectangle. I started laying down straight like a solid rectangle. Then I rolled over and got up to run in a circle and froze in a triangle shape at the end. I tried the dance 2 times to help me remember the parts.

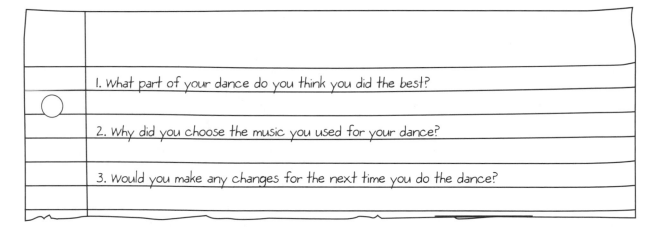

start shape   circle pathway   end shape

Figure 6.7 Student writing explaining the student's choreographic process.

1. What part of your dance do you think you did the best?

2. Why did you choose the music you used for your dance?

3. Would you make any changes for the next time you do the dance?

Figure 6.8 Student-constructed questions for a peer assessment.

each other. Additional questions may include the following:

- What movements did the students use to show the dance idea?
- What direction, speed, or type of force did they use?
- Was there a change in level?
- Did he or she perform the movement the way you expected?
- What changes would you recommend? Why?
- What ideas can you add to the dance?

- How is this dance the same or different from yours?
- What question would you like to ask the dancer?
- How did the dance begin and end?
- Where did the dancer move in space? Can you draw the pathway?
- What about the dance did you think was creative?
- How do you think the music went with the dance?
- What was the purpose of the props in the dance?
- What effect did the costumes have on the dance?
- Did you observe that the dancer or dancers focused on the dance?

Young children who are not proficient in reading and writing a response can draw a pathway or shape that they observed, demonstrate a part they liked, or tell their peer what they remembered about the dance. The teacher can provide a question to focus the observation and facilitate the assessment.

The link between assessment and learning becomes strengthened when students have the opportunity to revise their work after peer assessment (Goodrich 1997). In this way, children can reflect on the assessment and make changes to improve their dance or their performance of a dance. Through peer assessment, students take responsibility for their learning, become autonomous learners, and develop transferable personal skills needed for lifelong learning. This shared activity promotes the interaction of ideas and discovery of one's own preferences about dance.

Student Self-Assessment

In self-assessment, the students evaluate themselves on what they know about dance, how well they learned or created a dance, and how they feel about dance. Students can assess their learning through a variety of tools that include completing a questionnaire, writing a journal entry, having a personal conference with the teacher, writing a letter about their experience, drawing a picture, or recording comments on a tape recorder. These activities all take considerable time and can occur during or outside of the session. The classroom teacher can also be asked to help with the writing and drawing portions of the assessment. We find that the students' responses to the self-assessment inform us about what the students were experiencing and learning. It also contributed to our revision of lessons and units. Sometimes the questions are announced at the beginning or end of a unit or lesson whereas others are asked throughout the lesson. We have developed a question bank as a resource that can be useful in a variety of self-assessment situations (see figure 6.9). We select one or two key questions from the bank that will provide us with the information we are seeking and design a tool that is easy for students to read and complete.

Portfolios are an approach that teachers use that provides children and teachers with a comprehensive view of learning. This assessment tool is a chronological collection of student work gathered throughout the year and used to document progress and achievement. McTighe (1997) describes portfolios using this analogy: "If a test or quiz represents a snapshot (a picture of learning at a specific moment) then a portfolio is more like a photo album—a collection of pictures showing growth and change over time" (p.12). A dance portfolio might include writing samples, journal entries, drawings, notations of dances, list of dance ideas or music, tests, audiotapes, photographs, videotapes, peer reviews, collections of articles and news items, and artwork. Establish and communicate the purpose of the portfolio to the students and take time to review and reflect on its contents frequently. In addition to providing a useful method to document student work, portfolios also provide a tangible way for students to view and celebrate what they have accomplished.

When portfolios are taken home, students can share their work with parents and other adults, which facilitates the school-to-home communication about what is learned in the dance program. Management and storage of portfolios can be overwhelming and take time for review

1. What did you learn about dance today?
2. Is the dancing you did today like any other dancing you have done before?
3. What did you do best in your dance?
4. What was the hardest part of this assignment?
5. What was the most important thing you learned in doing this assignment?
6. Did you pay attention during the whole lesson?
7. Did you cooperate with your partner as you moved together?
8. What movements did you do well?
9. What movements could you practice so they are better the next time?
10. Did you learn anything new about dance from the lesson today?
11. What was your favorite part of the learning experience? Why did you like this part?
12. Would you like to do this dance lesson again?
13. How would you describe your dance to someone at home?
14. What part of your dance should be changed? How would you change it?
15. Did you choose to use music? If you did, why did you choose that piece of music for your dance?
16. What was your purpose in adding a prop or costume to your dance?
17. Name three different movements you performed in the dance.
18. Why do people dance?
19. Describe how directions and levels are used in the dances.
20. What movements are similar in the two folk dances we learned today?
21. Describe one movement from each dance that you feel was strong and powerful.
22. What do the movements in the [name a specific dance] tell us about the culture?
23. Describe the sequence of the [name a specific dance]. How does it begin? What happens next? How does it end?
24. What parts of the learning experience did you like most? Why?
25. Would you like to perform this dance again? Why?
26. What do you like most or least about dancing?
27. How do you feel when you are dancing?
28. Do you feel you can be creative in dance?
29. Do you enjoy dancing with others as part of a small group?
30. Did you feel uncomfortable in any part of the dance learning experience? What part and why?

Figure 6.9 Sample bank of questions for student self-assessment.

and filing. We suggest that you provide each child a folder and organize the folders by class in a basket or box. Then, bring the box to the dance session for students to place their work and review the portfolios at the end of each unit. You will gain valuable insights into what your students think and how they can express themselves in a variety of ways.

Summary

Assessment in dance can be a challenge to design and facilitate. However, for dance to be viewed as an important component of the arts or physical education curriculums, it must provide evidence of student learning. Remember that assessments need definitive criteria and practical rubrics to be effective in helping students understand learning expectations. The content and type of assessment we choose convey a strong message to students about what is important for them to learn. Assessment can be addressed using a variety of approaches. We have discussed four different approaches: assessing the teaching effectiveness, student learning, peer assessment, and student self-assessment. Each tool provides a strength of its own, and in combination they provide a comprehensive view of what students know and can do. The value of feasible and relevant assessments is evidenced in increased appreciation and understanding of dance as a language for expression and communication.

Questions for Reflection

⊚ What type of assessments would you use to evaluate a student's ability to perform a dance with a specific sequence of movements?

⊚ How would you use assessment to determine a student's grade?

⊚ Small groups frequently work together to create a dance. What would be criteria to assess a group dance?

⊚ Consider a format for recording notes or writing in a journal after each class. How would a teacher use the format to reflect on the teaching and learning experience?

Learning Experiences for Children's Dance

The second part of the book presents 20 exciting and practical dance learning experiences. These ready-to-use experiences are written in a style that clearly depicts what the experience will be like when a class of children is actively learning. The descriptions provide the teacher with the language needed to present the learning experience initially and then shape the content to his or her own style of teaching. Bracketed notes guide the teacher along the way. Although these learning experiences focus on creative dance, we suggest that teachers use other resources focused on social and cultural dances to present a comprehensive dance program (please refer to the suggested readings at the end of the book).

In this book, the term *learning experience* is used to describe a sequence of tasks, beginning with an introduction and ending with a culminating dance, that focus on a set of learning objectives. Depending on the amount of time students attend dance sessions, the learning experience may be presented in one or more dance sessions.

In part II, you will find two chapters, each with 10 learning experiences. Chapter 7 contains learning experiences that are appropriate for children in kindergarten through second grade. The content and flow of the learning experience is interesting to and developmentally appropriate for young children. Chapter 8 focuses on students in third through fifth grade, who are able to create and learn dances more independently than younger children. Ideas from either chapter, however, can be adapted for all grade levels. For many years, these learning experiences have been part of the physical education and dance program at the Brunswick Acres Elementary school. They are practical learning experiences that the children have found to be enjoyable yet challenging. When a dance unit is announced, the children gladly welcome the opportunity to express themselves through dance and experience the joy of dancing with others.

The learning experiences in part II are organized to help you easily gain access to the information needed to make a teaching selection. Each learning experience is formatted as follows:

1. Name—The name of the learning experience.
2. Objectives—Objectives that explain what children will gain as a result of participating in the learning experience.
3. Organization—The organization of the children during the learning experience, describing if they will participate individually, in partners, and/or in small groups.
4. Equipment Needed—The kinds and amounts of equipment needed for presenting this learning experience to children.
5. Introduction, Development, Culminating Dance, and Closure—A description of the total learning experience that includes these four components.
6. Look For—Key points for teachers to keep in mind when observing informally children's progress in the learning experience. These points are related to the learning experience objectives.
7. How Can I Change This?—Provides ideas for extending the lesson or presenting a variation.
8. Assessment Suggestions—Ideas for developing assessment tools for student self-assessment, teacher assessment of student learning, and peer assessment.
9. Interdisciplinary Connections—Provides suggestions for linking the dance experience with content in other subject areas.

Explore, experiment with, and enjoy using these learning experiences. They are for you and your students to share as you all discover the excitement of creating, performing, and responding to dance. Our hope is that, because of your willingness to teach dance, more children will have the opportunity to learn about this meaningful form of expression. The skills and knowledge they gain will last a lifetime.

chapter 7

Learning Experiences for Kindergarten, First, and Second Grades

Young children delight in dances that use vivid imagery, stories, and familiar characters. Several of the dance experiences in this chapter provide opportunities for children to express their ideas about circus characters, animals, and real or imaginary experiences. The teacher plays an important role in planning tasks that are appropriate to the physical, cognitive, emotional, and social needs of the particular age group. In these creative dance experiences, the teacher guides students to create and expand their movements within the planned structure of a culminating dance. To facilitate your selection of learning experiences, we have summarized each learning experience in table 7.1.

Table 7.1   Kindergarten, First-, and Second-Grade Learning Experiences Index

Name of dance learning experience	Description of dance learning experience
Neighborhood friendship streamer dance	Children use colorful streamers to dance a story about celebrating friendship in a community.
Floating clouds and rain showers	The shapes and movements of clouds are explored and expressed in a dance depicting how individual clouds connect and form a huge rain cloud.
Run, hop, jump, skip	A poetic text serves as the accompaniment to four dances that express the words that form a rhythm through rhyme.
The playground	Children recreate the activities of playing on a slide, the swings, and a seesaw through moving on different levels and in different directions.
Ocean waves and swimmers	The dancing space is transformed into an ocean and beach in this dance, which uses the level changes of the waves and actions of swimmers to create a dance about a day at the beach.
Spaghetti dance	Are you ready for a bowl of spaghetti? This dance experience, which focuses on creating straight and curved shapes and pathways while varying levels and tempo, concludes with a dance about the adventure of a box of spaghetti.
Balloons	Inflating, deflating, floating, and popping are the actions explored in a learning experience that uses the image of a balloon to create a dance about small and big shapes and movements.
Percussion instrument dance	Light and strong forces are the focus of this dance experience that uses the sounds of a drum, a triangle, and maracas to create three dances that express the quality of the sounds.
The hungry cat	In this learning experience, children dance the slow and fast movements of a cat who wakes up, chases and then captures a mouse, and goes back to sleep.
Circus dance	Welcome to the circus! A suite of dances portrays the actions of four circus acts: the galloping horses, the tightrope walkers, the lions and tigers, and the funny clowns.

Handwritten annotations:

1st - 3rd

Neighborhood friendship streamer dance — Initially seems hokey. Keep reading. It's good!

Floating clouds and rain showers — 2nd s. up or 3rd s. up

Run, hop, jump, skip — NO

The playground — K - 3rd as is or as an introduction to movement = stories w/ 4-8th but substitute something for the slide

Ocean waves and swimmers — 4-8th. There is room for artistic inovation w/beach dancers & ocean unison movement

Spaghetti dance — NO

Balloons — K-8 could have visual intro of child w/balloon walking. Ties it to something & joins dancers (or just sits & watches)

Percussion instrument dance — NO

The hungry cat — NO

Circus dance — ? 2nd + 3rd ?

NEIGHBORHOOD FRIENDSHIP STREAMER DANCE

Objectives

As a result of participating in this learning experience, children will do the following:

- Explore different ways to move in circle pathways on the floor and in the air
- Make straight, twisted, and curved shapes using their whole bodies
- Use a prop while dancing
- Gain an understanding of how a community celebrates friendship through dance

Organization

Students begin the lesson by exploring movements individually; then they dance with a small group; and, finally, all the groups dance together.

Equipment Needed

Tape/CD player • music for accompaniment • 3-feet-long paper or plastic streamers equally divided into four different colors—blue, green, yellow, and red—with enough streamers for each child to have one • four cones to mark the corners of the space

Introduction

Today, we are going to do a friendship dance that uses circles. You will find ways to travel in a circle, turn in a circle, and use a streamer to make circles in the air. The streamer will be your dancing partner. After I give you a streamer, find a personal space and begin to draw circles in the air.

Find all the places around your body that you can draw a circle with the streamer. Can you draw a circle over your head, on the side of your body, around your waist, in front of you, and in back of your body? Try another way.

Draw the largest circle you can. Reach up high, far out to the side, and down to the floor. Make sure you draw circles with each hand. Can you draw a big circle very slowly? Now, a small circle as fast as you can?

Next, travel in a circle by skipping, galloping, or sliding sideways, while making circles with your streamer. Choose one of the ways to travel you didn't select the first time, and make a circle with your streamer in a different way. Now, move the same way you just did, but this time circle the streamer in another different way.

Development

Now, you are going to make circles using your streamer by learning four different ways to turn. In your personal space, make a circle with your body by turning on one foot. How can you use your streamer as you do this turn? Next, try a jump turn. This turn can go all the way around or just part of the way. Be sure to land on your feet, and bend your knees as you come down. Now, find a way to turn using a wide stretched shape. The fourth turn is to turn as slowly as you can. Can you change levels while you slowly turn?

Next, you are going to practice the four different turns, but now you will add a skip before your turn. Here is the pattern. Skip, skip, skip, skip and turn around. Try this pattern using each turn. [Gallops can be used in place of skips, and the teacher can designate an order for practicing each turn instead of the children choosing the order.]

In the next movement, I want you to toss the streamer high above your head, let it go (making sure not to hit anyone), and watch it fall to the floor. What is the shape of the streamer as it lies on the floor? Is the streamer twisted, folded, straight, or curled?

Find a way to make your body into the same shape as the streamer. Toss your streamer into the air again, let it fall, and see what shape it makes on the floor now. Try out this new shape with your body. Try tossing and making shapes a few more times.

Culminating Dance

Now, we're going to combine all the ideas we explored with the streamer into a dance. This is a dance about celebrating friendship in a neighborhood. In this neighborhood, there are four streets. All the students with blue streamers will live on Blue Street in one corner. Students with red streamers will live on Red Street in another corner, yellow streamers on Yellow Street in the third corner, and green streamers on Green Street in the fourth corner of the room. (See figure 7.1.)

Each group will take turns skipping to the middle of the room, doing a turn, and skipping back to their corner. Red group, you will do a one-foot turn, the blue group will do a slow turn moving high and low, the green group will do a jump turn, and the yellow group will do a turn in a wide stretched shape. [Provide time for each group to practice moving together toward the center of the room while skipping and turning.]

Now, I will tell the story about the neighborhood friendship dance as you dance each part. Everyone decided to have a neighborhood friendship dance that lasted for three days. On the first day of the neighborhood dance, the people living on Red Street skipped to the middle of the neighborhood to show everyone their one-foot turn and then they skipped back home. Now, Red Street dancers, show us your skipping and turning. Then, the students living on Blue Street wanted to show the rest of the

neighborhood their slow turn, so they skipped to the middle of the neighborhood, did their slow turn and skipped back home. Okay, Blue Street, we are ready for you. Next, from the third corner, the students on Green Street skipped to the middle of the neighborhood to show their jumping turn and skipped back home. Okay, ready, Green Street dancers? It is your turn. And the Yellow Street dancers said, "Don't forget us! We want to show our wide stretched turn to the neighborhood." So the Yellow Street dancers skipped to the middle, did a big stretched turn, and skipped back home. It is your turn, Yellow Street dancers.

On the second day of the dance, the students on Red Street looked far across the neighborhood to the students on Blue Street and wondered what it would be like to live over there. At the same time, the students on Blue Street looked across at the students on Red Street and also wondered what it would be like to live on Red Street. Both groups decided to go and visit the other street. The red and blue groups slid sideways, leading with their right side, across the middle of the neighborhood to the opposite street, waving to each other with their streamers as they passed by. [Children slide to the opposite corner, passing the other group on the way.] Then the students on Green Street looked at the students on Yellow Street and wondered what

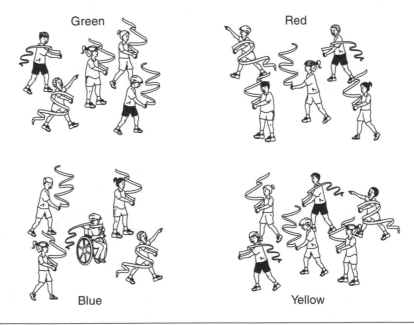

Figure 7.1   Students with streamers begin the dance in four corners in the room.

it would be like to live on Yellow Street. And, at the same time, the students living on Yellow Street had the same feelings. So both groups slid sideways across the space to the opposite corners, waving their streamers as they passed by the other group. [Children slide to the opposite corner.] Next, the Red Street students became lonely for their street and wanted to go home, and the Blue Street students felt the same way. So both groups slid sideways back to their own corners, waving to each other as they passed by. [Children return to their original corner.] Then the students from Green Street and Yellow Street wanted to go back home. So they slid sideways back across the neighborhood to their own corners, waving to each other as they passed by. [Children return to their original corner.]

On the third day of the party, the Red Street group decided to have their own party and invite the whole neighborhood. [Assign two students to be the leaders for the Red Street group.] Now, Red Street group skip over to the Green Street group, stop, wave to them, and say, "Hey, come with us." [Red Street group skips to the Green Street group.] Next, everyone in the red and green groups, skip over to the students on Blue Street, stop, wave to them, and say, "Hey, come with us." [Red and Green skip over to Blue, and Blue joins in to make one large group.] And, finally, everyone skip over to the students on Yellow Street, stop, wave to them, and say, "Hey, come with us." [The yellow group joins the others.] Now everyone skip in a big circle around the room, waving your streamers in the air.

Next, the Red Street group leaders stop, face each other, and hold the ends of each other's streamers to make a doorway into the party. Now, each student take turns walking under the doorway and into the party. At the party, everyone is turning and circling their streamers. You can dance by yourself or dance with another person who has a different color streamer. Okay, begin. I see some students turning slowly, some turning very fast, and some students holding hands and skipping. [Students improvise for 1 or 2 minutes.] Now, everyone stop—the party is over. The dance ends with everyone tossing his or her streamer into the air and making the same shape like we did earlier in the lesson.

Ready? Toss. Let the streamer fall to the floor, and now you slowly fall to the floor and make your body into the same shape as the streamer. [The teacher can signal the end of the party, or a student can create a signal that everyone can follow.] Nice job! Let's try the whole dance again. This time I will not tell the story as you dance. Express the story through your dancing.

Closing

That was great fun. What part of the dance did you like the best? What did you like about it? [Ask several students to share their comments.] How do you think the dance showed friendship? [More students respond.] Take your streamer home with you tonight and talk about our dance with your family. You can show them your turn and the shapes you made with the streamers.

Look For

- How children were able to coordinate the skip-and-turn sequence and maintain good balance. Some children may skip too fast and will not be able to change from the skip to the turn without falling.
- Children who need extra help to match their body shapes to the shape of the streamer. Some children will surprise you with their unique interpretations, and others will not be able to match the shape of the streamer with their bodies. You can ask these children to reproduce only a part of the streamer shape.
- Children who need help avoiding sliding into others when exchanging corners. Ask for suggestions on how to solve the bumping problem.

How Can I Change This?

- Try galloping or walking instead of skipping.
- Ask the street group to collaborate and choose a way to travel to the middle of the neighborhood. They could be connected, low to the floor, or changing directions.
- Allow children to choose the streamer color. This may lead to uneven groups in the corners, but having some streets

with more students can make the dance interesting.

◑ In the section of the culminating dance where two students hold hands to make a door, you can have everyone in the red group hold hands with a partner to make several doors for the other three groups to use as entrances to the party. This strategy will also alleviate waiting in line a long time to enter the party.

Assessment Suggestions

◑ Ask students to describe verbally what happens on each day of the Friendship Streamer dance to assess their recall of the dance sequence.

◑ Students can create a vocabulary list of words that describe the shapes of the streamers and their bodies after the toss. They can also make drawings of the shapes.

◑ Students, organized by their street group, can share with each other the different ways they made circles with the streamers.

◑ Students can draw a picture of friends dancing together with the streamers.

Interdisciplinary Connections

◑ Use this dance to initiate or conclude a social studies unit on communities or friendship.

◑ Integrate the dance with visual arts by having the students draw pictures of the circle pathways or the shapes of the streamers as they were lying on the ground.

FLOATING CLOUDS AND RAIN SHOWERS

Objectives

As a result of participating in this learning experience, children will do the following:

- Create shapes with their bodies inspired by moving clouds
- Demonstrate the contrast of slow and light movements with fast and strong movements
- Move in different relationships—with a partner, in a small group, and in a large group
- Use coordination and control in movement transitions

Organization

Students dance individually and then with a partner. Next, partners join other sets of partners to form small groups, and, finally, the whole class joins together in one formation.

Equipment Needed

Tape/CD player • slow and fast music for accompaniment or use a percussion instrument • paper and crayons for drawing • a chalkboard

Introduction

Today, we are going to do a dance called floating clouds and rain showers. This dance is about the shapes and movements of clouds. How can you describe the cloud shapes you have seen? Amy said they are round; Tim said long. I also heard puffy, big, soft, oval, and straight. [The teacher writes these shape words on chart paper or a chalkboard.] How do clouds move across the sky? I hear fast, slow, floating, twirling. Yes, sometimes they are still or move up and down. [The teacher writes movement words on chart paper or chalkboard.] Now, we are going to use the cloud shapes and the different ways clouds move to create a dance. Find a personal space in the room for our warm-up.

Begin your warm-up following me. I will use slow movements while we are standing in our spaces and then faster movements as we travel in the space. [The teacher slowly moves different body parts, bending and stretching in different directions. Then, the teacher asks students to walk around the room, followed by galloping, and finally running.]

Development

The cloud-shape words that you described in the beginning of class are on the chalkboard. Standing in your personal space, make your body into one of those shapes. Try another one, and now another. Let's try making a round-shaped cloud. Can you make the round shape with only your arms? Try making a wide cloud shape, now a long straight shape, and now a small shape. Can you make a cloud shape that uses another body part touching the floor, other than your feet? Meredith has made a long shape on the side of her body, and Tamika is in a wide stretched shape supported by her hands and feet. Try another cloud shape and one more different cloud shape.

Choose three different cloud shapes and then decide which one you will do first, second, and third. Let's practice changing from the first shape to the second shape and then to the third shape. Ready! Slowly make your first shape, quickly get into your second shape, and slowly make your third shape. Try the three cloud shapes again using the slow, fast, slow tempos. This time try a different tempo sequence for your cloud shapes such as fast, fast, slow or fast, slow, slow. Practice this cloud shape dance a couple times.

Choose a cloud shape and find a way to make it travel around general space slowly; now quickly. Choose another cloud shape and decide the speed it will travel. I see round clouds walking slowly, wide clouds sliding sideways, and fast and long straight clouds rolling on the floor.

Feel like your cloud is floating across the sky, changing shapes and tempo as it moves. Be careful to move around the other clouds. [Children practice their cloud movements. The teacher plays music or a percussion instrument while children practice.]

Does anyone want to show us her or his cloud dance? Let's watch and see what shapes the dancers are making and if they change the tempo. [Three or four students demonstrate, and the teacher asks observing students to comment on what they see.]

Now, I will assign you a cloud partner, and I want you to find different ways you can connect your cloud shapes to each other and float across the sky. [The teacher organizes students into partners and provides time for exploration.] What are the different body parts you can use to connect to another cloud? I see these two students are using their hands; others are using their feet. I see elbows connected to shoulders, hands connected to a back, and heads connected.

Next, can you and your partner combine your two cloud shapes and make a new cloud shape? Try making three different cloud shapes. Remember to stay connected. What other cloud shapes can you make connected together?

Now find a way to move your new cloud across the sky. Decide if one person is going to lead or if you are going to take turns as leaders. Can you continue to stay connected as you travel?

Find another cloud and connect together into a larger cloud. What are the different body parts you can use to connect to each other? Can you find a way for this cloud to travel across the space? Who will be the leader? What is the shape of your large cloud? When you have a large cloud, move slowly so everyone can move together and stay connected. Let me see how you move slowly in your cloud shape and stay connected. [When children move as connected clouds, you want them to enjoy the challenge of moving with another person and remaining safe. Take this opportunity to discuss cooperation in decision making. Make sure the students agree about how and where they are going to move before they begin. Remind them to move slowly.]

Now, all the small groups of clouds are going to join together into one really, really big cloud. Before we move, we need to talk about what shape the large cloud will be, how we will be connected to each other, and how the cloud will move. What shape should we use for the large cloud? Carmen suggests a long straight cloud. How will we be connected to each other? Joe suggests holding hands. How will the cloud move? Constantine says that walking will work best. Let's all join hands in a long line with Carmen as the leader and Joe at the end of the line. [Children get assembled.] Carmen, begin to lead the cloud around the room as everyone walks slowly. Bring the cloud to the middle of the room to form a circle, and now close the cloud shape by holding Joe's hand. Now, let go of your hands. Let's try it again with a new leader. Can anyone suggest another large class cloud? [The teacher can try several ideas, with suggestions from the students about the shape and how to move.]

Culminating Dance

Now, we are going to use all the cloud shapes in a dance. The dance will begin with your individual cloud shape and then move into partner or trio cloud shapes. Next, everyone will join together in one giant cloud. Now, each person find a personal space to begin the cloud dance. Begin to slowly make your body into one of your individual cloud shapes and travel in the space. As you move, find another person and connect. Remember to connect with different body parts. Now, find another cloud; connect and travel together across the sky. Move slowly so everyone can stay connected and travel together safely. Now all the clouds join together by holding hands in a long line with Gary as the leader and Rae at the end of the line. I see everyone is moving slowly and holding hands as you follow Gary around the room. Gary, bring the group into a big circle and join hands with Rae to make a large round cloud. Now, let's try the dance again from the beginning with a new leader.

Closure for Cloud Dance

To end the lesson, lay down on the floor and rest while you think about the cloud dance. Pretend you are watching a movie of the cloud dance. Watch yourself make different cloud shapes. What shapes are you using? Now you are connecting to another cloud. What body parts did you use to connect? Next, partner clouds are connecting to other partner clouds, and you are all moving across the sky. Are you moving slowly? And, finally, everyone connects into one giant cloud. What is the shape of the giant cloud?

[The learning experience can conclude at this point, or you can continue to add the next section, the rainstorm.]

The next part of the learning experience begins with everyone standing in a large circle like a big round cloud. In this part of the dance, the cloud is going to fill up with rain and burst open. How can we make this cloud become bigger and bigger? I hear from Sari that we can let go of hands and move backward, and Brad suggested that we make big stretching shapes. Let's try both ideas. Let go of hands and move backward four steps, growing into a big stretched shape. (See figure 7.2.) Ready! 1, 2, 3, 4. Hold your big shape still. Let's try it again.

Once the cloud is full of rain it will burst open. What are some other words we can use instead of burst? I hear explode, break open, pop, bust apart. How can your body move to show a bursting movement? I hear up, open, stretched, jumping, turning. What kind of force is needed? Yes, strong. Where will you move in space? Okay, up and forward, up and backward, or up and sideward. Create three different burst-

Figure 7.2 The cloud becomes bigger and bigger, filling up with rain.

ing movements. Ready! Burst, burst, and burst. Try each burst in a different direction. Burst, burst, and burst. Practice your three bursting movements each in a different direction.

Now, let's combine the cloud filling with rain and the bursting. First, the circle becomes bigger 1, 2, 3, and 4, and now burst, burst, and burst. Let's try that part again. 1, 2, 3, and 4, and burst, burst, and burst. [The teacher can ask several students to demonstrate their bursting movement while the children observe the different directions of the burst.]

After the cloud bursts open, it begins to rain all over the room. What are some different ways we can use movement to express the rain? Jennifer suggests that we run all over the room with big leaps in the air, like the wind is pushing the rain all over. Trevor suggests that the rain falls straight down and we should show the falling rain by using our arms, starting high and moving low several times quickly. You may use either of these suggestions or create your own movement for the rain. Will your movement travel around the space or stay in your personal space? Let me see what choices you have made to show the rain. [Children practice being the rain falling while the teacher observes.]

In the last part of this dance, the rainstorm stops and the last drop falls slowly to the ground. Stop your rain movement and hold your body still. Now slowly, very slowly, fall to the floor. Can you add a turn to your slow falling? Keep your body in control as you fall. What shape will your body be in at the end of the fall? Think about it! Now combine your rain movement with the stop and slow fall to the floor ending in a shape. Ready! Rain, rain, rain, rain, rain, rain, rain, rain, and stop. Now slowly fall to the floor, ending in a shape. [Students can practice this sequence several times to coordinate the transitions between movements.]

Now let's put the whole rainstorm dance together. Begin with everyone holding hands in a large circle. Now, let go as the cloud fills up with rain. Step backward, 1, 2, 3, 4, and make a wide big shape and hold it still, 1, 2, 3. Now burst and burst and burst; and now rain, rain, rain, rain, rain, rain, rain, rain, rain, and stop; and slowly fall to the floor and end in a shape. [The sequence of movements can be noted on a chalkboard or by drawing picture symbols to indicate the order of the movements.]

Now, let's combine the cloud dance with the rainstorm dance. Ready! Find your personal space to begin your individual cloud. Slowly make your body into the shape of a cloud and begin to travel in the space. Find another cloud and join together. Now find another cloud and join together to form a bigger cloud. Everyone join in one large, long cloud with Carmen as the leader and Joe at the end. Carmen, lead the cloud around the room and come to the middle of the room to form a circle by taking Joe's hand. Let go of your hands as the cloud fills with rain. Step backward and make a wide stretched shape. Now burst and burst and burst; and rain, rain, rain, rain, rain, rain, rain, and rain; and stop; and slowly fall to the floor and end in a shape.

Closure for Rainstorm

What are the different types of energy you used to express different parts of the rainstorm? What part of the rainstorm did you enjoy dancing? Why did you like that part?

Look For

- ⊙ The different shapes the students create. Are they able to make a variety of different cloud shapes?
- ⊙ How children control their movements in the cloud and rainstorm segments. Specifically, can they coordinate the transitions between each part of the dance?
- ⊙ How children use different directions for the bursts in the rainstorm segment. Do you see the whole body or body parts moving in a specific direction?

How Can I Change This?

- ⊙ Students can create smaller clouds that fill up with rain and burst instead of the one large cloud.
- ⊙ Add creating a rainbow at the end of the rainstorm with the sun shining. Students can make small-group shapes representing the curved line of the rainbow in a variety of ways. Ask them for ideas.

Assessment Suggestions

- ⊙ Children can draw and label shapes they used in the cloud dance.
- ⊙ Partners can write a list of body parts they used to connect to each other in the cloud dance.
- ⊙ Teacher checklist records observations to assess if children can burst in three different directions using control by landing on their feet.

Interdisciplinary Connections

- ⊙ Connect to visual arts by having children observe and draw clouds on a large piece of paper.
- ⊙ Integrate children's literature by using the book *Little Cloud* (Carle 1996) as a guide for making different cloud shapes and developing a dance to accompany the story.
- ⊙ Integrate children's literature by using the book *Listen To The Rain* (Endicott 1988). The text and illustrations will stimulate ideas for creating dance movements.
- ⊙ Use this dance to reinforce science concepts about the water cycle, cloud formations, or different types of weather.

RUN, HOP, JUMP, SKIP

Objectives

As a result of participating in this learning experience, children will do the following:

- ☉ Perform locomotor movements of run, hop, jump, and skip
- ☉ Use movements that enhance balance and strength
- ☉ Perform a sequence of movements
- ☉ Connect rhyming words to movement.

Organization

Students will move individually in their personal space for the run dance, the skip dance, and the hop dance. The jump dance begins individually and ends in a small group.

Equipment Needed

Chalkboard or chart listing the locomotor words and the rhyming words (see figure 7.3)

Figure 7.3 Rhyming words listed on chalkboard.

Introduction

Today, we are going to dance to words that rhyme with run, hop, jump, and skip. [Words are written on the chart or chalkboard.] Can you suggest words that rhyme with run, hop, jump, and skip? [The teacher writes down children's suggestions.] We will use all these words in our warm-up and then select a few words for the dance.

In your personal space, begin to jog in place as we say the words you listed under run. Run, bun, pun, fun, nun, sun, and stun. Now hop on your right foot as we say the words listed under hop. Now we will repeat the words while we hop on our left foot. Hop, pop, mop, bop, cop, drop, flop, clop, lop, chop, top, plop, stop, and prop. Next, jump in place while you say the words listed under jump. Bump, clump, stump, rump, dump, frump, grump, hump, lump, mump, pump, and plump. The last movement in the warm-up is to skip while saying the words listed under skip. Blip, clip, sip, dip, flip, drip, grip, slip, lip, nip, and rip.

Development

I have selected a few words from the list to use in the warm-up for the dance. I am going to read the first poem that uses the words *run, fun,* and *sun* and then we will create different ways to move to each word. [The teacher reads the run poem.]

> Let's all begin to run
>
> And run, and run, and run.
>
> Everyone stop,
>
> And have some fun
>
> Some fun, some fun, some fun
>
> In the sun, in the sun, in the sun.

First, let's find different ways to run. What are some other different ways to run? Jessica suggests that we run with tiny steps. Let's try Jessica's suggestion. Can we think of any other different ways to run? Miguel is running with his arms stretched out to the side. [Students try the suggestion.] Now try your own idea for running. Now try another idea. [This would be a good time for children to rest and share their running explorations either with the whole class or with a partner.] Think about choosing your favorite way to run for this dance. We will use it in a few minutes.

For the word *fun,* we will create movements that show us doing something fun, like playing ball, jumping rope, petting a dog, roller skating, or playing catch. Think about some other things you do for fun. How can you express them through a movement? Show me now. Exaggerate your movements; make them very big. Choose one you would like to use in this dance. The last rhyming word is *sun*. Create a shape with your arms that is round like the sun. Move your arms from right to left, beginning low on the right side of your body, stretch your round arms high over your head; and end low on the left side of your body. Do you know what this arm movement is like? This movement shows the movement of the sun rising in the morning, moving across the sky, and setting low at night. Try this movement again, starting slowly on the right, reaching up high, and going low to the left. Keep the movement smooth and slow.

This time, as I read the poem, move using the run movement you chose, then the fun movement you selected, and then we will all do the sun movement together. Ready! Do your run movement. "Let's all begin to run, and run, and run, and run." Now use the fun movement. "Everyone stop and have some fun, some fun, some fun, some fun." What are your fun movements? Everyone does the sun movement all together. "In the sun, in the sun, in the sun." Try it again, but I'm not going to tell you when to do things. [The teacher reads the poem again while the students perform their dance.]

Our next dance uses words that rhyme with *hop*. I will read the poem, and you listen carefully for the words that rhyme with hop.

> One day we all went out for a hop
>
> With our hands placed on our top.
>
> Then someone came by and yelled "stop!"
>
> We then did a pop and a drop.

What were the words that rhymed with hop? Yes, *drop, stop, top,* and *pop.* Good listening!

Let's begin with the word *hop*. What are the different directions you can use for your hop? I see some students hopping forward, some backward, and others sideward. When you hop, remember that one foot is doing the hopping and the other foot is up off the floor. While you are hopping, can you place the leg that is off the floor in front of your body? What about stretched in back of your body? Out to the side? Give each leg a turn to hop.

The next word is *top*. Create different shapes with your hands when they are on the top of your head. Pretend your hands are like a hat on top of your head. I see some pointed hats, round hats, flat hats, hats that look like horns, and some that look like a crown. Do you think you can hop with your hands on your top? Choose a hat shape and a way to hop, and give it a try.

The third word is *stop*. Create a still shape. Make a round shape, a twisted shape, a stretched shape, a shape with many angles in the body. Each time I clap my hands I want you to make a different still shape and freeze. Ready! [The teacher claps 6 to 8 times.] Remember your still shapes; we will use them when we dance to the poem.

The fourth word is *pop*. We are going to explore different ways to pop up in the air. It is like a jump. Make sure you land on your feet with your knees bent. Can you pop in the air and make a stretched shape? Can you take off on two feet and land on one foot? Can you add a turn to your pop? Try a pop where you jump high into the air and a pop that does not go very high.

The last rhyming word is *drop*. I want you to be safe and drop slowly as if you are melting down to the floor. Show me how you can slowly lower your body to the floor very carefully. Use your hands to help you as you become lower and lower. Can you add a turn as you drop? Let's practice combining the pop and drop. Ready and pop! And now drop very slowly. I see you can change from a strong, fast movement to a light, slow movement.

Now, I will read the whole poem, and as I say the words I want you to dance the movements you created. Here's the poem: "One day we all went out for a hop with our hands on our top." [Children hop with hands on the top of their head in a hat shape.] "Someone came by and yelled 'stop!'" [Children freeze in a shape.] "We then did a pop and a drop." [Children jump into the air for the pop, and slowly drop to the floor.] Try the dance again as I read the poem. [Repeat the poem again.]

Our next dance uses words that rhyme with *jump*. Here's the poem:

We all went out to jump
And jump and jump and jump.
We jumped so close together
We all started to gently bump
And bump and bump and bump
And slowly fell into a clump.

What words rhymed with *jump?* Good, Alyssa, one is *clump.* Yes, Min-Su, another one is *bump.* The first word we will use is *jump.* When I say go, I want you to find a space and try different ways to jump in place. Go! Can you jump so your feet move together and apart? What are the different shapes you can make with your arms as you are jumping? Try jumping forward in a zigzag pathway. Find a way to take small jumps and then large jumps, first moving forward, then backward, and finally sideward. As I read the first part of the poem, choose your favorite way to jump. [The teacher reads the first two lines of the poem while the children jump.]

The next word is *bump.* We are going to use different body parts to lightly bump against another person. As you walk around the room and come close to another person, lightly bump them with your arm. I want Curtis and Tamika to demonstrate a light bump with their arms. [Students demonstrate.] They are using a soft touch for the bump. Now everyone try the soft bump with your classmates. Try bumping with another body part, like maybe your foot, knee, elbow, hand, shoulder, hip, back, or finger. The bumping will be a big change of force from the jumping. Let's combine the jumping with the bumping. Make sure you have a place in the room where you have lots of space around you. I will read the poem, and I want to see how you change from the strong force used in the jumping to the light force used for the bumping. Get ready to move! [The teacher reads the first five lines of the poem while children jump and bump.]

The last word in this poem is *clump.* What is a clump? Ryan says it is a lot of things bunched up together. We are going to be a clump of children at the end of the poem. To make the clump we will slowly fall to the floor and end in a round shape. In your own space, try slowly falling to the floor in a round shape. Now I want two, three, or four people to get together in a group and together, using a slow tempo, fall to the floor. Can all of you stay together in a small space and fall slowly at the same time? Try it again.

Now, I will read the whole poem. I want you to end the dance in the clump with the same people you were just with. Start the dance far apart from each other and move toward each other on the jumps, then gently bump the people in your group, and then slowly fall into a clump. [The teacher reads the whole poem as the children dance.] Nice job jumping, bumping, and clumping!

This last dance rhymes three words with the word *skip.* Listen to the poem for the words that sound like skip.

We all began to skip
And skip and skip and skip.
Then tried to do a flip
A flip, a flip, a flip.
Instead we began to trip
And fell upon our hip.

Begin the dance with exploring different pathways for skipping. First try skipping in a straight path. Now try a curved pathway. Can you skip backward on the straight or curved pathway? Try different ways to move or make shapes with your arms as you skip. I will assign you a partner, and I want you to show each other your favorite pathway to use in the skip. Tell your partner what kind of pathway you observed while they skipped. Now, I will read the first two lines of the poem and you can skip using your pathway or the pathway your partner used. [The teacher reads the first two lines as the students skip.]

The second rhyming word in the poem is *flip.* We are not going to really do a flip. That would be too dangerous; however, we are going to create a turn that changes levels. Find a way to turn on one foot or two feet so your turn starts on a high level, changes to a low level, and ends on a high level. [Students practice turning while the teacher cues the movements.] Ready! Turn high, low, and high. Try another turn using high, low, high levels. As I read the third and fourth lines of the poem, try your flip turns that change levels. [The teacher reads the poem.]

The third word is *trip*. We are going to slowly fall to the floor using your hands to help you lower your body to the floor. Can you add a turn to your slow fall? [Students practice slowly falling to the floor.]

The last word in the poem is *hip*. Point to your hips. Can you lie down with your right hip touching the floor? Now try your left hip. Find another way to lie down with your hips touching the floor. Try one more way. Now, let's combine slowly falling to the floor and ending the fall in one of the ways you created to lie on your hips. Ready? Slowly fall and have your hips on the floor. Now, as I read the last two lines of the poem, do the falling movements ending on your hips. [The teacher reads the last two lines of the poem.]

This time, as I read the whole poem, perform the movements you created to represent the words *skip, flip, trip,* and *hip*. Let's review all the movements first. Here's the first line: "We all began to skip, and skip and skip and skip." Show me the pathway you chose for your skip. "Then we tried to do a flip, a flip, a flip, a flip." Now do your high, low, high turn. "Instead we began to trip." Slowly fall to the floor. "And fell upon our hip." End in a shape with your hip touching the floor. I will read the poem again. I want you to dance the movements you created as you hear the rhyming words, but I'm not going to tell you what to do. Ready? [The teacher repeats the poem again.]

Culminating Dance

Each of these poems can be performed individually as a culminating dance, or you can combine two, three, or all four poems to form a longer sequence as the culminating dance.

Closure

What was your favorite poem? Raise your hand when I call out the one you liked the best. The run poem. The hop poem. The jump poem. The skip poem. Does anyone have another movement that we could use to create a poem dance?

Look For

๏ Children who are not ready to perform the skip. You can substitute a gallop or present the dance when everyone has learned how to skip.

๏ Children who tire easily when performing many repetitions of locomotor movements that require strength and balance. Provide more frequent moments to rest.

๏ Changes in the students' use of force in all four dances. All dances begin with strong force and end using light force.

How Can I Change This?

๏ Students can choose their favorite poem (run, skip, hop, jump) and perform the dance while other students accompany the dancing by playing percussion instruments.

๏ Use other locomotor or nonlocomotor movements as the inspiration for rhyming words and creating movements.

Assessment Suggestions

๏ Students organized into partners or small groups select two of the poems, practice the movements while they say the words, and perform the poems for another set of partners or another group. The teacher can provide a question on which the observers can focus their observation. Use the question bank (see figure 6.9) for assessment ideas.

๏ Use a teacher checklist to note how well each child performs the locomotor movements in the poem dances. Also, use the checklist format to assess how well children can change from one movement to another in the dance sequence.

Interdisciplinary Connections

- Ask the classroom teacher about vocabulary words students are learning that could be used for rhyming dances.

- Students can write poems using action verbs and then create movements to express the words.

- This dance supports language arts content focused on rhyming.

- Add children's books that use locomotor movements as content such as, *Hop Jump* (Walsh 1993); *Jump, Frog, Jump* (Kalan 1981); or *In The Small, Small Pond* (Fleming 1993).

THE PLAYGROUND

Objectives

As a result of participating in this learning experience, children will do the following:

- Perform locomotor and nonlocomotor movements
- Create movements that represent the different ways children play on a playground
- Apply the different elements of movement emphasized at each area of the playground: range and unison movement on the swings dance, levels for the slide dance, and relationships using opposition for the seesaw dance

Organization

Students move individually, in partners, and with a large group as they visit the different imaginary playground spaces.

Equipment Needed

Tape/CD player • lively music for accompaniment • signs indicating the different playground spaces • tape

Introduction

Today, we are going to create a dance about the playground. Pretend this room is a playground. What are the different ways you play at the playground? I hear sliding down the slide, going on the seesaw, swinging on the swings, playing on the climbing bars (monkey bars). Let's choose three areas to visit on the playground today: the seesaw, the sliding board, and the swings. I have a sign for each of these areas, and I will place the signs on the walls. The slide will be at this end of the room [place sign on wall], the seesaw will be in this corner [place sign], and the swings will be in the middle of the room around the center circle [place sign on the floor].

For our warm-up, we are going to find different ways to travel to the playground. Let's pretend we are walking to the playground.

sand box
rocking toys

Try walking fast in a curvy pathway; now walk backward slowly. Can you pretend to be riding a bicycle, steering to the right and to the left? Next, let's warm up our arms by swinging them forward and backward, now side to side. Start with small swings and make them bigger and bigger and as big as you can, then smaller and smaller and as small as you can.

Development

Now that we have arrived at the playground, let's go on the slide first. Everyone begin in one end of the room. Pretend the space in front of you is a giant slide. Let's start by using our arms and legs to climb up the ladder using 8 counts. Begin low and reach higher on each count. 1, 2, 3, 4, 5, 6, 7, 8. [The teacher demonstrates while counting to 8.] Now, let's try climbing to the 8 counts all together. Begin in a squat position low to the floor and climb a little higher on each count. [Children practice the imaginary climb while counting to 8.] Now, let's pretend to slide down the slide. Lower your body to the floor, and find a way to move forward as if you were going down a slide. I see some students on the front of their bodies pulling themselves with their hands along the floor, others are sitting and using their arms and legs to push and pull, and others are moving forward walking on their hands and feet. When you arrive at the other end of the room, go back to where you started. Climb up the ladder for 8 counts, and try another way to move down the slide. Can you travel backward or sideward down the slide?

Next, let's go to the swings. In this dance, we all move in unison. That means we all do the same movement at the same time. I want everyone to join together and make a circle. Now swing your arms forward and backward, forward and backward, using 4 counts. Let's try it all together. Forward, backward, forward, backward or 1, 2, 3, 4. [The teacher leads the unison practice with the students.] Now place one foot forward. Rock forward toward the front foot and then rock backward, shifting the weight to the back foot. Add the arms we just practiced to the rocking feet. All together, swing forward, backward, forward, backward. [The teacher leads the unison practice.]

Let's add a second part to this dance. This time make a giant arm swing forward, walk forward 4 big steps, and stretch up on the fourth step. [The teacher demonstrates the walk and stretch.] Ready, all together with me. Swing your arms forward and step, step, step, step, and stretch. (See figure 7.4.) What happens to the circle when we do this at the same time? Yes, it gets smaller. Now swing the arms backward and take 4 steps back. Let's try the swing and walk several times. Ready? Swing forward, 1, 2, 3, and 4; swing backward, 1, 2, 3, and 4. [The teacher and students practice the swinging forward and backward in unison several times.]

Let's combine the first and second parts of the swing dance. Remember, 4 swings with the arms (4 counts), 4 swings with rocking feet (4 counts), swing walking forward (4 counts), and swing walking backward (4 counts). The whole dance is 16 counts long. Let's try it all together three times.

Now, let's move over to the seesaws. I will assign you a partner or make groups of three. Can someone tell us how seesaws move? Marcos

suggests that when one side is up the other side is down and they keep changing. Face your partners and find a way for one person to start low and the other start high and then change at the same time. Can you hold hands and do the seesaw movement? Can you connect with another body part? Find a way to do the up and down seesaw movement while sitting on the floor. You and your partner create three different ways to move in opposition to show the seesaw movement. Practice each of the ways three times. Show me how you can change smoothly from the first way to the second and then to the third.

Culminating Dance

Now, we are going to combine the three short dances into one big dance. The first time we do the dance we will all go to the same place in the same order. The second time you perform the dance you can choose the order for your dance. Ready! Let's all travel to the playground by riding our bikes. Here we go. [Students can follow the teacher or choose their own pathway and meet at the slides.] Well, here we are at the playground. Let's all go on the slide first. Ready to climb? Start low. 1, 2, 3, 4, 5, 6, 7, 8, and slide down forward or backward. Go back to the other side of the room and try the counting and climbing again, and this time, choose another way to slide.

Now, let's go over to the swings. Make a big circle. Everyone ready? Let's do this dance together. Arm swings, 1, 2, 3, 4; rocking swings, 1, 2, 3, 4; swing walk forward, 1, 2, 3, 4; swing walk backward, 1, 2, 3, 4.

Now, let's go to the third area, the seesaw. Find your partner and do the seesaw movement, either standing high and low or sitting high and low. Count to 12, and then meet me near the chalkboard.

You now can do the dance by yourselves while I play the music. This time you choose what area of the playground you are going to play in first, second, and third. Perform the movements we practiced at each area. Start when the music begins, and meet me by the chalkboard when you are finished. [The teacher begins the music.] I see Danielle is on the slide—I can hear her counting to 8 as she climbs—and Hector is

Figure 7.4 Swing dance.

on the swings moving forward and backward, and Theresa and Steve are at the seesaw moving opposite each other going high and low.

Closure

Everyone show me your favorite movement of the dance. Next, show me the movement that was the hardest for you to perform. Can you think of another piece of playground equipment we could add to this dance? How would you create a dance about that piece?

Look For

- How students perform the skills based on their motor development and fitness level. Can students alternate hands and feet as they represent climbing? Do students demonstrate adequate strength to travel low to the floor as needed in the playground slide? On the seesaw, are students able to coordinate their muscles to move up and down with even rhythm?

- Students who may need help to make a decision about which playground area to play in during the second part of the culminating dance. These children may need to follow other students.

How Can I Change This?

- Students can make shapes with their bodies either individually or with others that represent the shape of the swings, the slide, and the seesaw.

- Students can draw pictures of the different areas of the playground and place them under the signs.

- Students can suggest different pieces of playground equipment for the dance.

- Take time before students try the second part of the culminating dance to have them plan the order, and write or draw pictures of which playground area they will go to first, second, and third.

Assessment Suggestions

- The teacher reflects on the three dances and reviews how well the children were able to perform the movements within the limitations of the task.

- The teacher videotapes the children performing the second part of the culminating dance. The tape is reviewed to see what parts of the dance children could perform without teacher direction.

Interdisciplinary Connections

- The dance sequences reinforce math concepts of counting and patterns.

- Students can use mapping skills to draw a playground map, arranging the playground equipment in different spaces to correspond to the dance or create a new playground.

OCEAN WAVES AND SWIMMERS

Objectives

As a result of participating in this learning experience, children will do the following:

- Move on high and low levels
- Coordinate arm and leg movements to express the ocean waves and the swimmer's movements
- Use locomotor movements in different directions and pathways

Organization

Students explore movements individually using levels, pathways, and directions, and in two large groups they perform the culminating dance.

Equipment Needed

Tape/CD player • music with the sound of ocean waves • pictures or video of waves or swimmers • drum or other percussion instruments

Introduction

Today, we are going to the beach. Did you bring your swimsuit and towel? The ocean will be in this half of the room, and the beach will be in the other half. (See figure 7.5.) In this dance, we will move high and low, and use different pathways and directions. Has anyone been to the beach? Can you describe how the waves move? Now, let's do our warm-up so we are ready for a day of fun at the beach.

Begin the warm-up by walking in the space. Let's pretend we are walking to the beach. I will play the drum with an even, steady beat. As you walk, match the tempo of the drumbeat with each step. Swing your arms as you walk. Can you walk and change levels reaching up high and bending down low? Now change the walk to a skip or a gallop as I change the drumbeat. Keep swinging your arms.

Development

In your personal space, let's first create some movements about the ocean waves. Using your hands and arms show me how an ocean wave moves. I can see that your hands and arms are moving up and down. Make the up movement bigger and higher, and reach the down movement low to the floor. Try both arms at the same time. Now add your whole body when you reach up high with your arms, and then

Lunge
couree
walk

Ocean wave dancers

Swimmers

Figure 7.5 Beginning places for the ocean waves and swimmers.

bend your whole body as you reach down low with your arms. Let your head follow the up-and-down movement too. Add these 4 up counts and 4 down counts to the movement as I play the drum. Take all 4 counts to move up and all 4 counts to move down. Up-up-up-up and down-down-down-down, and up-up-up-up and down-down-down-down.

This time, find a way to walk forward in the space and move your body high and low. Add the counts up-up-up-up and down-down-down-down. Remember these walks; we will use them later in the dance to represent the ocean waves.

Now, let's create movements that feel like the splashes of the ocean waves as they hit the beach. Keeping your body low to the floor, how can you use your arms and legs to show the movement of a splash? Where do your arms and legs move in the space? What kind of force will you choose? Can you splash in different directions?

What happens to the wave after it hits the beach and splashes? Yes, it rolls back into the ocean. Show me how you can roll your body sideways as if you are a wave going back into the ocean. Add some of your splashing movements as you roll.

Now, let's combine the three different ways the wave can move. First, in your self-space do the rising up-and-down movement of the waves. Ready! Up-up-up-up and down-down-down-down. Do it again. Now add walking forward, up-up-up-up and down-down-down-down, and end down on the floor. Let's repeat this from the beginning: in place, up-up-up-up and down-down-down-down, and, again in place, up-up-up-up and down-down-down-down; now walking forward, up-up-up-up and down-down-down-down, and end on the floor.

Now add the splashing movements in your self-space on the floor. Ready! Splashing, and splashing, and splashing, and splashing. You really have to use lots of force in your arms and legs. Now, splash in different directions.

The third wave movement is rolling back to the ocean with little splashes of your arms and legs. Ready! Roll, and roll, and roll, and roll, and add splashes each time you roll onto your back.

Remember the three different movements of the ocean. We will use them later in our dance. Now, let's create movements for the swimmers. What are the different ways your arms move when you are swimming? I see arms moving forward, backward, sideways. Try a movement in which you alternate your arms. Try another way to move your arms so they move together, then apart and together and apart. Now add walking to your swimming arm movements. Use forward, backward, and sideward directions in the walking and in the arm movements. Swim all over the room using curvy pathways, as if you are swimming in all parts of the ocean.

I am going to divide the class into two groups. One group will be the ocean waves, and the other group will be the swimmers. Each student will have a chance to dance as the waves and swimmers today. The swimmers and waves will begin the dance on opposite sides of the room.

Culminating Dance

[At this point the teacher tells the story, and the children listen without dancing.] This is a story about the ocean waves and the swimmers. First, the swimmers put on their swimsuits; grab their towels; and walk, skip, or gallop to the beach. They move on the beach side of the room. Next, they find a spot on the beach and pretend to place the towels down by using a swinging arm movement. They lay down on the towel to feel the sun. Think about what shape you will use when you lie down on the towel. It is a very hot day, and the swimmers decide to go for a swim. They stand up on their towels and look toward the ocean. While the swimmers are standing and watching, the ocean waves begin to rise up and down, and then move forward and splash. The swimmers walk in between the splashing waves, using their swimming arm movements. Some swimmers are swimming backward, some are swimming forward, and others are swimming sideward. Everyone is using different arm movements for the swimming. Some swimmers may be surfing. Then, the swimmers walk back to the beach for a rest and sit down on their towels, and the ocean waves roll back into the ocean. The ocean waves splash a little as they roll back. This is the end of the dance. Then the ocean waves and the swimmers change places.

Let's begin the dance. This time when I tell the story you will dance. [The teacher assigns each group, and the children go to the designated space. Children are assigned roles, and the teacher tells the story again as the children move. This process helps the students remember the sequence of movements and clarifies how the ocean waves and swimmers interact with one another.] Ready, swimmers move first. [The teacher relates the swimmers' part of the story.] Now, the ocean waves begin to move. Remember to count, up-up-up-up and down-down-down-down and up-up-up-up and down-down-down-down. Now, walk forward up-up-up-up and down-down-down-down, and move to the floor for the splash. Be sure to have a big space around your body, so the swimmers will be able to move around you. Now, the swimmers move around and between the ocean waves. Swimmers return to their towels, and the ocean waves roll back into the ocean. [The teacher cues children for the movement when needed.] Now, switch roles. Can you do the dance by yourself without me telling you the story? Try it to the sounds of the ocean waves.

Closure

Move up and down like the ocean if you liked dancing the part of the ocean waves. Move like you are swimming if you liked dancing the part of the swimmers. How many different ways did you use your arms as the swimmers?

Look For

- Students to exaggerate the stretching up and bending low for the ocean waves. Are they doing the ocean movement with a big change of level?
- Coordination of the up-and-down counts with the movement. Can they take all 4 counts to stretch up and all 4 counts to move down?
- The ability of the swimmers to keep the arm movements continuous as they walk between the spaces of the splashing waves. Can the swimmers use different directions?

- Ample space around each student when they perform the splashing waves. Discuss with students why this safety concern is important.

How Can I Change This?

- You can elaborate on the story by adding playing in the sand before students go in for a swim. You could have swimmers lie on beach towels on the front, side, and back of their bodies, and have the swimmers dry off different body parts after the swim.
- Use real towels or towel-size pieces of plastic for the swimmers' props. The ocean waves can use blue streamers as props.
- The ocean waves can be performed with the children dancing in partners and moving in unison. Partners can also be assigned for the swimmers to move together.
- You can give students the choice of performing the dance sequence without teacher cues. Discuss with the students how they will know when to initiate the different parts of the sequence.
- You can emphasize the concept of unison movement with the waves in the up-and-down sequence. Talk about what unison means and how students will be able to use it in the dance.
- Add ocean fish, crustaceans, and birds as characters living in the ocean (e.g., pelicans, dolphins, crabs, seagulls, lobsters, clams).

Assessment Suggestions

- The children draw two pictures of themselves in the dance. One picture shows them in the role of the swimmers, and the second picture shows them in the role of the ocean waves. They can label the picture or write a sentence about what is happening in the picture.
- The teacher observes how well the children can count for the level changes in the ocean wave part of the dance and if they exaggerate the level changes.

◐ The teacher observes the swimmers' movements as they move around and between the ocean waves. Notice what pathways the students are using, if there is any change of directions, and if the children can continue to move their arms in a swimming motion as they walk.

Interdisciplinary Connections

◐ Connect this dance to science concepts focused on water forms or ocean study.

◐ Connect to music when songs and music compositions about the beach or ocean are added as accompaniment to the dance.

◐ Introduce the dance using poetry or stories focused on ocean life or experiences at the beach.

SPAGHETTI DANCE

Objectives

As a result of participating in this learning experience, children will do the following:

- Move their arms, legs, and whole bodies to create straight and curved shapes
- Travel in space using straight and curved shapes and pathways
- Change from a straight shape to a curved shape
- Perform the dance sequence without teacher cues

Organization

Students move individually in their personal space for the introduction and development sections of the experience. In the culminating dance, students begin in small groups, and then dance as part of a large group.

Equipment Needed

Tape/CD player • music with a steady beat • drum or woodblock

Introduction

Today, we are going to dance about straight and curved lines. Look at your clothes. Does anyone have any straight and curved lines on their clothes? I see Becka has straight lines on her shirt, and Michael is showing us the straight lines on his pants. Sydney has found lots of curvy lines on her shirt, and Tinesha is pointing to her belt that makes a curved line around her waist.

For our warm-up, let's go on a trip around the room and find all the straight lines. As you walk around the room, I want you to look for straight lines on the ceilings, the walls, the floor, and the objects in the space. When you see a straight line, stop and make your body into a straight shape. I see Kelly has made a straight shape lying next to a line on the floor. Fernando is standing in a straight shape near the door. Now go to another place, and find more straight lines.

Try making curved lines where you see a curve in the room. Lana has found the round clock and is making a round curved shape on the floor, and Mario is standing with his back curved to the side next to a chair with a curved back. Go and find other places to make curved shapes.

Development

Now, you are going to make straight shapes with your arms, legs, and then your whole body. Stand in your personal space. Make a straight shape with your arm. Find another way to make a straight shape with your arm, now with both arms. Each time I beat the drum, make your arms into a different straight shape. [The teacher beats the drum 8 times.] Try making straight shapes with your legs on each of the 8 drumbeats. Now make your whole body straight. Use your legs, your arms, and your back. Make a straight shape on each drumbeat. [The teacher beats the drum 8 times.]

This time I want you to make a curved shape with your arms. Use all 4 drumbeats to make the curve. [The teacher plays 4 beats on the drum as the students slowly make the arm shape.] Now, make a different curved arm shape and another and one more different curved shape. Now use the whole body to make a curved shape. Make the shapes at different levels—some high, some medium, and some low to the floor. Ready and begin. Make a whole-body curved shape, now another, and another, and one more curved shape. [The teacher plays 4 beats on the drum each time as the students slowly make the whole-body shape.]

Now, I am going to ask you to change your body from a straight shape to a curved shape using this sequence: Make 4 straight shapes with a body part or the whole body and then one curved shape. The first 4 drumbeats are for the 4 straight shapes and the second 4 drumbeats are for the one slow curved shape. The straight shapes will be quick and sharp, and the curved shape will be slow and smooth. Ready? Straight-straight-straight-straight and curved.

Let's repeat it again using different shapes at different levels.

Now, we will explore moving our shapes on straight and curved pathways. This time I want you to find a way to keep most of your body parts straight and walk using a straight pathway. Can you keep your straight shape and change the direction to backward? Try another straight shape and travel sideways. Can you find another way to travel that is different from walking? Remember to use straight pathways.

Let's create different ways to travel in a curved shape on a curved pathway. Can you travel forward, backward, and sideward? Now try making many different curved shapes as you travel, sometimes reaching high in your curved shape and sometimes letting the curved shape take you low. Keep the body moving into different curved shapes. Change the speed and run and jump into the air as you make curved shapes with your body. See if you can keep your body curved as you jump into the air. This movement looks like someone tossed a rope into the air.

Culminating Dance

We are going to use all the movements you created in a dance about spaghetti. First, let me tell you what happens to the spaghetti in this dance.

The dance begins with the spaghetti in a box. This is straight spaghetti. The box is opened and the spaghetti jumps out and travels from the box to a big round pot of boiling water in the middle of the kitchen. The spaghetti jumps into the water and begins to cook. It changes from a straight shape to a curved shape and travels in curved shapes through the pot of water. Then slowly a big bubble appears in the center of the pot. It becomes bigger and bigger, pushing the spaghetti pieces to the edges of the pot until they jump out of the pot and fly all over the kitchen. The spaghetti gets stuck to the wall in a curved shape and then slowly falls from the wall back to the middle of the kitchen and onto the dinner plate.

In this dance, you will be the straight and curved spaghetti. The dance begins with four boxes of spaghetti, one in each corner of the room. (See figure 7.6.) I will assign you a box of spaghetti for the beginning of the dance. When you get to the corner, organize the group into a line. Everyone is standing in a straight shape. On my signal, the first piece of spaghetti from each box travels from the box to the giant pot of water—the taped or painted circle in the middle of the room—keeping its body in a straight shape moving on a straight pathway. As soon as the first person begins, the next person can start until everyone is standing around the circle.

Figure 7.6   Children begin the dance pretending they are uncooked spaghetti standing in four boxes.

Next, the spaghetti will take a small jump into the pot when I hit the drum. Ready and jump! Very slowly begin to change your straight shape into a curved shape beginning with your feet; then your legs; waist; back; arms; and, finally, your head. Travel slowly in the circle, moving in between each other without touching. Keep changing into many different curved shapes. Use high and low levels as if you are swimming all through the pot of water. I see Krista is really curving her back in different ways as she cooks in the water. Theo is moving high and low as he changes curved shapes.

Now, just listen as I explain how we will add the part where the giant bubble appears. I will be a slow bubble that begins to grow in the middle of the pot. I will start low in a curved shape in the middle of the pot, then begin to make my shape bigger and bigger until I am stretched out in a wide shape. [The teacher demonstrates how she or he will perform the bubble movements.] The spaghetti will begin to move to the edges of the pot until I wave my arms at you as if I am pushing you out of the pot. When you get to the edge, jump out. When everyone is out, the bubble spins around and the spaghetti runs and jumps as it flies around the kitchen. Everyone needs to run and jump in one direction around the circle. Remember to keep your curved shapes as you move around. Ready? Let's try the bubble. I want you to keep cooking as the bubble begins to grow. I am beginning to grow bigger and bigger, and now I stretch out into a wide shape. Begin to move to the edges of the pot and as I wave my arms, jump out. First, these pieces of spaghetti jump out, now these pieces, and these pieces over here. Oh, I cannot forget these pieces! Now everyone is out, and I begin to spin around. You begin to run and jump in curved shapes.

Now, the spaghetti becomes stuck to the wall. On the drumbeat, I want you to find a place to stick to the wall in a curved shape. What body part will you use to connect to the wall? Great, look at Andrew. He is standing on one foot in a curved shape and his arm is stuck to the wall. Find another way to stick to the wall and keep your curved shape. Now very, very slowly find a way to keep your curved shape and travel from the wall to the center of the room, where the pot of water has now become the dinner plate. Slowly fall to the floor onto the plate and end in a curved shape. And that is how the dance ends. [The teacher can repeat this section for additional practice.]

Let's go back to the beginning of the dance and try all the parts together. [The teacher conducts a review by asking the following questions.] Who can tell me how the dance begins? What shape are you in? What happens next? When does the spaghetti change from a straight to a curved shape? How can you move in the pot of water and not bump into your friends? What happens to the spaghetti when the bubble appears? What movements do you use when you are flying around the kitchen? When you hear the drum, what happens? What shapes are you in? How will you move from the wall to the plate? What shape will you be in for the end of the dance? This dance starts slowly, becomes a little faster, then very fast, stops, and ends slowly. Any questions? Ready?

Let's try it from the beginning. The first time I will tell the story as you move, and the next time you can do the dance without my directions. [Students dance the story while the teacher provides needed cues.]

Closure

Ask the students to identify which parts of the dance use light force, strong force, large movements, small movements, slow tempo, and fast tempo. Ask students to talk to another student about their favorite part of the dance.

Look For

- The many different ways children create curved and straight shapes.
- How children move around and among one another when they are cooking in the pot of water. Can they do it without bumping into others?
- The transition from a straight shape to curved shapes. Does this change occur gradually or all at once?

How Can I Change This?

- Use two or three pots of water in the culminating dance, and the students can choose which one they want to use. You can also use two or three plates at the end of the dance.

- Repeat the section of the culminating dance where the spaghetti flies around the kitchen and sticks to the wall several times, instead of only once, so students can find different places to stick to the wall.

- Students can travel to the pot of water connected. They can also stick to each other instead of the wall and then travel connected from the wall to the plate.

- Three or four children can dance the part of the bubble instead of the teacher.

- Introduce the dance reading the poem "Spaghetti" by Shel Silverstein (1974).

- Bring in a box of uncooked spaghetti and a pot of cooked spaghetti to use when you are telling the story.

Assessment Suggestions

- The teacher videotapes the class performing the dance, then shows the videotape to the children and asks them to observe how they each performed the straight and curved shapes. The teacher asks the children to write about the part that they feel they performed the best.

- The children can also choose a part they would like to perform better and then perform the dance again and talk about what changes they made.

- Children can draw themselves in a straight or curved shape that they used in the dance and label the drawing.

Interdisciplinary Connections

- Introduce the dance using the humorous poem "Spaghetti" (Silverstein 1974).

- Connect to visual arts concepts on how straight and curved lines appear in paintings and sculptures.

- Include social studies concepts that discuss how noodles are part of the cuisine in a variety of cultures.

- Read from the book *Noodles* (Weeks and Carter 1996) as an introduction to the dance.

BALLOONS

Objectives

As a result of participating in this learning experience, children will do the following:

- Change the range of their movement from small to big and big to small
- Dance together with a partner and a small group
- Create a short dance

Organization

Students dance individually, with a partner, and in small groups.

Equipment Needed

A balloon • tape/CD player • slow music for accompaniment • a drum

Introduction

Today, we are going to dance using small movements that become bigger and bigger. What are some things that start small and become bigger? Our warm-up includes movements that are small and big. Find a personal space and make small movements with your fingers that open and close. Now make the movement bigger by opening and closing your whole hand several times. Now the open and close movement is bigger and uses your arms. Try the open and close movement jumping with your feet apart and then together. First, start with a few small jumps; then make your jumps wider and wider. The last part of the warm-up uses running, skipping, or galloping. Choose one of these three ways to travel in the space. Take 10 small steps, 10 medium-sized steps, and 10 giant steps. Now do those 30 steps again. [The teacher directs the students to repeat the warm-up movements several times.]

Development

Sit on the floor and make a small round shape using your whole body. Great! I see that you have rounded your back, legs, arms, and head to make the shape. I am going beat on the drum 8 times. On each count, make your shape become bigger. [The teacher plays the drum and counts aloud as the students move.] 1, 2, 3, 4, 5, 6, 7, 8. Now, go back to your small round shape in 4 counts, becoming smaller and smaller. 1, 2, 3, 4. Let's try making the round shape big and small again. Ready to become bigger on each count? Now make a different small shape. Choose a high, medium, or low level as you get smaller. As I play the drum, make your shape grow bigger in 8 counts and then smaller in 4 counts. Ready! Big 1, 2, 3, 4, 5, 6, 7, 8, and small 1, 2, 3, 4. This time, make your shape grow big in 4 counts and smaller in 2 counts. This will feel faster. Ready! Big 1, 2, 3, 4, and small 1, 2. Can you suggest a number of counts for becoming bigger and smaller? Sanam says to use 3 counts to get bigger and 13 counts to get smaller. Let's try it. I will beat the counts on the drum.

We are now going to explore small and big movements with one or more partners. You will face your partners and mirror each other's movements. One partner is the first leader, and then the others will take a turn as the leader. Brian and I will demonstrate. I will be the first leader, and Brian will mirror my movements. As the first partner, I will create movements that start low and small and become big and high. Be sure to go slowly so your partner can follow. [The teacher demonstrates with a student.] Then, the next partner will create movements that start big and high and change to small and low. I will tell you when to switch partners. [Use slow music to accompany this exploration.] I will assign you a partner, and you can choose who will go first. Then begin when the music starts and change leaders when the music stops.

Now, I will organize you into groups of four or five students and you will stand in a circle. I want you to work together to find a way to make your circle become bigger and smaller. See if you can all move at the same time, as you did when you were mirroring your partner. Select a leader in the group who will tell the group when to begin moving and when to stop. Make sure you listen to everyone's ideas, then try the ideas out, and choose how your circle will move from small to big and back to small. After each group has practiced, we will share our dance with another group.

Culminating Dance

For this next part, you'll stay in your small groups. You are going to create a dance about a balloon that inflates and deflates and, when it is fully inflated, all the air fizzles out. Your dance will be like this balloon I am going to blow up. [The teacher blows up a balloon using the following sequence.] First, I blow just a little air into the balloon and then let the air out while holding onto the balloon. The second time, I blow more air into the balloon so it is bigger and then let all the air out. Then, I blow the balloon up a third time so it is bigger than the first two times and, again, let the air out. Then, the fourth time I inflate the balloon to its fullest and let it go so it flies around as the air comes out. Watch to see how it flies around in the air. How does it move? Show me with your hand. [The teacher lets go of the fully inflated balloon.]

Use this sequence for your group dance. Your group will need to decide what movements you are going to use to show the balloon inflating and deflating four times, with the balloon becoming bigger each time before the air goes out. Then, choose what movements you will use to show the balloon flying around as the air comes out. How will the balloon land on the floor? Listen to each person's ideas for the dance, try them out, and choose the movements for the group. One person will need to be the leader to tell the group when to inflate and deflate and when to let all the air out and fall to the floor. I will come by each group to see if you need any help. Practice your sequence several times to make sure everyone is moving together. Can you add any voice accompaniment to your dance? When you are ready we will stop and show the dances to the other groups. [The teacher visits all the groups as they create their dances.]

Each group will share their balloon dance with the class. Before you perform, tell the class how your group chose the movements for the dance. The observers need to look for the pathway of the fizzle movement.

Closure

I want your group to sit together and talk about how you worked together to create the dance. Each person needs to say something about the dance. Then, make up a name for your balloon dance. [Students spend a few minutes talking, and then they are asked to share some of the comments and tell the rest of the class the name of their dance.]

Look For

- How students perform the mirroring activity. Are the movements too fast to follow, or are students moving slowly?
- How well the students use unison movements in the small group as students find a way to move from small to big. Can they all make their movements grow bigger at the same time?
- How well the groups work together sharing ideas.

How Can I Change This?

- The dance can be taught as a full-class experience with everyone as part of one balloon circle. Working as a single large group may be more appropriate for young children.
- The students can add a floating part to the dance after the balloon is fully inflated and before the air fizzles out. They can move slowly up and down like they are floating in the air.
- The dance can end with the balloon popping instead of the air fizzling out.

Assessment Suggestions

- During the time when students are creating their dances, the teacher observes how each group collaborates. Does each person have an opportunity to voice his or her idea? Does the group try different ideas and then choose one or more for the dance? Are they using the time to practice the dance moving in unison?

◉ As the groups are involved in the closure discussion, the teacher visits each group and asks this question: How did you change your movements to show that the balloon was getting bigger each time it inflated?

◉ The teacher creates criteria and a holistic rubric to assess each group's balloon dance (see figure 7.7).

Interdisciplinary Connections

◉ Introduce the dance by reading aloud the poems "Eight Balloons" (Silverstein 1981) or "Balloons" (Chandra 1993).

◉ Connect to science concepts on air currents, flight, or force.

◉ Include a discussion on how people use balloons to celebrate events to connect with social studies concepts on celebrations and traditions.

Rubric	Criteria
Excellent	All students performed the dance in unison, and the movements clearly demonstrated a gradual change from small to big.
Good	Most of the students performed the dance in unison, but the movements did not demonstrate a gradual change from small to big.

Figure 7.7 Balloon dance assessment tool.

PERCUSSION INSTRUMENT DANCE

Objectives

As a result of participating in this learning experience, children will do the following:

- Match different movements to the sound of a drum, a triangle, and a set of maracas
- Move using contrasting light and strong force and fast and slow tempos
- Balance while moving and while freezing in still shapes

Organization

Students will begin the lesson moving individually and then divide into three groups for the culminating dance. The room is set up with each instrument in a different space (see figure 7.8).

Equipment Needed

A drum • a triangle • a set of maracas

Introduction

Today, we are going to create movements to the sound of a drum, a triangle, and the maracas. I will show you the instruments and then demonstrate the different sounds each one can make. [The teacher plays each instrument to demonstrate the sounds it makes. First, a light drumbeat is played 8 times and then a strong drumbeat 8 times. Next, the triangle is tapped once, and then after the sound ends it is tapped again. Next, the triangle is played lightly and rapidly. Finally, the maracas are shaken slowly and lightly and then strongly and rapidly.]

We will use each instrument in our warm-up. First, we are going to begin with the sound of the drum. As I play slowly and lightly, lie on the floor and slowly stretch your arms and legs as if you are just waking up. Now, sit and stretch, and then slowly rise to standing and continue to stretch. Let's repeat the stretching with the drum. Now, I am going to play the drum strongly and quickly, and I want you to reach in different directions on each beat. Next, we'll do the triangle. On each tap of the triangle, take one giant slow step forward. [The teacher taps the triangle 8 times.] This time go backward as I tap the triangle. As I shake the maracas, I want you to take small running steps in the space. When you hear the maracas stop, freeze in a shape. [The teacher plays and stops the maracas several times.]

Development

Everyone move to the space where the drum is placed. We will begin to explore movement using

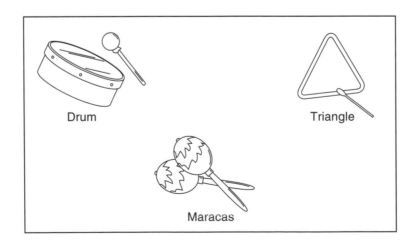

Figure 7.8 Instruments are placed in three spaces in the room.

the light and strong beats of the drum. Begin standing in a frozen shape. When I play the drum lightly, you will find a way to do small light leaps, hops, or jumps in different directions and stop when the drum stops. [The teacher plays the 8 light beats in a medium-paced tempo and the students explore light leaps, hops, and jumps.] Let's try this a few more times. Can you change your movement and the direction?

Next, I will play 8 strong drumbeats, and on each beat I want you to take a big strong leap, hop, or jump and then freeze in a shape. [The teacher gives the ready cue and then plays the 8 strong beats at a medium tempo.] Let's try this again. This time mix up the leaps, hops, and jumps while you move to the 8 beats. Remember to make the frozen shapes when you land. [The teacher plays the 8 strong beats.] Let's try this again.

Now, I will play 8 light drumbeats, then 8 strong drumbeats. Take small light leaps, hops, or jumps, then big strong leaps, hops, or jumps adding the frozen shapes. [The teacher plays 8 light beats then 8 strong beats.] Now, let's try this with 6 light beats and 6 strong beats. Now, move using 4 light and 4 strong beats. Finally, move with only 2 light and then 2 strong beats. This is the drum dance. Let's put it all together, first using 8 light and strong, then 6, then 4, and then 2. Can you do it? [The teacher plays the drum while the students perform.]

Now, everyone walk over to the triangle. Listen to how long the sound lasts after each tap. Sit on the floor, move your arms slowly, and keep them moving until you can no longer hear the triangle after the first tap. [The teacher taps the triangle.] Let's try again. Now, stand up and take one step each time you hear me tap the triangle. [The teacher makes 4 taps.] Step-step-step-step. Try taking the steps backward or sideward this time. [The teacher taps the triangle.] Step-step-step-step. This time, combine the steps and the slow arm movement for 4 beats. [The teacher taps the triangle.] Now, as I play the triangle faster, find a way to turn your body around quickly; you can choose any level. [The teacher taps the triangle quickly 8 times.] Try a different turn. [The teacher quickly taps the triangle 8 times.] Now, combine the 4 slow steps using the arms with the 8 fast taps for

turning. [The teacher plays 4 slow taps, then 8 quick taps.] Let's repeat this triangle dance again. Remember to take 4 slow steps and then do your quick turns.

Let's move to the third space where we will dance to a set of two maracas. Listen to how the sound changes when I shake them lightly and then strongly. I will start with a light shake as I move the maracas just a little. [The teacher plays the maracas to demonstrate the different sounds.] Begin a small shaking movement in your fingertips as I shake the maracas lightly. Keep the movement small and light. Now, let the shaking go to your hands, forearms, elbows, and all the way up your arms to the shoulders. Now, try the shaking beginning with your toe, then your whole foot, your leg, and then up to your hips. Is there another body part where you can begin shaking and then let it move to other parts of your body? I see Cole and Jenny have chosen their heads, others are beginning the shaking in their bellies, and Carmen chose to start in her shoulder. This time, listen as I change the sound from light to strong and show that change of force in the shaking of your arm. Begin the shaking small and light and let it become strong and big as the maracas become louder. [The teacher shakes maracas.] Try light-to-strong shaking in your legs, starting with your toes and going all the way up to your hips. Now, begin shaking your whole body, going from light and small to strong and big. Try this lying on the floor, then sitting, and now standing. Each time I play the maracas from light to strong, start the shaking with a different body part. Also, choose if you will be lying down, sitting, or standing. [The teacher shakes the maracas for about 10 to 15 seconds.] Find a way to travel with the shaking movement, beginning with light and small movements and increasing the movements to strong and big. Can you take the strong shaking up off the floor into a jump? [The teacher shakes maracas for 10 to 15 seconds.]

Now, let's combine the light and strong shaking into a dance. Ready? [Students move as the teacher tells the story.] The students are sleeping on the floor. They wake up slowly by shaking lightly. Then they stand up and continue to lightly shake. The shaking begins in one body part, and then more body parts begin to shake until the whole body is shaking. The students go out to play. The shaking grows stronger and the students shake with big and strong movements as they travel in the space. The shaking suddenly stops, and the students freeze in a shape. The students resume the shaking as they return home and slowly fall to the floor and go back to sleep.

Culminating Dance

Now, when you perform the three dances, you may choose which one you want to dance to first, second, and third. Think about your order for the dances. Now, everyone who wants to dance first to the drum go over to the drum space. Those who are dancing to the triangle first go to the triangle place. And those who are dancing first to the maracas go to where the maracas are placed. Only one group will dance at a time while the other two groups sit and observe.

I will play the drum first. Ready, drum dancers? Remember to make clear changes between the light and strong movements as I play the light and strong drumbeats. [The teacher plays the sequence of beats while the students dance.]

Now, I will play for the triangle dancers. Who can tell us what type of dance goes with the triangle? Juwon explains, "You take four slow steps on each tap, then fast turns on the fast taps." Okay, ready, everyone? Let's try it all together. [The teacher plays the triangle sequence while the students dance.]

The third dance is the maracas. Here, the dancers perform a story about waking up, going out to play, and then going back to sleep—all through shaking movements. Observing students, watch how the shaking starts small and light and becomes bigger and stronger. I will tell the story as I play the maracas. The dancers begin to wake up by lightly shaking. Now, they stand up and begin the light shaking in one body part and now more body parts begin to lightly shake. Next, they go out to play as the shaking becomes bigger and stronger. They begin to travel in the space shaking and shaking, sometimes jumping into the air. The maracas

suddenly stop, the dancers freeze, and then they lose their strong shaking energy and lightly shake all the way home and go back to sleep.

Now, I want everyone to point to the next instrument you want to dance to and walk to that place. [Remind the children to walk as they change from one instrument area to another. Excited children will tend to begin running to an area.] I will play the instruments in the same way, beginning with the drum dance, and then the triangle dance, and ending with the maraca dance. When you are not dancing, I want you to notice how your classmates are showing light and strong force as they dance. [Students perform their second dance and then move to the third instrument to perform their third dance.]

Closure

I will assign partners, and I want you to tell each other the order of your dances and your favorite dance. [Children spend a few minutes sharing their experiences with each other.] Now, I would like to hear about your favorite dance. [The teacher asks a few children to talk about their favorite dance.]

Look For

- How children perform strong and light movements. Are they able to demonstrate the difference in the force clearly?
- What dances the children choose first, second, and third. You may want to discuss with them why they chose a certain order. Which dances did they like to perform or which one did they least prefer?

How Can I Change This?

- Play different instruments.
- Use more or fewer instruments.
- Add a specific rhythm to each instrument instead of playing the regular beats.
- Students can develop their own stories to accompany the instruments for their dances.
- Ask the students to play the instruments.

Assessment Suggestions

- ๑ Students draw a picture of the instruments or themselves dancing in the order they performed the three dances.
- ๑ The teacher records anecdotal notes about children who demonstrate difficulty with balance in the slow movements and frozen shapes. For example, Shanida was unable to hold the frozen shapes still, and she lost her balance several times.
- ๑ The teacher uses a checklist to note if the children can demonstrate strong and light movements. At the end of the learning experience, the teacher asks four students at a time to show a strong movement, then a light movement.

Interdisciplinary Connections

- ๑ Connect to music concepts focused on types of percussion instruments, timbre, and tempo.
- ๑ Have the children work on language arts skills by asking them to write stories inspired by the dance sequences or to write stories and then express them through dance and percussion instruments.

THE HUNGRY CAT

Objectives

As a result of participating in this learning experience, children will do the following:

- Perform movements clearly using fast and slow tempos
- Move a body part in isolation
- Perform a dance without teacher cues

Organization

Students will dance individually throughout the entire learning experience.

Equipment Needed

Percussion instruments—a drum and a triangle

Introduction

In this dance learning experience, we are going to find different ways to move fast and slow. We will then do a dance about a hungry cat who moves fast and slow. We'll start with a warm-up using slow and fast movements.

When I say go, find a personal space and run in place as fast as you can. Go! Now run in place as slowly as you can. Now find a different way to travel through general space as fast as you can. Find another way. What are some of the ways you traveled fast? [Students share their answers with the class.] Now move through space as slowly as you can, taking a long time for each step. Find another slow way to move. How slow can you go? Can someone show the class how slow they can travel in the space? [The teacher selects several students to demonstrate moving slowly.]

Think of some things that you do to get ready for school in the morning. [Students answer with morning routines such as brushing teeth, getting dressed, eating cereal.] We are going to try pretending to do some of these slow and then fast. Ready? Let's all do the movement of brushing our teeth as fast as we can, now as slowly as we can. Now try slowly putting on your clothes; now get dressed as fast as you can. The third

movement is about eating a bowl of cereal very slowly. Shake the cereal into the bowl slowly, pour the milk slowly, take your spoon and scoop up the cereal slowly, and put it in your mouth slowly. Now eat the cereal as fast as you can. Feel the difference in your muscles when you move fast and slow. Can someone tell us what that feels like?

Development

Today, I am going to play a triangle for all of our slow movements. Listen to how long the sound lasts after I hit the triangle. Now, begin to move your arms when I hit the triangle and continue to keep them moving until you do not hear the triangle. [The teacher taps the triangle once.] Keep your movement smooth and slow. Feel your arm moving for a long time. Can you keep the movement going? Now try this with another body part. I want to see if you can listen to the sound and move one body part slowly until the sound of the triangle stops. I see that some of you are moving your arms forward and backward, some are moving their arms together and apart, and some are moving one arm and then the other. Some students are moving their shoulders, their legs, and their whole bodies. Notice how each movement takes a long time when you move slowly.

I will play fast drumbeats to accompany the fast movement. See if you can move your arms as fast as you can until you hear the drum stop. [The teacher plays fast drumbeats for a few seconds.] Try moving your arms high and low, forward and backward, together and apart. [The teacher again plays fast drumbeats for a few seconds.] This time, point with your arm to a different corner of the room as fast as you can on each of the 4 drumbeats. [The teacher plays 4 drumbeats as students point.] Try pointing with the other arm. [Again, the teacher plays 4 drumbeats as students point.] We will use this movement in our cat dance.

This time, run as fast as you can and stop when you no longer hear the drum. [The teacher plays fast drumbeats for 10 seconds.] This time, add a leap or jump to the run as I play the fast drumbeats. [The teacher plays fast drumbeats for 10 seconds.] Try this again and make sure you land on your feet with your knees bent at the end of the jump or leap. [The teacher plays fast drumbeats for 10 seconds. Children practice this movement several times.]

Culminating Dance

Now, it is time for the hungry cat dance. Everyone find a personal space and lie on the floor. We are going to practice each part of the dance first and then put them all together. In the first part, the cat is sleeping. What are the different shapes a cat uses for sleeping? Yes, curved, perhaps stretched. Find another sleeping cat shape and another. I see many of you in round curled shapes, some of you are on your backs, others are sleeping on their sides. (See figure 7.9.) Change slowly from one sleeping shape to another each time you hear the triangle sound. I will tap the triangle four times. Ready? [The teacher makes four taps on the triangle.] Make your first sleeping shape, now slowly change to your second shape, now take a third shape, and finish by moving slowly into the fourth and last shape. That was great! You used four different sleeping shapes and moved very slowly into each shape.

Next, still lying on the floor, the cat begins to wake up and stretch slowly. On each tap of the triangle, I will tell you a body part to stretch. [The teacher makes one tap on the triangle.] The cat stretches one arm reaching high with

its paw. [The teacher makes a second tap on the triangle.] Now, the other arm stretches high. [The teacher makes a third tap on the triangle.] Now, the cat stretches one leg up high reaching with its foot. [The teacher makes a fourth tap on the triangle.] Then the cat stretches up the other leg. The cat sits up and slowly moves its head, then its back, and then its shoulders. [The teacher makes three taps on the triangle: one each for the head, back, and shoulders.] The cat stands up slowly onto two feet. Make sure you take your time as you stretch each part of your body as you wake up. This is the beginning of the dance. All the movements are smooth and slow. Let's practice this part again.

Now, in the second part, we will change to make fast sudden movements on each drumbeat. The cat will move fast when it suddenly sees and points to a mouse. Move your arm quickly to point to a corner of the room. The cat sees a mouse over there! Now, the mouse has moved to another corner; point to that one. Oh no, the mouse moved to another corner! Point to it! And now point to the last corner as the mouse moves one last time. Make your pointing movements strong and fast. I will beat the drum once for each pointing movement. Ready? Point, point, point, point. [The teacher beats the drum.]

In the third part, the cat chases the mouse around the room. I will beat the drum very fast, and you will run adding leaps and jumps. Ready? [The teacher beats the drum fast for about 10 seconds while the children run after the imaginary mouse.]

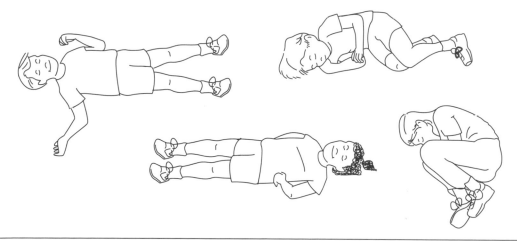

Figure 7.9   In the beginning of the hungry cat dance, the "cats" are sleeping.

In the next part, the cat catches the mouse by taking one big jump. The cat slowly bends forward to pick up the mouse by the tail, opens its mouth, and drops the mouse in. Now, the cat is so tired after chasing and eating the mouse that it slowly moves back to the place where it was sleeping. I will play one loud drumbeat to cue the jump. [The teacher plays one loud drumbeat.] Then, I will play the triangle to accompany the slow movements as you pretend to pick up the mouse, eat it, and go back to sleep. Let's try this part of the cat story. Begin with a jump and bend down slowly to pick up the mouse; pretend to drop it in your mouth, and add a stretch and yawn to show you are tired before you slowly go back to sleep. [The teacher plays the drum and triangle as the students dance the sequence of movements.] Let's try this part again.

Now, let's put all the story parts together into one big dance. I will play the instruments while I tell the story. Then, the second time you will do the dance by yourself. [The teacher plays the instruments and tells the story while the children dance.] Now, I will play the instruments and not tell you the story. You can dance the story because you have practiced it now a few times. Before we begin, can someone describe the dance? [One or more students describe all or part of the dance.] Be clear about making the slow movements slow and the fast movements fast. Feel the difference in tempo as you dance.

Closure

Can anyone suggest any new parts we could add to this cat dance? Are there any parts we should take out of the dance?

Look For

- ◑ How well children can change from fast to slow movements. Is the difference clear?
- ◑ How effectively children can move in the space without bumping into each other during the mouse chase.

How Can I Change This?

- ◑ During the development section, you can divide the room into two zones: the fast zone, where the students can perform the fast movements, and the slow zone, where the slow movements are performed.
- ◑ Develop short movement sequences that combine fast and slow movements. For example, students choose a movement and perform it using this sequence: slow-fast-slow or fast-slow-fast. Try different combinations with nonlocomotor and locomotor movements.
- ◑ Students are organized into partners. One partner does a fast or slow movement, and the other partner responds doing the same movement in the opposite tempo. For example, partner one touches the head with the hands, turns around, and makes a stretched shape using a fast tempo. Partner two responds by doing the same three movements using a slow tempo.

Assessment Suggestions

- ◑ Students are organized into partners. One partner calls out a nonlocomotor movement and chooses a fast or slow tempo, and the other partner performs the movements. For example, "Wiggle your whole body fast," or "Twist slow." Students take turns. Next, repeat this activity using locomotor movements.
- ◑ The teacher uses a checklist to observe if children can isolate body parts in the part of the dance where the cat wakes up. This part of the dance can be assessed while the children are dancing.
- ◑ The teacher videotapes half of the class performing the dance without teacher cues and then videotapes the other half. Later the tape is reviewed to assess if children can remember the sequence and demonstrate the fast and slow movements clearly.

Interdisciplinary Connections

- To introduce the cat dance, read the children stories or poems about cat adventures.

- Integrate this dance with science concepts focused on animal life.

- Add visual arts and music through creating cat and mouse masks and using music with an emphasis on slow and fast tempos.

CIRCUS DANCE

Objectives

As a result of participating in this learning experience, students will do the following:

⊚ Perform locomotor and nonlocomotor movements at different levels

⊚ Create a short dance sequence by themselves or with others

⊚ Balance while traveling and freezing in still shapes

⊚ Use their imaginations to dance about the characters and animals in a circus

Organization

This learning experience includes four dances: the galloping horses, the tightrope walkers, the lions and tigers, and the funny clowns. Three of the dances require students to dance individually, and one dance, the funny clowns, uses partners or small groups.

Equipment Needed

Tape/CD player • circus-type music or lively music • a stick with multiple streamers taped to the end for the circus leader • three hoops for the lions and tigers • lines on the floor for the tightrope walkers

Introduction

Has anyone been to the circus? What did you see? [Students share their experiences.] Today, we are going to turn our room into a circus with galloping horses, tightrope walkers, lions and tigers, and funny clowns. You are going to be the circus performers, and I will be the circus ringleader. [The teacher can share books or pictures about the circus.]

For our warm-up today, we will practice moving high and low and forward, backward, and sideward. I will organize you into groups of four or five, and each person in the group will have a number from one to four or five. Then, when I play the music, person number one will step into the center of the circle and create a

movement that moves high and low. You can use your whole body or only one body part. Everyone in the group follows the leader and does the same movement. Then, I will say "change" and person number two will do a different high and low movement and everyone will follow. Everyone will have a turn to create a movement. [The teacher plays the music and calls "change" after 15 seconds until everyone has had a turn as the leader.] The second part of the warm-up is just like the first except your movements will be forward and backward or side to side. Let's begin this time with person five and end with person number one. [The teacher plays the music and calls "change" after 15 seconds until everyone has had a turn as the leader.]

Development

This learning experience is composed of four short dances about the circus. The first dance is about the galloping horses. Let's explore different ways to gallop. First, make a shape with your hands and arms that are like two front hooves. Your hands can be close together, wide apart, or one high and one low. Keep the hand and arm shape as you gallop forward. Can you gallop in a large circle pathway? Now try a small circle. Can you pretend you are a horse leaping into the air as you gallop? Can two or three horses gallop in the space with one horse as the leader? Now change leaders and the pathway. [The teacher plays the music while the children practice.]

Next are the tightrope walkers. For this circus act, you will use the lines on the floor as the tightropes. Find a line and begin to walk forward. Can you change your level to low and high as you walk? How about walking backward? Can you walk and turn or hop or jump and stay on the line? Find a way to balance on one foot. Be still and count to 5. Can you find another way to make a still balanced shape? How about another balanced shape? Now you will choose three different tricks for your tightrope act. You will need a locomotor movement, a still balance, and a turn. You can change levels and directions but keep the movements slow. Now practice your tightrope act. [The teacher plays the music while the children practice. Also, the teacher can write the three components of the tightrope act on the chalkboard or on chart paper.]

Our next circus performers are the lions and tigers. In this circus act, the lions and tigers will stay low to the floor and walk on their hands and feet, stretch up as they let out a loud roar, jump through a hoop, and roll on the floor. Let's practice the walking on hands and feet. Show me how you can walk on your hands and feet using small steps, now big steps. [Students may need a brief rest due to the strength involved in using the arms to support the body weight.] Now, let's practice the lion and tiger roar. Kneel down and sit back on your heels with your hands touching the floor. This is the waiting shape. [The teacher is holding a stick with streamers attached, and when the stick is raised the children stretch up and use their voices to make a loud roaring sound.] When I raise the stick, this is the signal for the lions and tigers to stretch their front paws and let out a loud roar. When I move the stick down, the lions and tigers stop the roar and return to the waiting shape. Let's try this a couple times. How high can you stretch your arms and how loud can you roar? [The teacher moves the stick up and down a few times and the children follow the signal.] In the next trick, the lions and tigers jump through the hoop and roll on the floor while reaching with their paws. [The teacher or several students can hold hoops vertically as the children jump through the hoop and then do a sideward roll, similar to a log roll. The hoops can be held at different places in the space. Also, the teacher plays the music while the children practice.]

The final act of the circus is the fabulous juggling clowns. You are going to pretend that you are juggling. Let's create many different ways to juggle. [A light juggling scarf can be added as a prop.] First, put a big smile on your face and move your arms and hands to show a juggling movement. Can you juggle while walking forward or backward? Try juggling lying on your back, kneeling, sitting, standing on one foot. What other ways can you juggle? Turn and face another person and pretend you are juggling together. Can you move high and low at the same time or opposite each other? Can you

move apart and then together while you juggle? Select three different juggling ideas, choose the order, and practice the first idea, the second, and the third without stopping. [The teacher plays the music while the children practice.]

Culminating Dance

Welcome to the circus! Now, we will combine the four dances into one dance. The first time we perform the dance everyone will do all the dances in the order we learned them. The second time, you may choose which dances you would like to perform. When you are not performing, you will be the audience. On the chalkboard I have drawn a picture of each circus act in the order we will perform them. (See figure 7.10.)

The galloping horses will start. I want everyone to make one line. When I introduce the galloping horses, you will gallop in a large circle. Then, listen for my directions to show your horse tricks. Here we go! And now for the talented galloping horses! [The teacher uses the stick with streamers to direct the first student in line to lead the gallop. This is also a good time to play the music.] Watch them as they gallop together in a big circle. Now, for their first trick, horses take small gallops in their own small circle. Can you gallop in the other direction? Next, gallop and jump or leap into the air. Horses stop, turn in place, and take a bow.

Figure 7.10 Students can refer to the drawings on the chalkboard to see the order of the circus acts.

In our next circus act, I ask you to look high above the crowd to see the amazing tightrope walkers. [The teacher asks everyone to take his or her starting place on a line.] The tightrope walkers will do three tricks today: traveling forward and backward, a still balance, and a turn. Here they go. [The teacher plays the music while the students perform their movements.] Everyone is staying on the line—great balance and control! What an awesome group of performers. Amazing! Tightrope walkers, take a bow.

The third circus act introduces the fabulous lions and tigers. I want everyone to sit side by side, on a line, facing me. When I introduce the lions and tigers, I want you to walk forward on your hands and feet taking 10 steps and then kneel down in the waiting shape. We will do the roaring stretch three times, jump through the hoops, and roll back to the line where you started. [The teacher assigns three students to hold the hoops. One-third of the performers are assigned to each hoop.] And now for the fabulous lions and tigers—here they come! Don't be afraid, they are friendly. Now, watch them roar when I lift my stick. And roar! [The teacher lifts the stick up and down three times.] Now, watch how skillfully they jump through the hoops and roll. Will my assistants please hold the hoops? [The students make three lines and jump through their assigned hoop. The jumping may be repeated several times.] Okay, lions and tigers, take a bow.

Our final circus act is the super juggling clowns. They will perform their many different juggling tricks. [Students stand around the perimeter of the room and begin their imaginary juggling when the music starts.] Some are juggling low to the floor, some are moving backward, and some are juggling with other clowns. Wow! Look at all the super juggling! That was great! Now, take a bow.

This time, I will introduce the circus act and you may choose to perform or be in the audience.

Closure

Each student will show one movement from any one of the dances and the rest of the group will guess which circus act the movement is from.

Look For

- Ways to encourage leadership in the dances by assigning students a specific role or asking students to take responsibility to lead a small group or the whole class.

- Students who may need help structuring their sequences in the tightrope and clown dances. They can write or draw the sequence to help them organize and remember their dance.

How Can I Change This?

- Use different circus acts such as the balancing elephants, swinging trapeze performers, dancing bears, jumping and turning seals, or galloping equestrians.

- Students can work in small groups to create their own galloping horse dance using circle pathways moving right and left and forward and backward.

- Tightrope walkers can perform in partners using a leading and following relationship.

- Lions and tigers can create different ways to jump through the hoops using different directions or shapes.

- The juggling clowns can create funny bows at the end of their act.

- Props and costumes can be added, such as scarves and streamers.

- Use a different piece of music for each circus act. Use popular music or look for music that traditionally accompanies a circus.

- The culminating dance can include a circus parade with the students choosing a character for the parade.

Assessment Suggestions

- Students draw a picture of their favorite part of the circus. They can include a movement they performed or draw the circus character.

- The teacher completes a checklist noting if students can organize and perform a sequence of movements alone or with another student.

๑ Students write a list of the locomotor movements they used in each of the dances.

๑ Students are organized into groups of three or four and show each other the different balances they performed in the tightrope walkers dance.

Interdisciplinary Connections

๑ Connect to children's literature using the illustrations in *Circus* (Wildsmith 1970) or *Circus 1-2-3* (Halsey 2000).

๑ Integrate the circus dance with a circus thematic unit in social studies or science.

๑ Use the dance to initiate writing stories about the circus acts.

๑ Create vocabulary lists based on words connected to the dance such as *tightrope walkers, galloping, lions, tigers, rolling, balance, hooves, clowns, juggling,* or *roar.*

chapter 8

Learning Experiences for Third, Fourth, and Fifth Grades

Students in third through fifth grade have experienced the basic locomotor and nonlocomotor movements and can use these movements to create dances as individuals, partners, or in small groups. They can recall sequences of movements, move in unison to counted phrases of movements, and organize movements when composing a dance. The teacher can conduct discussions regarding the historical, social, and cultural contexts of the dance content and ask students to assess themselves and their peers. Although you may find some students in this age group reluctant to dance, the learning experiences in this chapter offer nonthreatening ways to engage in dance using familiar movements. To facilitate your selection of learning experiences, we have summarized each learning experience in table 8.1.

Table 8.1 Third-, Fourth-, and Fifth-Grade Learning Experiences Index

Name of dance learning experience	Description of dance learning experience
Dancing homework machine	A learning experience that begins with students individually exploring the concept of repetition and concludes with a collaborative effort using repetitive movements to create parts of a moving homework machine.
Creative square dance	This creative dance experience is a wonderful addition to a traditional unit on square dance. Students have the opportunity to use their knowledge of square dance to create new movements and call their own contemporary square dance.
Action words	Students explore directions, levels, shapes, ranges, and tempos through creating different ways to run, pause, spin and collapse. The words are then linked together to form a movement sentence. Students also create their own action word dances using words they select.
Float and punch	These words are two of the eight effort actions defined by Rudolf Laban (1976). We chose float and punch because they express the scope of how time, force, and space are used in movement. Students enjoy the contrast in movement and are challenged to create a dance that clearly demonstrates the opposing qualities.
Baseball dance	This popular learning experience is a great way to celebrate the opening of baseball season or the World Series. Students create adaptations of pitching, running, batting, and catching movements emphasizing tempo, levels, and direction. These movements are then combined into a dance performed in unison using a double-circle formation.
Bubbles	In this learning experience, students explore how descriptive words are expressed through movement. The characteristics of bubble movements and shapes become the content for individual, as well as small-group, dance compositions.
Birthday celebration	Birthday celebrations are part of the traditions of many cultures. This learning experience focuses on expressing the events at a birthday celebration such as traveling to the party, blowing out the candles, unwrapping gifts, playing a game, and traveling back home. The culminating dance is performed in unison in a circle formation with each section of the dance performed as a specific sequence of movements.
Partner dance	Learning to collaborate with another person is the focus of this learning experience. Students learn four partner relationships—mirroring, shadowing, echoing, and call and response—and then use the relationships to choreograph a dance using the ABA choreographic structure.
Sport dance	The sport dance is a great learning experience to introduce to students who may be reluctant to dance. The sport dance uses sport actions familiar to the students and explores different ways to perform the actions using time, range, and levels. Three different ways to create sport dances are addressed. Each way can be taught as a single session, or they can be combined to form a complete creative dance unit.
Dance maps	Students create shapes and pathways that result in drawn maps of their dance. Initially, students create an individual map and then collaborate with a small group to combine their dances into one dance. This learning experience offers a step-by-step process for creating the dances and requires the students to work independently with the teacher in the role of facilitator.

DANCING HOMEWORK MACHINE

Objectives

As a result of participating in this learning experience, children will do the following:

- Create repetitive movements using the whole body and isolated body parts
- Perform repetitive movements that vary in levels, directions, tempos, ranges, and amounts of force
- Create repetitive movements using a machine part as inspiration
- Collaborate with a small group to create a machine part using repetitive movements

Organization

Students move individually, in partners, and then in small groups.

Equipment Needed

Tape/CD player • music with a steady beat • a drum or woodblock • chalkboard • signs attached to cones naming parts of the machine: in slot, smoother, computer, checker, out slot, homework

Introduction

Today, we are going to create movements that are repeated exactly the same way over and over and over and over again. These are called *repetitive* movements. We will use these movements to create a dance about a machine that does your homework. Now, let's warm up.

In your personal space, move your arms up and down exactly the same way each time as I play the drum. [Students move their arms on each beat of the drum.] Now, take a step forward on each drumbeat. Make each step exactly the same. Now, move backward. As I play the drum at different tempos, see if you can take one step on each beat. [The teacher alternates the drumbeat between fast and slow tempos.] Change the direction of your steps as you move fast and slow.

Now, I will play a steady beat on the drum. I want you to use your head to create a repetitive movement that moves at the same tempo as the drum. Now try a repetitive movement with your shoulders, now one arm, alternating arms, now the legs.

Choose a body part that can repeat the same movement as I play the drum faster and then slower. Make the movement faster as you hear the drum played faster and then slower as the drum is played slower.

This time, choose two different body parts and alternate them as you do a repetitive movement to the drumbeat. For example, if you choose head and arms, move your head up and down for 8 beats, then move your arms apart and together for 8 beats, then repeat the head movement, and then the arm movement. [Students choose body parts and practice to the drumbeat.]

Create a repetitive movement that uses your whole body and changes levels. Can you travel forward while changing levels?

Development

I will assign partners, and then you will create a repetitive sequence of movements that you can perform in unison. Your sequence should have three different movements you both can do. Each movement moves to 8 counts before you change to the next movement. [Students explore, select, and practice their sequence of movements.] Now, you and your partner will perform your sequence for another set of partners, who are the observers. Then you will switch places. The observers will be looking to see how well you can perform in unison. After the performance, the observers will talk with the performers about their observation. [The teacher can call on two sets of partners to model the performance and observation task.]

Today, we are going to build a human homework machine using repetitive movements. I have listed the five parts for our homework machine on the chalkboard: the in slot, which pulls the homework into the machine; the smoother, which smooths out the homework after it comes out crumpled from your backpack; the computer, which does the homework; the checker, which makes sure the homework is correct; and the out slot, which pushes the homework out of the machine. We will also need some human homework to travel through all the parts of the machine. First, everyone will create a repetitive movement for each part of the machine. I will play the drum to provide a tempo to accompany your movements.

Let's begin with the in slot. Create a movement that repeats a reaching and pulling movement to pull the homework into the machine. Begin small and make the movement bigger and bigger. You may need to take a few steps forward and backward as you reach and pull. [The teacher plays a medium-tempo steady beat as students practice a pulling and reaching repetitive movement.] Can someone share her or his in slot movement? Let's observe how the movement repeats over and over again. [Several students share their movements.]

The next machine part is the smoother. Show me a movement that demonstrates how you would smooth out the crumpled homework. Choose a level for the movement—high, medium, or low. Make sure you can keep repeating the movement. What different body parts can you use to smooth the homework? [The teacher plays a medium-tempo steady beat as students practice a smoothing repetitive movement.] Let's share your ideas like we did for the in slot.

The next machine part is the computer. What kind of movements can you create that would show the inside of a working computer? Make this movement very big, using your whole body; exaggerate the size of the movement. Keep repeating the movement over and over again. Again, let's share ideas.

Next is the checker, which is going to make sure the homework is done well. Create two different movements for the checker. Can you alternate the movements every 8 beats of the drum? I will play a steady beat while you create your movement and practice. [Students share their ideas, either with the whole class or with another student.]

The last machine part is the out slot. Create a movement that pushes the homework out of the machine. Try this move using light force. Now, try the same movement using strong force. How does the change of force change the way the movement feels? Can you use different body parts to push? Let's share again.

Now we need to work on making the homework that travels through the machine. What are some ways you think the homework will move? [Students offer different locomotor movements.] Let's all try Sarina's suggestion to skip. Can you change levels as you skip? Now, let's try Jamal's idea to walk in a curvy pathway. Can you start low and become higher as you walk and then go lower again? [The teacher can ask for additional responses and use the elements of space, time, and force to create variations.]

Culminating Dance

Now, you are going to work with others in a small group and put together the movements you created for each machine part. Each group will be a different part of the homework machine. I have placed cones around the space in a semicircle with a sign marking the area for each machine part. (See figure 8.1.) The first time we do the dance, I will choose the machine part or homework for you; the second time, you can choose where you would like to dance. [The teacher assigns students to a machine part and asks them to work together to create a repetitive movement for their part. Next, the teacher assigns a few students to be the human homework.] While the groups are creating and practicing their machine movements, the students who are the human homework should work on creating a way to travel through the machine parts.

Now, each group will share what they have created and practiced. [The teacher has each machine-part group demonstrate while the remaining students observe.] Now, let's start up the machine and all dance together. The machine parts begin in a still shape. [The teacher plays the music and directs the students when to begin moving.] First, one piece of homework begins to travel to the in slot. Now, the in slot begins and keeps working as

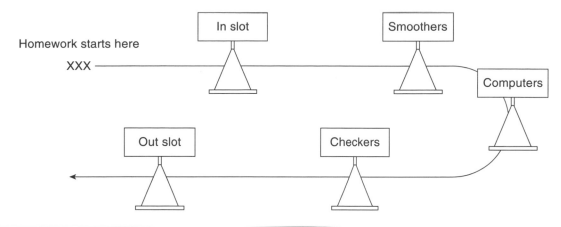

Figure 8.1 Space plan for the dancing homework machine.

each piece of homework passes through. Next, the second piece of homework begins as the first piece travels to the smoother. Next, the smoother begins. Each part of the machine begins to move as the first piece of homework travels by; the parts keep moving while the other pieces of homework move by. Now, the computer starts to move, then the checker, and then the out slot—all perform their repetitive movement. Keep going! I want the homework to show us different ways you would move as you pass each machine part. As the homework approaches the smoother, show me what shape you would be in before you are smoothed out. Start curved and then stretch out as you pass through the smoother. When all the homework has gone through the machine once, stop. Let's try that again.

Now, I am going to add a story to the homework machine. Listen to the sequence first, and then we'll do it. The machine starts up slowly beginning with the in slot, then the smoother, the computer, the checker, and the out slot. As the machine is moving slowly, homework begins to travel through the machine parts. After all the homework passes through the first time, the machine picks up speed, and the homework travels through again, this time a little faster. There is a lot of homework that needs to get done. So, the machine begins to move faster and faster until it explodes and breaks apart! The machine parts travel all through the space in individual pieces, stopping in different places to perform the movement they did when

the machine was all together. The homework calls the machine parts back together, and the machine parts slowly reassemble in their original places. The homework travels through the machine once more, and the machine slows down and comes to a complete stop. The parts freeze in a shape.

Let's try the story with our machine. I will tell you the story again as you dance. This time you can choose which machine part you would like to be. Some groups may have a lot of people who need to work together. We will get organized, create the machine part, practice, and then dance the story.

Closure

This activity makes you think about how a machine works, doesn't it? All the parts have to work together. What are other times when you need to work together with others? Let's talk about repetition in movement and how we use it in our daily lives. When do we need to use repetitive movement to accomplish a task? What machines have been invented to replace human movement?

Look For

- ☙ How well students can perform repetitive movement in an isolated body part and alternate body parts

- ☙ How well students can coordinate a change in the tempo of their movements

๑ Groups that need to develop collaborative skills to share ideas and practice together

๑ The variety of locomotor movements performed by the homework dancers as they travel through the machine

How Can I Change This?

๑ The dance can be repeated several times with students choosing to dance a different part each time.

๑ Small groups of students can design smaller homework machines instead of designating the whole class as one large machine.

๑ Students can create their own stories about what happens to the machine in the dance.

๑ Students create their own list of machine parts and then create repetitive movements that express each part.

๑ Students can add props, costumes, and vocal sounds or percussion instruments to accompany the dance.

๑ Students create a dance about another type of machine.

Assessment Suggestions

๑ The students write in their physical education or dance journals about how to perform the movements in their favorite part of the machine. They name the machine part and describe how they used one or more elements of dance.

๑ The teacher completes a checklist of performance criteria that assesses the partner sequence and checks off the corresponding level of performance for each student. (See figure 8.2.)

๑ Individually, students complete a recording sheet that reflects how their group's machine part performed. The sheet should include the following information:

• Names of group members.

• Machine part.

• Describe a movement that changes levels.

• Describe a movement that changes direction.

• How would you describe your group's level of cooperation when you created and performed the machine part?

• What changes would you suggest for this dance?

Student name	1	2	3	4

Criteria

1 = Student can perform a sequence composed of three different repetitive movements each performed a minimum of four times. No hesitation between movements.

2 = Student can perform all three movements with hesitation between movements or does not repeat minimum of four times.

3 = Student performs only two of the three movements.

4 = Student performs only one movement.

Figure 8.2   Dancing homework machine assessment tool.

Interdisciplinary Connection

๑ Read Shel Silverstein's (1981) poem "Homework Machine" as a way to introduce the dance.

๑ Display books or pictures of different types of machines. Talk about how repetition is used in the machine parts.

๑ Connect to science concepts focused on different ways force is exerted such as push, pull, squeeze, swing, twist, and lift.

CREATIVE SQUARE DANCE

Objectives

As a result of participating in this learning experience, children will do the following:

- Apply their knowledge of square dance movements and formations to create their own square dance
- Teach others the movements they created
- Perform a creative square dance called by the teacher or a student
- Cooperate as a group to learn and perform a creative square dance
- Move using different partner relationships
- Demonstrate respect for individual ideas and take responsibility as a contributing member of a group

Organization

Students are in a square dance formation in partners. When a class does not have complete sets of eight, you can use fewer or more students on a side of the square or use a triangle formation.

Equipment Needed

Tape/CD player • music that is either chosen by the students and appropriate for use in a school environment or traditional square dance music • chalkboard or chart paper • microphone for calling the dance cues

Introduction

Today, we are going to create, teach, and perform a new square dance using movements you create. [This learning experience can be connected to a unit on traditional square dancing.] First, we need to warm up. Find a personal space. What are some different ways you can travel while moving on 8 counts? Lisa suggests running. I want you to run through general space taking one run on each of the 8 counts and then stop. Ready, run, 1, 2, 3, 4, 5, 6, 7, 8. Try it again.

What other ways can you travel? Nick suggests skipping, Yuh lin says sliding, Evan says walking, and Keisha suggests jumping and hopping. Choose one of the ways to travel that was mentioned and move using 8 counts and stop. Choose another way to travel.

Development

Now, I will organize you into groups of four. Stand in a square or circle formation and practice the following movement phrase that has 32 counts. Slide to your right for 8 counts and then left for 8. Next, take 4 steps forward into the square and 4 steps backward out of the square, and repeat the 4 steps forward and 4 steps back. The goal is to move in unison by finding a way to begin at the same time and perform the movements at exactly the same time. After you practice a few times, add arm movements while performing the slides and the steps forward and backward. [Before students practice, the teacher calls on one group to demonstrate the sequence of steps.] How did you decide when to start all together?

Next, I will combine two groups of four to make a group of eight and ask you to choose a leader to signal the group to start and move in unison to the 32 counts of movement. [Students practice working on the same sequence of movement they performed as a group of four.]

Now, I will join all the groups of eight to form one large group performing the movement sequence. [The teacher organizes the class and selects a student to be the leader who signals for the group to start and counts out the sequence to keep everyone moving in unison. Each time the class dances this sequence, a new leader can be selected.] We have been moving in unison using the same movements; now, I will organize you into sets of six or eight and you will create, teach, and practice your own square dance. [It is helpful if students have had some experience with traditional square dancing to provide a reference for creating a new dance.]

Next, each set of partners will create a movement and a name for the movement in one of the following four categories written on the chalkboard:

⊚ Honor your home partner and corner partner. [This is a movement that greets and acknowledges the home partner and corner partner.]

⊚ Circle right and left. [Students can choose a way to travel such as running steps, jumping, walking steps, grapevine steps, or a combination of traveling steps. They can also add arm movements.]

⊚ Turn in place. [Students can create different ways to turn by changing levels, supporting themselves on different body parts, and adding movements as they turn such as wiggling or moving their arms up and down.]

⊚ Exchange partners. [This exchange is similar to the do-sa-do/do-si-do in traditional square dance. Students can jump, walk, skip, move at different levels, or connect using different body parts as they change places and then return to their original spot.]

Your group can choose a way to select the category for each set of partners; however, all four categories need to be used. [The teachers can also assign categories to partners.]

After you have created your category movement, each set of partners will teach their movement to the other students in the group, so everyone knows how to perform all the movements in each category. [Students establish an order to teach and practice the movements.] Now each group will show the rest of the class the movements they created. Also, tell us the name you have given to the movement. The group on my right is first. Please show us your honor-your-partner-and-corner movements. [Students demonstrate.] Now, let's see the circle-right-and-left movement. [Students demonstrate.] Now, the turn-in-place movement. [Students demonstrate.] And, the partner-exchange movement. [Students demonstrate.] Next, let's see another group's movements. [Each group of students demonstrates the movements they created.]

Culminating Dance

In the next part of the session, I will call a dance sequence that I have designed using the four categories. [The teacher points to the chalkboard or chart paper where the sequence is written.] When I call the category your group will perform your movement that corresponds to the category. Ready? Stand in your square formation and number each set of partners. Remember from our square dance lessons how each set of partners has a number like this diagram on the chalkboard. (See figure 8.3.) Ready, here's the first call:

⊚ Partners honor each other.
⊚ Corner partners honor each other.
⊚ Everyone circles 8 counts to the right.
⊚ Everyone circles 8 counts to the left.
⊚ Partners turn in place.
⊚ Corner partners turn in place.
⊚ Partners one and three, move to the middle and do partner exchange.
⊚ Partners two and four, move to the middle and do partner exchange.
⊚ Partners one and three, move to the middle and do partner exchange.

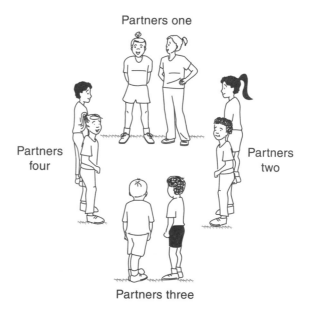

Figure 8.3 Numerical arrangement for square dance partners.

- Partners two and four, move to the middle and do partner exchange.
- Everyone go to the middle and do the turn in place.
- Everyone go back home and say, "Good-bye."

That is the end of the dance. Now, let's try it to music as I call the dance again.

Next, each group will practice their dance using the sequence on the chalkboard; however, this time substitute the names of your movements instead of using the category term. For example, say "happy high five" instead of "honor your partner," or "the tornado twirl" for "turn in place." Select one person in your group to call the dance. They will also dance at the same time. [After students practice, they can share their dances with the class. The caller can use a microphone to call the dance, and another student can take his or her place in the dance.]

Closure

Did you observe any movements in another group that you thought were creative? Can you describe or show the movement and tell us why you thought so? How did your group show respect for one another?

Look For

- How well students can perform the 32-count sequence in unison. You may need to offer cues to help them start the sequence.
- How partners collaborate to create a movement in the assigned category.
- The strategies that students use to teach their movements to others. Do they use words, do they demonstrate, or do they combine words and demonstrations?
- The process students use to choose leaders. Did they vote? Share the leadership? Change leaders? Did students volunteer eagerly?

How Can I Change This?

- As the teacher, you can suggest other square dance sequences. Look at the sequence of steps from other square dances for ideas.
- Students can design their own sequences.

Assessment Suggestions

- Assessment Station—While students are practicing their dances, each student can audiotape their response to a question at a preset assessment station. They will state their name and the response. Examples of questions are as follows: Describe the name and how to perform a square dance step that you created. How did you feel your group worked together to learn and practice your dance?
- Each student draws a diagram of their dance group and labels the partners by number and writes the name of the movements they created.
- The teacher writes anecdotal notes about how well the group collaborated to teach and practice the movements in their dance.

Interdisciplinary Connections

- Use children's literature focused on square dance as a way to introduce the dances. Try *Barn Dance* (Martin and Archambault 1986), *Barnyard Dance* (Boynton 1993), or *Pigs in the Corner* (Axelrod and McGinley-Nally 2001).
- Introduce music through showing and talking about the instruments that are used for traditional square dance music.
- Include social studies through discussing the history and cultural contributions of square dance.
- Tell students about the Square Dance Legislation collection (1975–present) at the Library of Congress American Folklife Center (www.loc.gov/folklife/guides/squaredance.html). This site documents the history of legislation to designate square dance as the national or state folk dance. Include a discussion on other national symbols that are representative of the United States.

ACTION WORDS

Objectives

As a result of participating in this learning experience, children will do the following:

- ◐ Explore and create variations using the elements of dance for the action words *run, pause, spin,* and *collapse*
- ◐ Perform locomotor and nonlocomotor movements using different directions, levels, range, tempos, and shapes
- ◐ Work alone and with a small group to create a dance using a sequence of selected action words

Organization

Students dance individually, then participate in small groups.

Equipment Needed

Chalkboard or large sheet of paper to list action words • smaller pieces of paper and pencils for students • a list of action words for each student (See figure 8.4.)

Introduction

Today, we are going to explore four action words using different directions, levels, shapes, tempos, and body parts. The words are *run, pause, spin,* and *collapse.* We will use these words to create a dance.

The warm-up today is called "Quick Response." I will call out a word, and I want you to show me a shape that you feel represents the word. Find a personal space and begin standing in a straight shape. Ready? Reach, twist, stretch, bend, reach, twist, stretch, bend. Now, let's try jump, swing, squeeze, inflate, jump, swing, squeeze, inflate. Can you suggest other words we could do in our personal space for our warm-up? [The teacher writes the words on the chalkboard and then calls them out.]

Development

The first word we are going to explore is *run.* [The teacher writes the word on the board.] Begin running in a forward direction at a medium tempo. Now change the direction to sideways—right then left. [To prevent falling, we

Run	Shake	Wiggle	Skate	Wait	Freeze
Jump	Bend	Stretch	Spin	Turn	Pop
Skip	Vibrate	Shiver	Twirl	Burst	Open
Hop	Swing	Reach	Sneak	Close	Slink
Leap	Squirm	Fidget	Shuffle	Prowl	Fling
Walk	Twist	Wring	Roll	Grow	Rise
Step	Bounce	Spring	Pounce	Swell	Shrink
Slide	Fall	Collapse	Squeeze	Explode	Flick
March	Drop	Melt	Dab	Tap	Press
Stamp	Fold	Crumple	Punch	Float	Glide
Crawl	Compress	Contract	Slash	Splatter	Stab
Slither	Inflate	Deflate	Flip	Bump	Push
Gallop	Recede	Advance	Pull	Slam	Kick
Dart	Lift	Dash	Stop	Pause	Pump

Figure 8.4 List of action words.

do not recommend that children run backward.] Change direction after 8 runs in one direction. You can choose to run sideways right, then forward, and then sideways left, or choose another order. Now, change direction after 4 runs. [The teacher can play a drumbeat or use music with a clear steady beat.] Now, run using 8 small steps and then 8 large steps. Repeat this running pattern a few times and add different directions.

The next word is *pause.* [The teacher writes it on the chalkboard next to the word *run.*] What is a pause? Gina says it is a short stop, and your body is still. Can you think of any other words that mean the same as pause? Now, I want you to make a different paused shape on each drumbeat. Can you make shapes that are wide? Narrow? Twisted? Curved? Balanced on one foot? Low to the floor? Stretched up high? This time you will add a pause shape to the run. Begin running when you hear the drum, then pause on the one loud drumbeat. [The teacher plays the drumbeats faster for the run and then one loud beat to signal the pause.] Hold your body still. Notice your shape. What is the shape of your arms? Are you leaning in a particular direction? Where are you looking? How are your feet placed on the floor? After the next run, pause in a different shape. [The teacher plays the drum.] Is your shape straight? Twisted? Round? Tall? Wide? Stretched? Balanced on one foot? Run again, changing the direction and size of the steps and pause in a different shape. Keep your body very still. [The teacher plays the drum.] Try the run and pause again. [Again, the teacher plays the drum.]

The next word to explore is *spin.* [The teacher writes the word on the chalkboard next to the word *pause.*] Spin while changing to different levels. Can you spin low to the floor? What are the different ways you can spin low? What other levels can you use to spin? How high off the floor can you spin? Is there a way to start your spin low to the floor and end on a high level? Can you do the opposite? Now, we will combine run, pause, and spin into a sequence, like a sentence of movements. I will play the drum for the run, the one loud beat for the pause, and fast light beats for the spin. Each part will be 8 counts. [The teacher plays the drum and calls out the words while the students perform

the sequence.] Let's repeat this sequence again making the movements different each time.

The last word is *collapse.* [The teacher writes the word on the chalkboard next to *spin.*] What happens to your body in a collapse movement? Yes, Kareem, that's it. I see your body carefully falling to the floor; your muscles look loose. Now, everyone raise your arm up high and let it collapse. Try the collapse with both arms at the same time. Now, let your head collapse forward. Now, collapse the top of your body forward from the waist. Stretch your whole body reaching up to the ceiling, and then slowly collapse to the floor. Which direction did you use? Try the collapse forward, backward, and sideways. I'm going to watch as you collapse; remember to keep it slow and controlled.

When you perform the four words in this order, you are creating an action word dance. The order is run, pause, spin, and collapse. Let's do this dance all together using the same movements. Which direction will we run and for how many counts? Sue suggests we run forward at a fast speed for 12 counts. What shape and counts will we use for the pause? Aaron suggests a 5-count stretched shape. At what level and counts will we do the spin? Kara suggests we spin at a high level that takes us off the floor for 3 counts. How will we collapse and how long will it take? Travis suggests the whole body collapses slowly in a forward direction for 10 counts. [The teacher writes the counts under the words and reviews the sequence before the students dance.] Everyone find a place to begin the dance. Ready? [The teacher plays the drum or uses music to accompany the dance.] Run forward for 12, pause in a stretched shape for 5, spin high off the floor for 3 counts, and slowly collapse forward to the floor counting to 10. Let's try the dance again. [The students practice the dance.]

Let's try the same dance, but now we will do it in a different order, using the same counts for each word. [Students suggest this sequence: spin, collapse, pause, and run.]

I will assign partners and you will create your own dance using the four words—run, pause, spin, and collapse. You can change the order of the words and the tempo, direction, level, size, shape, and counts of each movement.

Make your decisions, write the word order and number of counts on a piece of paper, and then practice your dance. I will ask one set of partners to share their dance while another pair observes. [Students work together to write and practice their dance.] Now, one set of partners will demonstrate their dance and when the dance is over, the students watching will tell the dancers the order of the words they observed. Then switch places.

Culminating Dance

In the next part of this learning experience, you will collaborate with a group of three or four people to make your own choice of action words for your dance. I have provided you with a list. (See figure 8.4.) Choose four words, decide how you will perform the words, and choose how many counts each word will take. Each person selects a word for the dance. Write each word on a separate piece of paper and rearrange the words until you find an order you like. Try several different orders before you make a final choice. Then, practice your dance.

Decide how your group will be organized in the space. Will you use a circle, a line, or a scattered formation? Will the dance be performed in unison, or will different people start and end the dance at different times?

Each group will perform their dance for another group. Then, you will switch. The observers will write down the sequence of action words they observed.

Closure

What did you like about this learning experience? Can you suggest any changes for the next time? Describe a new way you learned to move.

Look For

- The variety of different shapes students create for the pause
- Spins with control at different levels
- How carefully students control their body on the collapse (safety is important when children use action words such as *fall, melt, deflate, drop,* or *sink)*

- How smoothly students can transition from one movement to another
- Students who need help choosing action words from the list
- Strategies that groups use to cooperate as they create their action word dance

How Can I Change This?

- Select a category of words for the action word dances such as words associated with traveling, sports, animals, food, clothing, or words used in comics.
- Read a story or poem to the students and select action words from the text.
- Choose more or fewer words for the dance.
- Add descriptive adjectives to the word list.
- Students can create a story that uses the order of the words in their dance: One day, three girls were running to the playground. They paused when they saw a beehive. The bees came out and the girls began to spin around, waving their arms to get away from the bees. They all got stung in the arm and collapsed to the ground.
- Encourage students to explore many possibilities of how the action words can be performed. Provide a list of the elements of dance to help them make choices of how to vary the action words.
- Students can add percussion instruments or sounds to accompany the movements.

Assessment Suggestions

- Each student in the group records the order of the words for their dance. Next to each word is the number of counts and a description of how the group performed the word.
- Students and the teacher compose criteria and a rubric to assess the dance for a peer assessment (see figure 8.5).
- Teacher checklist notes how well the students make transitions between movements. The "+" symbol can denote

Rubric	Criteria
Super great	The dance had four words. Everyone showed a lot of energy.
Needs more practice	The dance was missing a word, or some of the dancers did not show energy.

Figure 8.5 Action words assessment tool.

smooth transitions using control, and the "?" symbol can denote a performance where the child loses balance, falls, or uses an inappropriate amount of energy to maintain control.

Interdisciplinary Connections

- Integrate language arts concepts about verbs, adverbs, adjectives, and nouns. Include books such as *To Root, To Toot, Parachute: What is a Verb?* (Cleary and Prosmitsky 2001).

- Use the concept of a sentence in comparison to a dance sequence.

- Ask the students about spelling words they could use for their dances.

- Students can use writing and composition skills to write stories that reflect the action word dances they created.

- Students can create dances based on the action words used in novels and poems they are reading in the classroom or at home.

FLOAT AND PUNCH

Objectives

As a result of participating in this learning experience, children will do the following:

- Move using float and punch effort actions (Laban 1976)
- Move with direct and indirect use of space, strong and light force, and fast and slow tempo
- Create a dance made up of floating and punching movements

Organization

Students work individually, then in partners.

Equipment Needed

List of the effort actions (see figure 8.6) • percussion instruments (drum and triangle or gong) • slow and light music for floating movements and strong and fast music for punching movements

Introduction

Today, we are going to dance using two opposite ways to move. One is a strong, fast, and direct punch-type movement, and the other is a light, slow, and indirect float-type movement. Punch and float are two of the eight effort actions listed on the chalkboard. Each of the eight effort actions uses space, time, and force in a differ-

ent way. That's what makes them so interesting. [The teacher can talk about and demonstrate each of the effort actions.]

Let's begin the warm-up by running on a straight pathway for 8 counts and then freezing in a shape for 8 counts. [The teacher plays the drum or percussion instrument.] Try running again and then freeze in a different shape. [The students repeat this pattern of 8 runs and a freeze several times.] Next, I will play the triangle, and on each tap you will slowly stretch your body for 6 counts. Start with your right arm for 6, left arm, both arms; bend your body forward and reach for your knees for 6 counts, bend sideways to the right, and then to the left. Move slowly and lightly. Repeat the stretching sequence again. [The teacher taps the triangle and counts to 6 for each stretch.]

Development

We're going to start today by creating punch movements. This movement will use space directly, which means the movement follows a straight pathway from beginning to end. A punch movement uses strong force and a fast speed. Find a way to do a punch movement with your hands on each beat of the drum. [The teacher plays 8 to 10 beats.] This time, make the punch go in different directions: up, down, to the side, forward, and backward. [The teacher plays 8 to 10 ten beats again.] Now, alternate punches

Effort actions	Time	Space	Force
Wring	Slow	Indirect	Strong
Press	Slow	Direct	Strong
Glide	Slow	Direct	Light
Float	Slow	Indirect	Light
Flick	Fast	Indirect	Light
Slash	Fast	Indirect	Strong
Punch	Fast	Direct	Strong
Dab	Fast	Direct	Light

Figure 8.6 Effort actions.

with your right and left hands, using a different direction for each punch. [The teacher plays 8 to 10 beats.] What other body parts can do a punch movement? Yes, your head, foot, hip, knee, shoulder, chest. On each drumbeat, try a punch movement with a different body part. [The teacher plays 8 to 10 beats.] How can you make the whole body do a punch movement? Try another whole-body punch movement and another. [The teacher plays 8 to 10 beats.] Create a short punch dance in your space using two different body parts and two different directions to this rhythm. Punch . . . punch . . . punch, punch, punch. Punch . . . punch . . . punch, punch, punch. Let's see you put it together. Ready? [The teacher plays the rhythm on the drum while the students create and practice their dances.] Let's share the punch dances. Half of the class will show us their dance while the other half observes, and then we will switch places. The performers need to be clear about using different body parts and directions. After the performance, the observers will describe the body parts and directions they observed.

The second effort we are going to explore is float. In this type of movement, space, time, and force are used in the opposite way from punch. The space for a float is indirect, which means the movement wanders in the space between the beginning and the end. The force is light, soft, and easy, and the speed is slow and sustained. Begin the float with your arms. Let them float up and down on each tap of the triangle, first right then left. [The teacher taps the triangle once for each movement.] Try the floating movement with other body parts. See if you can make your head move slowly and lightly. Now use a foot, a knee, your back, shoulders, and elbows. Use your whole body to float and travel in the space. Keep the tempo slow and the energy light. Change levels and directions as you float in the space. Now, I will play music that is light and slow. I want you to create a float dance that has four parts. You begin in a frozen shape, then different body parts float in your personal space, and then you float while traveling in general space and end in another frozen shape. You can choose how many counts you will have for each part of the dance. Try your dance a couple times and make changes each time.

Culminating Dance

Now, each person will create a short dance combining the punch and float movements. Your dance will follow this sequence: punch, float, punch. [The teacher shows students the sequence written on the chalkboard.] Decide which body parts you will use, the direction of your movement, and the level of your movement. You will use 4 beats for each word. Remember the punch is strong, fast, and direct, and the float is light, slow, and indirect. [The students create and practice their dances while the teacher observes.]

This time, create your own sequence combining punch and float. Choose three or four movements for your sequence. I have written two examples on the chalkboard: float, punch, punch, punch or punch, punch, float. You can use these examples or create your own sequence. While you are practicing your sequence, be clear about how you use space, time, and force in the punch and float movements. Feel the differences in the tempo and force of the movements. [Students create and practice their dances.]

Next, each person will perform his or her dance for another student. When you perform, start and end the dance in stillness so the beginning and end are clear to the observer. The observers will tell the performers the sequence of the punch and float movements. They will also identify the directions and levels used in the dance. I will assign you one or more partners for the performance and observations. [Students observe and perform for each other.]

Now, you will teach your dance to your partner. [Students spend a few minutes teaching and learning the dances.] Next, add the two sequences together into one long sequence. One partner's sequence will be first, and the other partner's sequence will follow. You'll need to choose whether you will do your long dance sequence face to face, back to back, side by side, or one behind the other. You can change these relationships during your dance. Practice the dance several times so you can perform it in unison. [Students practice their dances.] Now, you will perform your dance for another set of partners and then switch places.

Closure

Ask students to describe how the punch and float movements feel in the muscles of the body. What images can students use to describe how it feels to perform punch and float movements? For example, they might say, "When I punch with my hip, I feel like _____," or "Floating reminds me of _____."

Look For

- Clear use of the effort action in how space, time, and force are used.
- How students demonstrate the effort action in different body parts.
- Different ways students create to travel using the effort action.
- Smooth transitions between effort actions.
- The various strategies students use when they teach their sequences to each other. How did they use words and demonstrations in their teaching?

How Can I Change This?

- Use the other Laban effort actions: press, flick, glide, slash, tap, and wring.
- After the students are familiar with several effort actions, they can create dances using three or more different effort actions. For example, they might choose punch, flick, and press.

Assessment Suggestions

- Teacher observes each student performing her or his sequence. Criteria include inclusion of a three-part sequence; smooth transitions; and clear change of tempo, force, and space in each of the three parts.
- Observing partners assess a performance of the combined sequences (see figure 8.7).
- Students write about the parts of the combined sequence dance that they found hard or easy to learn.

Criteria:	Both dancers remembered the sequence.
Rubric:	Great—both remembered everything. Okay—they need more practice.

Criteria:	Dancers performed in unison.
Rubric:	Great—they were together the whole time. Okay—they need more practice.

Figure 8.7 Float and punch assessment tool.

Interdisciplinary Connections

- Connect with science concepts based on how force is exerted. How do Laban's (1976) efforts apply to functional movement, such as turning on a light, getting dressed?
- Use music that expresses the qualities of Laban's efforts. What music pieces express or remind you of floating or punching?

BASEBALL DANCE

Objectives

As a result of participating in this learning experience, children will do the following:

- Perform movement sequences based on baseball skills: running, pitching, batting, and catching
- Move in unison with others to the same rhythm
- Understand how dance can be used to celebrate an event

Organization

Students will learn the dance movements individually and with a partner, and then the whole class forms a double circle for the culminating dance.

Equipment Needed

Tape/CD player • music (locate a version of "Take Me Out to the Ball Game") • pictures of baseball players using the movements in the dance: pitching, catching, running, and batting

Introduction

Today, we are going to celebrate the opening of baseball season across America by learning a new dance that uses baseball movements. I have selected pitching, batting, running, and catching for the dance. Look on the chalkboard at the pictures of players using these skills. What do you see? Can someone choose a picture and make their body into the shape in the picture? [Several students are selected to demonstrate the shapes. The teacher asks the students to describe the shape.]

Let's begin the warm-up pretending we are jogging around the bases. Stand on a spot that will be home plate, now point to a place for first base; now point to second base and third base. When I say go, everyone will take 7 jogs to each of your bases and 1 jump on the base on the count of 8. Ready, go. Jog, 1, 2, 3, 4, 5, 6, 7, and jump on 8. Let's repeat. Remember to take one step on each count. Ready, and jog, 1, 2, 3, 4, 5, 6, 7, jump 8! Let's try that again.

The second part of our warm-up is stretching movements you do before a game. Can anyone suggest a stretch? [One student demonstrates and the other students perform the stretch.] Can anyone else suggest a stretch?

Development

The first baseball movement is the pitch. First, show me how you would pitch a ball to the batter. Try it several times and think about how your arms move, how your feet move, and how the movement starts and ends. [Students practice pitching overhand.] Now, do the pitch as slowly as possible. Make the movement big, with a feeling of stretching. Practice several times, and hold your shape at the end of the pitch. [Students practice.] Add the following counts to the pitch: 4 slow counts for the windup and 4 slow counts for the follow-through. Ready! Windup, 1, 2, 3, 4, 5, 6, 7, 8. Remember to keep the movement slow and continuous and lean back on the windup and forward on the follow-through. Let's try again, and hold your shape still on count 8. Ready? Windup, 1, 2, 3, 4, 5, 6, 7, and hold 8. I can see that you are coordinating your movement with the counts and are moving slowly. We will use this slow pitch in our dance.

Now, let's change our movement to batting. First, bat the way you usually do. Remember how your feet are placed, your knees are bent, the body twists, your hands hold the bat with elbows lifted, and your eyes look at the pitcher. Try a few swings. [Students practice.] You are going to take 3 swings. The first 2 swings take 2 counts each, and on the third swing you will follow up with a complete one-foot spin for 4 counts. Now, add a stop at the end of your spin and hold your body still. Ready? Swing, swing, and swing and spin, hold. One more time. Ready? 1, 2, 3, 4, 5, 6, 7, and 8. Let's practice this part again.

The third movement you will need to learn for the dance is running. This part you already know. I want you to repeat the 7 runs and 1 jump from the warm-up. Can someone show us how they performed the runs and jump? Yes, Isabel, it is 7 runs and a jump on the eighth count. Do the runs and a jump four times through. The first jump lands on first base, the second jump on second base, the third jump on third base, and the fourth jump on home plate. I want you to practice the runs and jumps in a circle of six to eight students. See if everyone can run and jump on the counts at the same time. Designate a leader to count out loud for the group. See if your group can do the entire sequence of 32 counts with everyone running and jumping at the same time. [Students practice as the teacher observes and helps where needed.]

The fourth movement is catching. We are going to do four catches in a sequence. Show me a catch reaching up high, now a low catch, a catch reaching to the right at a medium level, and then reaching to the left at a medium level. Together, let's practice the sequence. Ready? Catch high, catch low, catch right, and catch left. Use 2 counts for each catch. Try it again using the counts 1, 2, 3, 4, 5, 6, 7, and 8. Now, I will assign you a partner. You and your partner will face each other and perform the 8-count catching sequence in unison. Practice several times with your partner.

Now, let's review all the movements in the four sequences. Everyone find a personal space. Ready? Pitching, 1, 2, 3, 4, 5, 6, 7, and hold 8. Now, the batting sequence. Swing, 1, 2, swing, 3, 4, swing and spin, 5, 6, 7, hold 8. Next, 32 counts

of running and jumping. Run 7 counts to each base and jump on 8 four times through. Ready, go. And now, the 8-count catch repeated two times. Catch high, low, right, and left; catch high, low, right, and left.

Culminating Dance

We are going to combine all the movements we practiced today into a dance. The dance will not be exactly like a baseball game; however, parts of the game will be in the dance. The formation for the dance is a double circle. (See figure 8.8.) I will assign you a place on the inside circle or the outside circle. The dancers standing in the inside circle are the pitchers, and the dancers standing in the outside circle are the batters. You are facing a partner. Let's combine the pitching and batting sequences. First, the pitcher will pitch for 8 counts and hold still while the batters perform the batting sequence. Then, the pitchers go again and hold, and then the batters perform. Alternating sequences with a partner in dance is called "call and response." The pitcher's sequence is the "call," and the batter's sequence is the "response." Pitchers get ready, and batters get in your batting stance. Pitchers, begin the 8-count pitch and hold your follow-through at the end. Ready, pitchers? Pitch, 1, 2, 3, 4, 5, 6, 7, and hold on 8. Batters, now do the batting sequence you practiced. Swing, swing, swing, and spin. Now, the pitchers go again and repeat their pitch. Keep the movement slow, stretched, and continuous as you look the batter in the eye. Batters go again.

Figure 8.8 The dancers are organized into a double circle for the baseball dance.

The next part of the dance uses the 32-count running phrase with a jump on the eighth count. Turn to your right, and get ready to run on my signal. Remember, the inner circle will need to take smaller runs and jumps because you have less space to move in, and the outer circle can take a little bigger run and jump because you have more space. Everyone ready! Run, 1, 2, 3, 4, 5, 6, 7, and jump. And, 1, 2, 3, 4, 5, 6, 7, and jump. And 1, 2, 3, 4, 5, 6, 7, and jump. And 1, 2, 3, 4, 5, 6, 7, and jump! Turn and face your partner at the end of the running and jumping. If you are not standing in front of your partner, the inner circle should stay still and the outer circle can take a few more running steps until you meet your partner. Let's try it again, and see if you can coordinate your runs and jumps with my counts. [The teacher can play the music and count with the students.]

The third part of the dance uses the catching sequence: catch high, catch low, catch right, and catch left. This sequence is repeated two times by everyone as you face your partner. You and your partner try to move in unison. Practice as I count. Ready? Catch high, 1, 2, catch low, 3, 4, right, 5, 6, and left, 7, 8. Again, high, low, right, and left.

Next, the pitcher and batter change places. On the change, they give each other a high five or another type of greeting. If you were the batter, you are now the pitcher; and, if you were the pitcher, you are now the batter. [Students switch places and take their new positions.] Let's try the dance again in these new positions. [Students repeat the dance again.] At the end of the second time you complete the dance, freeze the high five instead of changing places so that we end the dance in a still shape.

Let's try the dance from the beginning. Return to your original places.

Closure

Conduct a discussion about how baseball is part of the American culture and how it affects our lives. Explore the concept that dance is a way of recording and representing one's culture. What other events that occur annually as part of our lives could be represented in dance form?

Look For

- A slow and exaggerated pitching movement. Use the image of a slow-motion instant replay.
- How the batters coordinate the three swings and spin. Can they maintain their balance on the spin?
- How well the students can run in a circle in unison and maintain appropriate spacing. When students run in a circle, the circle tends to become smaller, and they may bump into one another.
- Clear level changes in the catching sequence.

How Can I Change This?

- Any of the movement phrases can be varied. For example, in the pitching phrase you can have the pitchers do slow pitches the first time and fast pitches the second time.
- Before the students begin the dance, add 16 counts of stretching movements as a game warm-up.
- Ask the students to greet each other using different ways they have seen in athletic events, such as different handshakes or bumping elbows.
- Assign different students to do the counting for different sections of the dance.
- Create a dance using movements from a different sport.

Assessment Suggestions

- The dance is videotaped, and the students observe themselves performing the dance. They reflect on their performance and write about what part they did well and what part they would like to improve. They perform the dance again while it is videotaped. They watch the second videotape and write or talk about how they improved their performance. The teacher observes the video and notes how well the whole class moves in unison to the same rhythm.

⌕ The teacher asks students to write about one of their real-life baseball experiences as a player, fan, game attendee, umpire, manager, scorekeeper, or coach.

Interdisciplinary Connections

⌕ Introduce children's literature by reading books on baseball such as *Ballpark* (Cooper 1998) or other children's novels.

⌕ Integrate music through using the song "Take Me Out to the Ballgame," with lyrics by Jack Norworth and music by Albert Von Tilzer, composed in 1908. Use the book *Take Me Out to the Ballgame* (Gillman 1999) as a companion to the music.

⌕ Connect math by adding the number of beats for each movement to complete a total of beats for the entire dance.

BUBBLES

Objectives

As a result of participating in this learning experience, children will do the following:

- ❧ Demonstrate word meaning through movement
- ❧ Develop a short dance using a sequence of movements that emphasize time, force, shape, range, and levels

Organization

The students move individually in the beginning of the experience, then create dances in small groups of three or four.

Equipment Needed

A list on a chalkboard or large piece of paper of vocabulary words that describe the characteristics of bubbles such as *shimmer, burst, float, circles, connected, spatter, oblong, pop,* and *sparkle* [the students can also develop the list of descriptive words] • tape/CD player • music with strong and light qualities • a drum or percussion instrument • container of bubbles • paper and pencils

Introduction

We are going to create a dance about the shapes and movements of bubbles. Some of the movements will be slow and light, fast and strong, and fast and light. The warm-up will include movements that show these qualities. There will be three warm-up areas with a leader in each area. (See figure 8.9.) I will organize the class into three groups. Each group will start at one of the warm-up areas, then after 1 minute, switch to the next area. The leader will improvise movements that reflect the movement quality for his or her area, and the group will follow the leader. The warm-up movements are nonlocomotor such as bending, stretching, twisting, reaching, swinging, shaking, wiggling, or turning. The first warm-up area, led by Kate, is the slow and light area. When you are in her area, she will do only slow and light movements and her group will follow. The second area, led by Tahreem, is fast and strong; and the third area, led by Anna, is fast and light. [The teacher assigns the three groups, plays the music for 1 minute and then switches the groups to the next area. This process is repeated until everyone has visited each area. The leaders do not switch.]

Leader 1

Leader 3

Leader 2

Figure 8.9 Three warm-up areas with a leader in each area.

Development

I am going to blow bubbles and I want you to observe the shapes and movements. Now, tell me what you observed. I will write a list of words that describe the shapes and movements of the bubbles. [The teacher writes words suggested by the students.] Look at the list of words describing the bubbles. Today, we are going to create movements that express each of the words. Later, you will select three or four words and create a dance.

Let's begin with *shimmer*. How would you express the word *shimmer*? [Maria says, "I would move like this, a little shaking all over."] Maria's movements are small, light, and quick. Now, everyone find a way to make all of your body shimmer, using very small, light, and quick movements. Make only one body part shimmer while the rest of the body is still. Try another body part. Begin the shimmer movement in your feet and let it travel up to your legs, waist, chest, arms, and head. Can you shimmer as you change levels? Begin lying on the floor and move to standing while you shimmer.

The next word is *burst*. What type of force will you use to express the word *burst*? [Kevin says, "Very strong. You would move big and fast like a firecracker."] In your personal space, find a way to make your hands show a bursting movement. Now, burst with both your arms at the same time. Try your whole body, expressing what it feels like to burst open. Remember to keep the movement strong. Add a jump to your burst. Travel backward, forward, or sideward as you burst. Try a burst movement at a low level and then at a high level. Can you turn and burst open?

Now, let's explore the word *float*. Using light force and a slow tempo begin floating low and small and then gradually float higher and bigger, then low and small again. Try floating in a stretched shape. Try making different shapes as you float lightly and slowly. Let the shapes float around the space. Add a turn to the floating movements.

Pop is the next word. Try using hopping and jumping movements to express a pop. Try 3 light hops, and make a shape with your arms

to go with the hops. Now, try 2 strong jumps and make a different arm shape to go with the jumps. Combine 3 hops and then 2 jumps using the arm shapes. Hop, hop, hop, and jump, jump. As you repeat the pattern, change the shapes of your arms.

The *sparkle* word will be expressed with only one body part at a time. The movement will be light and quick. You can choose if it will be big or small. When I call out the different body parts, you make them sparkle. Ready? Head, hand, shoulder, foot, hip, elbow, knee, head, shoulder, hand, elbow, foot, hip, knee. Now, each time I beat the drum you choose a body part to sparkle. Keep the movement quick and light. [The teacher plays 10 to 15 drumbeats.]

Next, we will explore three descriptive words: *circle, oblong,* and *connected*. Begin by making your whole body into a circle. Find another way to make a circle. Now, another way. Have you tried a standing circle, a sitting circle? How about a circle shape lying on the floor? I am going to organize you into groups of three or four. Now, connect your individual circle shape to the others in your group. Can you connect with your hands, feet, elbows, your sides? Now, each person connects to another person using a different body part.

Let's share the connected shapes by showing them to the class. [Each group demonstrates their connected circles.] What body parts are they using to connect? Do you see three different ways to make a circle with the body?

Next, with your group, make one oblong shape low to the floor. Now, make an oblong shape at a medium level. Try a high level. Find a way to begin your oblong shape low to the floor, and slowly change it to a medium level and then a high level.

Culminating Dance

Now, you will create a dance using some of the bubble words. Each person in the group selects a word from the bubble vocabulary list. Decide on an order for your words. For example, your group may choose *oblong, sparkle, splatter,* and *float*. The first word is the beginning of your dance. The next one or two words are the middle, and the last word is the ending. Your group will perform all the movements in unison. Each word will be performed using a different formation. Will you begin in a circle, a line, or a scattered formation? Then, change to a different formation for the middle of the dance and then another formation for the ending. Use the paper to write your words and draw the formations. [While the students are creating and practicing their dances, the teacher plays the music and visits each group to see if they need any help.] After each group is finished, we will observe the dances.

Closure

How do you think the dancing expressed the movements and shapes of bubbles? Did you use any opposite forces, levels, tempos, sizes, or directions in your dance? Tell us about how they appeared.

Look For

- How well students can exhibit the different qualities of movement. Do students demonstrate the balance and strength needed to move slowly and lightly or fast and strong?
- Students using fast movements in the popping, sparkle, splatter, and burst movements.

- Students' responses to changing body parts on each drumbeat in the sparkle movements. Can students demonstrate the coordination needed to perform these movements?
- How the groups collaborate to connect their circle shapes and move the oblong shape at different levels.
- How students land on their feet with knees bent when they jump in the burst and hop or jump in the pop. Is the landing safe?
- How students round their spines to make circle shapes clearly with their whole bodies.

How Can I Change This?

- Students can add percussion instruments or vocal sounds to accompany their dance.
- Each group teaches their dance to the entire class, and then everyone performs it together.

Assessment Suggestions

- The teacher creates criteria and a holistic rubric to assess the group dance (see figure 8.10).
- Students record the words, a movement description, and the formations they used in the dance (see figure 8.11).

Rubric	Criteria
Excellent	Students perform in unison while changing formations. Force, range, and tempo for each section of the dance are clear, and transitions between sections are smooth.
Good	One or two of the criteria are missing. [Note which criteria are present.]
Needs work	The group was not able to complete the dance.

Figure 8.10   Bubble dance assessment tool.

Word:	Pop	Float	Burst
Movement:	Small and fast jumps	Big stretches w/ walking	Strong turns
Formation:	X X X X	X X	X
		X X	X
			X
			X

Figure 8.11   Student assessment for the bubble dance.

Interdisciplinary Connections

◈ Integrate with language arts as the students write poems or stories incorporating the words used in their dance.

◈ Combine the dance learning experience with a science lesson based on observations of how bubbles form.

BIRTHDAY CELEBRATION

Objectives

As a result of participating in this learning experience, children will do the following:

- Perform a dance created to reflect the events at a birthday party
- Move in a circle formation in a unison rhythm, maintaining an even space among dancers
- Move using the specific rhythms designated in each section of the dance

Organization

The dance uses a single large-circle formation. Students are assigned partners for one section of the dance.

Equipment Needed

Tape/CD player • music that has a steady beat • a list written on the chalkboard or a chart of events that are related to a birthday celebration such as traveling to the birthday party, blowing out the candles, unwrapping the gifts, playing a game, and traveling back home

Introduction

Today, we are going to learn a dance that expresses the events and feelings we experience at a birthday party. Does anyone have a birthday today? This week? This month? Let's celebrate everyone's birthday today. [The teacher asks students about how they celebrate birthdays. Also, before presenting this learning experience, the teacher checks with students to see if they are able to participate in a dance that celebrates birthdays. Not all cultures or religions celebrate birthdays.]

During the dance, all of you will be running in a circle for 32 counts—16 counts to the right and 16 counts to the left. For the warm-up, practice moving to the 32 counts; however, be sure to run in your own pathway. How shall we travel first? Mike says, "Let's jog." Okay, ready to jog to the right? [The teacher beats the drum for 32

counts.] Jog—1, 2, 3, 4, 5, 6, 7, 8, 9, 10, 11, 12, 13, 14, 15, 16. Turn left and jog—1, 2, 3, 4, 5, 6, 7, 8, 9, 10, 11, 12, 13, 14, 15, 16. What is another way we can travel? [Raina calls out, "Skip!" Everyone skips for 32 counts. The teacher asks for several more ways to travel in the warm-up.]

Development

Listed on the board are the different birthday party events that we will express in the dance. We will begin traveling to the party. I'd like everyone to organize themselves in a large single circle with a space in between each person. [Students assemble in a large circle.] We are going to travel to the party by riding a bicycle. How do you think your hands and arms will move? [Kevin says, "Our hands will hold the grips, and we will twist to show how we steer."] Good, good. I also want you to jog lifting your knees up high as if you are pedaling a bike. Turn so your left shoulder is facing in to the middle of the circle. Notice how much space is between you and the person in front of you. Now, take 4 jogging steps forward, holding your bike grips and keeping the same space between each person. Ready? 1, 2, 3, 4. Stop. Do you have the same amount of space between you and the person in front of you? Now, let's try 8 runs. Ready? 1, 2, 3, 4, 5, 6, 7, 8, stop. Now, look at the space. Is it still the same? Let's try 16 counts. Ready? 1, 2, 3, 4, 5, 6, 7, 8, 9, 10, 11, 12, 13, 14, 15, 16, stop. Now, look at the space. What did you do to keep the same amount of space as you jogged? At the end of our 16 jogs, we are going to turn our bikes around and go in the opposite direction just like in the warm-up. Then, your right shoulder will face in to the center of the circle. In your space, show me how you will turn your bike around. Will you use a jump turn? A one-foot turn? A two-foot turn? Let's practice adding your turn at the end of the 16 counts. Ready? All together, 1, 2, 3, 4, 5, 6, 7, 8, 9, 10, 11, 12, 13, 14, 15, 16, and turn on 1, 2, 3, 4, 5, 6, 7, 8, 9, 10, 11, 12, 13, 14, 15, 16, and stop. Great, you are all taking one step on each count and keeping a space between each person. Let's try it again. [The teacher can add the music or continue to use the drum.]

The second part of the dance is blowing out the candles. Pretend there is a giant cake in the middle of the circle. Show me how your body moves when you blow out candles on a birthday cake. How does your body move when you inhale? I see you are leaning backward. I want everyone to exaggerate the inhale movement and lean backward for 4 counts. Stretch and reach up and backward with your arms. Inhale and stretch backward, 1, 2, 3, and 4. Next, move this stretched shape toward the middle of the circle taking 4 steps, 1, 2, 3, 4. To blow the candles out, lunge forward and make a strong exhale movement for 4 counts. (See figure 8.12.) Then, take 4 large steps backward to where you began the inhale. Blowing out the candles uses 16 counts. Let's combine the inhale movement with walking 4 steps forward, then exhale, and then walking 4 steps backward. Ready? Inhale, lean backward, 1, 2, 3, 4. Walk forward, 1, 2, 3, 4. Lunge and exhale strong, 1, 2, 3, 4. Walk backward, 1, 2, 3, 4. Let's try the sequence again and move in unison.

The next part of the party is when the gifts are unwrapped. You will dance two parts—a gift and a child who unwraps the gifts. First, we will practice the gift part. I want each person to think about a toy for the gift and make your body into a shape that represents the toy. Is your shape low to the floor, at a medium level, or a high level? Each student will tell the class what toy his or her shape represents. Let's start with Trent and go around the circle. [Each student shows his or her shape and identifies the toy.] Remember your shape. Next, we will create movements that express the excitement you feel when you unwrap a gift. First, I will assign partners and you will take turns dancing the part of the gift and the person who unwraps the gift. [The teacher assigns partners by selecting students who are standing next to each other. One partner is identified as "happy," and the other partner is identified as "birthday."] The "birthday" people will be the gifts first, and the "happy" people will unwrap the gifts first. "Birthday" people, make your gift shapes. Now, the "happy" people skip in a circle around the gift, using fast arm movements that represent pulling off the ribbon and paper. You have 8 counts. [Students practice the unwrapping movements.] Now, switch parts with your partner so they can practice the unwrapping. Let's practice this section of the dance again.

Now, before we play the party game, let's see if we can combine the first three parts. You travel to the party on your bikes, blow out the candles twice, and unwrap the gifts twice. Start in a big circle with your left shoulder facing in to the center of the circle. Remember to keep the same space between each person and perform

Figure 8.12   Blowing out the candles during the birthday celebration dance.

the movements together to the music. [The teacher turns the music on.] Ready? Begin. [The students practice the first three parts of the dance while the teacher cues the counts.]

The next part of the dance is the party game. Today, we are going to hit a piñata. [The teacher shows the class a piñata, a decorated container filled with candies and gifts that is hung and broken open by hitting it with a stick.] Has anyone played this game at a party? In this part of the dance, the "happy" students take 4 walking steps toward the center of the circle and pretend they are holding a stick performing this sequence: swing, swing, and spin around for 4 counts. [The teacher or a student demonstrates the swing-and-spin sequence.] This movement sequence represents swinging a stick at the piñata. Then you will open your arms and reach up to catch all the candy for 4 counts and walk backward 4 steps to your place in the circle. Ready? "Happy" people walk forward, 1, 2, 3, 4, and swing, swing, and spin around, 1, 2, 3, 4, open your arms and catch candy, 1, 2, 3, 4, and walk backward, 1, 2, 3, 4. Now, the "birthday" people do the same. Now, each group will practice this part of the dance again.

Now, it is time to go home after the party. In this section of the dance, the "happy" people will go home first. They begin riding their bicycles to the right, weaving in and out of the circle among the "birthday" people without bumping into them. How would you describe the pathway they are traveling on? Keep jogging until you get back to your place. Next, the "birthday" people do the same. Let's try this once. [Both groups of students practice this weaving pathway.]

Culminating Dance

Now, let's combine all the sections of the dance we learned into one dance. Can someone tell us what happens first? What is one important thing to remember in the traveling-to-the-party section? What section is second? Can someone show us the sequence of movements for blowing out the candles? What happens in the third part? Can one set of partners demonstrate the gift and the unwrapping? Now, the piñata game. Can someone describe how to do it and then show the movements? Finally, the party is over

and the guests travel home. How is this part the same as traveling to the party, and how is it different?

Now, we are ready to put it all together. I will play the music and cue the counts for each section. [The teacher calls out the counts as the students dance.] Now, you perform the dance by yourselves. I will ask five students to count out loud so everyone can dance in unison. [The teacher selects a different student to count each section while she or he also dances.]

Closure

Ask students to describe the part of the dance they enjoyed most. Ask students what they learned about dancing in this learning experience.

Look For

- How well students can maintain an even space between each other as they travel in the circle
- How well students perform the movements in each section of the dance using the appropriate tempo and space
- Whether students can coordinate the 32-count run, with a change of direction after 16 counts
- How well students can move between each other without bumping

How Can I Change This?

- Suggest other means of traveling to the party such as driving a car, taking a subway, riding a skateboard, or flying in a plane.
- The whole group can represent the same gift instead of making individual choices.
- Use a different game played at a party.
- Students dance in small groups of eight to demonstrate different birthday parties.

Assessment Suggestions

- Students can draw a series of pictures on one sheet of paper that describes the correct order of sections in the dance.

- The teacher uses a checklist to note students who demonstrate difficulty with body control when changing directions and moving among others.
- Students draw a picture of themselves in the shape they used to represent the toy and write three words to describe the shape.

Interdisciplinary Connections

- Combine this dance with a social studies unit focused on cultural traditions. A birthday is one cultural tradition that is celebrated in many different ways. Incorporate these cultural traditions into the birthday dance.
- Integrate math concepts by adding together the ages of all the students, then use the total number as the number of counts for the dance. Students can assign a number of counts to each section of the dance. The total counts for the five sections will equal the total age of the students.
- Students can combine the dance with music as they sing "Happy Birthday" during the dance. The song can also be sung in different languages.

PARTNER DANCE

Objectives

As a result of participating in this learning experience students will do the following:

- Explore creating movements that use four partner relationships: mirroring, shadowing, echoing, and call and response
- Create a dance with a partner using the ABA choreographic structure
- Explore moving with a partner using contrasting tempos and ranges

Organization

Students will collaborate with different partners during the learning experience.

Equipment Needed

Tape/CD player • lively music in fast and slow tempos • chalkboard or chart paper listing the four partner relationships and the definition • paper and pencils for students to record their choreography

Introduction

Who can tell us what they know about the word *duet?* How is a duet used in music? Any other ideas about duets? In this dance unit, we are going to create duets with a partner. You will have the opportunity to create and explore different movements with many different partners.

First, we are going to warm up. Sit on the floor in a personal space. Pretend your arms and hands are partners. Can you move your arms so they both do exactly the same movement at the same time? Try using slow motion. Now, increase the tempo faster and faster. Can you move both legs exactly the same way in a leg dance duet? Can you move your legs far apart and close together? Can they change shape and levels? Now, try moving both your arms and legs in unison at the same time. [The teacher can play music that will be used during the lesson.]

In the next part of the warm-up, we will all stand in a circle. One student will volunteer to be the leader in the center of the circle, and everyone will follow. He or she will move using one of the elements of dance that I call out, and then another person will lead. Ready? Who will be first? Create a slow movement. Next person, do quick and light movements. [The teacher continues to change leaders after 15 seconds and calls a way to move such as one body part, twisting movements, changing frozen shapes, jumping apart and together, low movements, small movements using the hands, bending and stretching, turning, or strong and slow movements.]

Development

This unit will focus on four different ways to dance with another person: mirroring, shadowing, echoing, and call and response. These relationships are called partner relationships. You and a partner will explore each relationship and choose two of the relationships to compose a dance.

The first one is mirroring. In mirroring, you face your partner and move at the same time using the same movement. (See figure 8.13.) One person is the leader, and one is the follower. If the leader is using her or his right hand, the person following will use the left hand, like looking in a mirror. The leader moves slowly so it is easy to follow. [The teacher demonstrates mirroring with a student.] I will assign partners, and you decide who will lead first. Begin when I play the slow music, and stop and switch leaders when the music stops. [The teacher plays the music for 1 minute, and when the music stops students switch places.] Now, I will assign you a different partner, and we will try the mirroring again.

The second relationship is shadowing. In the shadowing relationship, the leader moves with his or her back facing the follower. The partners do the same movement at the same time. This time the leader chooses different ways to travel in the space, stopping occasionally to

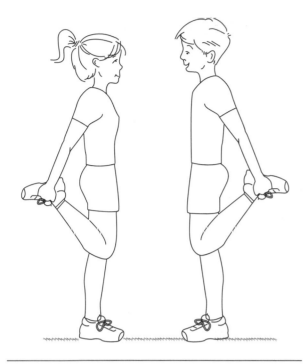

Figure 8.13 Mirroring.

freeze in a shape. [The teacher and a student demonstrate.] I will assign new partners, and, again, you decide who will lead first. When I play the music, you will begin, and when the music stops you switch places. [The teacher plays medium-tempo music.] Remember to stop and make a shape. [Students practice.] Now, I will assign you a different partner, and we will try the shadowing again.

The third relationship is echoing. Can someone tell us what you know about the word *echo?* What do you think it would look like in movement? [The teacher asks several students to share their responses with the class.] What can the leader do to make it easy for his or her partner to repeat the movement? How much time, after the leader performs the movement, should the person following wait before they do the movement? How many different movements do you think the leader should do for the echo? [The students and teacher discuss what makes the echoing relationship successful.] When you perform the echoing movements, make small and big movements and slow and fast movements. I will assign you a new partner; you decide who will be the first leader. When I play the music, you will begin, and when the music stops you switch roles. [The teacher

plays medium-tempo music while the students practice echoing.] Now, I will assign you a different partner, and we will try echoing again.

The fourth relationship is call and response. This relationship is like having a conversation with someone. First, one person briefly expresses a feeling or thought in movement, and when the call person freezes, the response person responds in movement. You may say something using small, light, and quick movements or strong, slow, and big movements. What are other types of movements you could use? I would like two students to demonstrate this relationship for the class. [Students demonstrate the call and response using a variety of different movements.] The movements can contrast with each other or be similar. Be creative and try different amounts of force and a variety of ranges of movement, body parts, tempos, and levels. I will assign new partners, and you decide who will start the conversation. When I play the music, you will begin, and when the music stops, freeze. [The teacher plays medium-tempo music while the students practice the call and response.] Now, I will assign you a different partner, and we will try the call and response again.

Culminating Dance

You will work together with your partner to create a dance that includes two of the four partner relationships using the ABA choreographic structure. The ABA structure is like a pattern. For example, if you chose call and response and echoing for the dance, the sequence in ABA would be call and response, echoing, call and response. You and your partner will create the movements and decide on the tempo for each part and the range of the movements. Let me know if you need help. Be prepared to write down the type of relationship you are using and how it follows the ABA structure. After everyone has created and practiced their dance, you will perform your dance for another set of partners who will be the observers. Then, you will become the observers as they perform.

Closure

What part of the dance did you practice the most before the performance? Why did that part need extra practice? I will call the four types of relationships; raise your hand when I mention the one you liked the best. Now, can someone share which one they liked and why they liked it?

Look For

- Smooth, slow movements in the mirroring relationship. Moving slowly is a challenge for some students.
- How children cooperate and relate to each other positively when you change partners.
- How well students can accurately reproduce the movements their partner is performing in the mirroring, shadowing, and echoing relationships.

How Can I Change This?

- Introduce different partner relationships such as connected, supported, or meeting and parting.
- Organize students in small groups of three or four instead of in partners.
- Assign different choreographic structures.

Assessment Suggestions

- Students identify the two relationships they used in their dance and write down the definitions.
- Students verbalize, draw, or write a definition for each of the four partner relationships experienced in the lessons.
- Peer observers write the partner relationships as they appeared in the ABA choreographic structure.
- During the partner performance, the teacher uses a checklist to record the accuracy of the selected partner relationships during the performance.

Interdisciplinary Connections

- Integrate the dance with a science lesson focused on the sun and shadows.
- Use this dance as a way to illustrate a social studies concept that looks at roles and responsibilities of leaders and followers in a community or partnership.
- Connect the choreographic structure ABA to the ABA music composition form.
- Use the dance as a way to illustrate the science concept of echoing.

SPORT DANCE

Objectives

As a result of participating in this learning experience, students will do the following:

- Create individual and group dances using sport actions as the theme
- Manipulate sport actions using the elements of dance
- Select and use pictures of sport actions to create dances
- Perform a dance in unison

Organization

Students dance individually for the sport web dance and as part of a small group for the sport add-on dance and the sport pictures come alive dance.

Equipment Needed

Tape/CD player • music with a clear beat • chalkboard or chart paper • sport web dance recording sheet • pencils • pictures of sport actions. The sport pictures can be obtained from magazines, the newspaper, the Internet, photographs, or a display of books.

Introduction

This dance unit uses sport actions and sport pictures as the idea for creating dances. Sports are part of our everyday world. We see sports in person or on television. We hear sports on the radio. We read about sports in magazines, books, on the Internet, or in the newspaper. We view sports movies, videos, photographs, or works of art. We wear clothing with sports logos. You may choose a career as a sports writer, a sports announcer, a sports official, or a coach, or participate as an athlete.

Can each person share her or his favorite sport they like to play or watch? [Each student in the class comments on a sport. The teacher can write the sports on the chalkboard or chart paper.] Before we start our dances, we need to warm up all parts of our body. Let's begin with jogging in place, and when I call out one of the sports you mentioned, I want you to freeze in an action shape from that sport. Ready, jog in place and freeze in a tennis shape. [The teacher repeats the sequence of jogging and still shapes several times, calling out different sports on the freeze.]

Development

During this unit, we are going to learn three different ways to create a sport dance. The first sport dance is called the sport add-on dance. I will organize you into groups of five or six, and I want you to stand in a circle. Give each student in your group a number that follows consecutively around the circle. Next, each student selects a sport and one action from the sport. Practice performing the action in 4 counts. [Students practice individually while in the group circle.]

I will demonstrate how your group will add the actions together. I'll use this group to demonstrate. The first student demonstrates her action to the group, and in unison the group members repeat the movement. [One student demonstrates, and then everyone in the group repeats the action.] Next, the second person in the group demonstrates his action, and in unison the group members repeat the movement. Then, the first movement is repeated followed by the second movement, which is added to the first. [Students demonstrate.] Then, the third person demonstrates her action, and in unison the group repeats the action. Now, the group combines the actions beginning with the first, then the second, and then the third. This pattern of demonstrating, repeating, and adding the movement on to the sequence is repeated until everyone in the group has contributed an action to the sequence. The goal is to remember the sequence, perform in unison as a group, and continue to do each movement in 4 counts. [The teacher directs the demonstration, adding two more actions.] The options for using the 4 beats are: one action is performed four times, once on each beat; one action is performed twice, taking 2 beats for the action; or one action is performed once, taking all 4 beats for the action. [The teacher observes the groups and offers help where needed.]

Now, each group will demonstrate their dance to the class. The other class members will observe the performance. After the performance, I will ask the observers to tell us what they saw. Here are the questions I will ask: Did the group perform in unison? What sport actions did you observe? How did the performers use their 4 beats?

Next, your group is going to revise your sport dance. Each person will make a change in the size or the level of his or her action. You will show the change to the group, the group members will try the change, and then the whole group will practice the dance again using the changes.

Next, I will combine all the groups into one large circle. You will maintain the same order you had in your small-group circle. As you become organized, notice that there will be people from the other groups mixed in between your group members. [The teacher organizes all the groups into one combined circle.] Point to the members of your group so you can see where they are. Now, all the group dances will be performed at the same time. Freeze in your last shape until all the groups have finished. Ready, begin. [Students perform their dances.] How did it feel to perform your dance while all the groups danced at the same time? Did you notice any of the other group's movements? [The sport add-on dance can be completed in a single dance session as a lesson in a unit on creating sport dances.]

The second way to create a dance using sport actions is called the sport web dance (Cone and Cone 2002). In this experience, you will create an individual sport dance using your favorite sport. First, we will create a dance together to demonstrate how you will create your dance. Let's select a sport, and I will write it in the center of the web. (See figure 8.14.) [The students and the teacher select a sport, and the teacher writes the sport in the center oval of the web drawn on the chalkboard or a large sheet

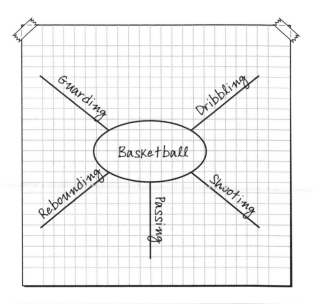

Figure 8.14   Sport dance web using basketball actions.

of paper.] On the lines of the web, I will write the actions performed by someone playing the sport. We selected basketball. Tell me some of the actions used in basketball. [Students respond with passing, shooting, rebounding, dribbling, and guarding.] I will write one action on each line of the web.

Now, make a still shape for each basketball action I call. This is similar to a photograph of a player caught in action. [The teacher calls out the actions, and all the students perform the same action at the same time in their own way.] Hold the shape for 8 counts. Ready? Shooting, 1, 2, 3, 4, 5, 6, 7, 8. [The teacher then calls out the actions of dribbling, guarding, passing, and rebounding and directs the class to hold each shape for 8 counts.] Now, can someone show us one of her or his shapes? [One student makes a shape.] Now look at Mariah's shape. Is the shape high, low, big, small, reaching forward, or leaning backward? What action do you think the shape represents?

Next, we are going to choose three of the basketball actions and create an action shape dance. [The students choose the actions jump shot, rebound, and dribble.] Everyone make three still shapes, one for each action. Freeze in each shape for 8 beats. [Students make the shapes while the teacher counts to 8 for each shape.] Next, you are going to connect the three shapes by moving in slow motion from one shape to another. Begin by making the first shape. Hold it for 8 beats, and then slowly move into the second shape. Hold the second shape for 8 beats, and end the dance by moving into the third shape and holding it for 8 beats. [Students practice their dance several times to music.]

Now, you will create your own sport dance using the same process we used for the basketball dance. I will give each of you a sport web sheet. Choose a sport and write the actions on the web. Then, create a shape for each of the actions. Next, choose three actions for your dance. You can select the number of beats to hold each sport shape. [Students complete the web, practice the actions, choose three actions, and connect the actions with slow motion.] You can travel slowly to another space between the action shapes. [Students practice while the teacher observes and helps where needed.]

To finish this web dance, I want everyone with the same sport to perform at the same time. I know you will all have a different dance using the same sport. Can all the football players perform? Now, swimmers. Now, ice hockey players. What other sports have you selected for your dances? [The sport web dance can be a lesson within a unit on creating sport dances or taught as an individual dance lesson.]

The third way to create a sport dance is called sport pictures come alive. I have a box of sport action pictures that I have collected. They are from newspapers and magazines and show one or more players caught in the action. The dance is composed of three parts. In the beginning of the dance, movements are performed that represent actions that may have occurred prior to the photo. The second part is a frozen shape that represents the player's shape in the photo. In the third section of the dance, create your own movements that may have occurred after the photo was taken. Before you choose a photo, let's look at a picture and talk about what you see. What are the players doing in the picture? What shapes are the players using? Are the players in a high, medium, or low level? In what direction are they facing? What type of energy do you think the players are showing? Can you make your body into the shape of the person in the picture? Now hold that shape for 8 counts.

I will organize you into different groups of two, three, or four people. Your group will choose one photo from all the photos I have displayed on the floor. First, make the shape of the person in the photo and count to 8. This is the middle of your dance. Then, create movements that would express what you think happened right before the photo was taken. Use 8 counts. This is the beginning of the dance. Then, create the third part of the dance using movements that you think happened after the photo was taken. Use 8 counts. The whole dance takes 24 counts: 8 counts of what happened before the picture, 8 counts showing what is in the picture, and 8 counts of what happened after the picture. [Students choose pictures and collaborate to create the dance. The teacher observes and helps where needed.] Now that everyone is finished, half of the groups will perform their dance while the other groups observe, and then we will switch. Before you begin, stand with your group and hold up the picture. Observers, take a look at the pictures you will see come alive. [Students perform their dances.]

Culminating Dance

For your final sport dance, you will be in a group of four or five. The group will choose one of the three ways you learned to create a sport dance: sport add-on, sport web, or sport pictures come alive. Give your group a name and then create and practice your dance. When each group is finished, you will perform your dance for another group.

Closure

Which way of creating a sport dance did you find most interesting? Why? How did you change your sport action to make it different from the way it is performed in a real game?

Look For

- ๑ How children create variations for a sport movement. Do they continue to explore new ideas and new ways of performing the sport action?
- ๑ Children who need help with transforming a sport action or picture into a movement

or shape. They may need to see how another student has transformed words and pictures into movement.

How Can I Change This?

- ৩ Use categories of sports such as winter sports, Olympic sports, water sports, team sports, or extreme sports.
- ৩ The sport web dance can become a partner dance.
- ৩ Students can bring in photos of themselves playing sports or use drawings for the sport pictures come alive dance.
- ৩ Students create a dance that uses a group sport tableau (see Rovegno and Bandhauer 2000) using sport action shapes designed by the students.

Assessment Suggestions

- ৩ Teacher observes each group's sport add-on dance and records its ability to move in unison using a checklist (see figure 8.15).
- ৩ Teacher assessment of individual students' sport web dance performances (see figure 8.16).

- ৩ Peer assessment for the sport pictures come alive dances. The following questions are presented to the observing group. Their answers can be either spoken or written. What sport did the dancers use for their dance? What types of pathways did the dancers use in their dance? Did the dancers change level or direction during their dance? Can you suggest any variations for the dance?
- ৩ Teacher assessment of culminating performance. Teacher uses a checklist to note which of the three ways the group chose for their dance (see figure 8.17). The teacher can use the letter "A" for the sport add-on dance, the letter "B" for the sport web dance, and a "C" for the sport pictures come alive dance. The checklist also notes the level of cooperation that the teacher observed as the group selected, created, and practiced their dance. A rubric can be used, such as Excellent (E), which means that the group worked well together or independently to practice and perform their dance, or Needed Help (NH), which means the group needed teacher assistance to organize and practice their dance.

Excellent	All students remembered the sequence and performed in unison using 4 beats for each sport action.
Very good	Some students (one or two) had trouble moving in unison with the other members of the group.
Needs improvement	Most students in the group were not in unison.

Figure 8.15 Group assessment tool for the sport add-on dance.

Excellent	Student held still in all three shapes and clearly demonstrated slow movements between shapes.
Very good move	Student had trouble holding the shapes still, or she or he did not slowly to connect one shape to another.
Needs improvement	Student held only one shape still or was unable to hold any of the shapes still and could not move slowly from one shape to another.

Figure 8.16 Sport web dance assessment tool.

Student name	Group name	Type of sport dance	Cooperation used to create, practice, and perform
Sanam	Red Dogs	A	E
Bart	Magic Steppers	B	NH
Christos	Super Dancers	C	E

A = sport add-on dance, B = sport web dance, C = sport pictures come alive dance, E = excellent, NH = needed help

Figure 8.17   Sample teacher checklist for culminating dance.

◐ Student self-assessment of the culminating dance performance. Each student in the group writes a response to the following questions: Which way did your group choose to create their sport dance? Why did they make that choice? How did you feel about your performance in the dance as a part of the group?

Interdisciplinary Connections

◐ Discuss how using the web to develop the sport dance is similar to using a web for developing ideas when writing.

◐ Use the text and illustrations in children's literature books and poems based on sports, such as *Hoops* (Burleigh and Johnson 1997), for initiating ideas for a sport dance.

DANCE MAPS

Objectives

As a result of participating in this learning experience, students will do the following:

- ๑ Create an individual dance using pathways and still shapes as the theme of the dance
- ๑ Collaborate with a small group to create a group dance
- ๑ Choose a music selection to accompany their dance

Organization

Students will work individually and then as part of a small group.

Equipment Needed

Tape/CD player • three different selections of music (choose from a variety of styles such as classical, jazz, contemporary, new age, cultural, blues, or rock) • four place markers for each student such as rubber-spot markers, beanbags, construction-paper shapes, foam cylinders, or hoops • chalkboard or chart paper listing the map dance directions • paper and crayons for recording dance maps

Introduction

This dance experience will focus on how to make a map of a dance. The map will show the pathways, shapes, and movements that you use in your dance. You will also select music to go with your dance.

First, we are going to do a warm-up focusing on shapes and pathways. Find a personal space, and pretend you have a giant crayon in your hand and you are standing inside a huge cylinder of paper. Begin to draw curved pathways. Reach high, low, out to the side, and over your head. Place the crayon on another body part, perhaps your elbow, nose, knee, or heel, and draw straight pathways vertically, horizontally, and diagonally. Can you place the crayon in the middle of your back and draw zigzag pathways? What other body parts can

you use to draw? Each time you hear me call out the word "change," draw with a different body part using a different pathway. Ready, change, change, change, and change. [The teacher pauses for a few seconds before calling out the next change of body part.]

Now, step out of your cylinder and pretend you have a giant bucket of paint in front of you. Jump in and out of the paint bucket, and walk in a curved pathway in the general space. See if you are leaving a painted pathway behind you. Return to the bucket and jump in and out, and then travel in the space using another locomotor movement and a different pathway. Each time you hear me call out the word "change," travel using another locomotor movement on a different pathway. Ready, change, change, change, and change. [The teacher again pauses for a few seconds before calling out the next change of movement and pathway.]

The last part of the warm-up is pretending you are a rubber band. Stretch your body as wide as you can, and hold the shape still while you count to 5. You can make your shape standing, sitting, kneeling, or lying down. Now, try stretching as high as you can. This time stretch and hold a shape for a count of 5, and then slowly retract the rubber band and stretch into another shape. Move in and out of your shapes slowly. [The teacher can use a drum to keep an even beat for the counting.]

Development

The step-by-step instructions for completing the map dance are listed on the chalkboard. (See figure 8.18.) We will create each step and then you will have time to put the dance together. First, you will receive four space markers. These markers will show the places you will make still shapes in your dance. Find a different place on the floor to put down each marker. Now, identify each of your markers as one, two, three, and four. Stand on marker number one; now go to two; now, three and four. [The teacher can have students stand on the markers in numerical order a few times to help students establish a sequence for the

Step 1:	Make a different shape on each of the markers.
Step 2:	Create a pathway between each marker.
Step 3:	Choose a way to travel on each pathway.
Step 4:	Work on putting your dance together.

Figure 8.18 Instructions for the map dance.

dance.] This will be the order of the spaces you move to in your dance.

In step one, you will make a different shape on each of the markers. Shapes can be wide, tall, low to the floor, twisted, curved, straight, or a combination of different shapes. Hold still in each shape. You can choose the number of counts. [The teacher provides time for students to create and practice their shapes on each of the markers.] I want you to show the shapes you have created. This half of the class will observe, and this half of the class will demonstrate their

Homework starts here

shapes. Demonstrators, you will begin on your first marker, hold each shape still for the number of counts you have chosen, and then go to each of the next three markers. Sit down when you have finished. [The students demonstrate, and then the demonstrators and observers switch roles.]

Now, let's go to step two. Create a pathway between each marker. You can use straight, curved, zigzag, or a combination of pathways. Look at this example on the chalkboard. [The teacher shows the students a sample drawing. See figure 8.19.] Try a couple ideas and then

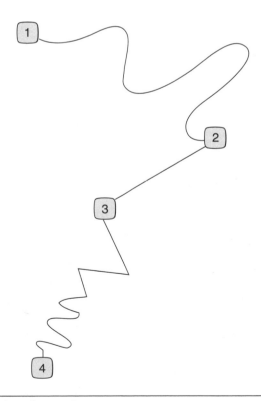

Figure 8.19 Teacher example of pathways connecting four place markers.

use a piece of paper to draw your pathways. You can use different colored crayons for the different pathways. [The students create and practice making the pathways, then they draw the pathways connecting the four markers as shown in the example.]

Next, we have step three. Choose a way to travel on each pathway. Incorporate a locomotor movement, a level change, and a direction for each part of the pathway. For example, you may walk backward slowly taking big steps on your first pathway, then quickly slide sideways to the third marker, and walk on your hands and feet while turning to the fourth marker. Remember to practice your shape when you arrive at each marker. [The teacher or a student can demonstrate the example. The students work on their traveling movements.] When you finish, write down how you are traveling next to the pathway on your map.

Last, let's work on step four. Work on putting your dance together by practicing the shapes and locomotor movements in your dance. Make your beginning shape on your first marker, then travel on your pathway to your second marker and make your second shape. Next, travel on your second pathway to your third marker and make a shape. And, finally, travel on your third pathway to your fourth marker to make your ending shape. Do you want to make any changes to your dance? Work on making the transitions smooth between the shapes and the traveling movements. [The teacher provides time for the students to practice and make changes to the dance.]

Culminating Dance

In the final dance, three or four students will combine their individual dances into one dance. I will organize you into small groups, and each person will demonstrate her or his dance to the others in the group. First, explain your map to the group and show them where you have placed your markers. Then perform your dance. [Each student in the group performs while the others in the group observe.] Now, I would like everyone in each group to perform her or his dance at the same time. As you dance, make eye contact with each other, and notice when others

in your group are in their still shapes and where they are traveling in the space.

Before you perform the dance again, your group will agree on a place to make a connected group shape and decide how many counts you will hold the shape. In addition, everyone will agree on one way to travel from the group shape to his or her first marker. A held group shape and a single way to travel to the first marker will be the beginning of the group dance. In the middle part of the dance, everyone performs his or her individual dance. To end the dance, the group returns to the same place they started using the same way to travel and freezes in the same group shape. [Students collaborate to create a group shape and a way to travel to and from their individual dance.]

The final decision your group needs to make is to select a piece of music to accompany your dance. You will listen to each piece of music, practice your dance to each piece, and then you will choose the one you want to use. I will play 30 seconds of three different pieces of music. [The teacher plays each music selection twice while the students listen.] Now, I will play each piece of music again, and I would like your group to perform their dance while the music is playing. [The students perform their dance three times, once to each piece of music.] Now, after listening and dancing to each selection, your group can make a decision on the music selection.

To conclude this learning experience, each group will perform their dance for the class. Tell us which piece of music you selected, and take your place in the group shape. When the music begins, start your dance. I will stop the music when everyone returns to the group shape. Which group would like to perform first? After each group performs, the observers will complete the group observation form. (See figure 8.20.) Before you perform, tell us why you chose the music piece for the dance. [Each group performs for the class, and the observers assign a recorder for their group and jointly complete the observation form.] Now, on one large piece of paper, each person in the group will draw their dance. Assign a different colored crayon to represent each person. At the end, all the pathways of each of your dances will overlap one another to form one drawing. Then, clip

Names of dancers:

Names of observers:

Write three words to describe the beginning and ending group shape.

What was the common locomotor movement the group used to move to their individual shapes?

List five different movements you observed the students performing.

1.

2.

3.

4.

5.

Figure 8.20 Group observation form.

your individual drawings to the group drawing and give them to me. [The teacher can display the drawings as part of a bulletin board display about dance maps.]

Closure

What part of this learning experience did you enjoy the most? What ideas would you add to this learning experience to make it different? What was the most challenging part of the learning experience?

Look For

- How students use different pathways and locomotor movements. Help students to expand their choices so all movements and shapes are not the same.
- Students who need help drawing the pathways and writing the words.
- Students who may have trouble getting started with the shapes and locomotor

movements. Ask guiding questions (see Pike 2000) such as these: What type of shape would you want to start in? What level do you want your shape to be in? What are some ways you like to move? These guiding questions can provide students with ideas yet still allow them to make their own decisions.

How Can I Change This?

- Reduce or increase the number of shapes and pathways.
- Students can work in pairs to create the dance.
- Individuals or groups can create stories to accompany their dance.
- Students can enlarge their paper maps by drawing them on the sidewalk or blacktop facility with chalk. They can label the movements and draw the markers and then move on the chalk pathways.

Assessment Suggestions

๑ Students complete a drawing of the pathways used in their dance and identify the locomotor movements. They may also include a description of each shape and the number of counts.

๑ During the performances, the teacher uses a checklist to note if the students have included the four shapes and three pathways in their dance.

๑ Students, organized into groups, complete an observation form after observing a performance of another group.

Interdisciplinary Connections

๑ Connect with social studies by discussing the purposes of maps. Bring a variety of different maps to the dance lessons.

๑ Use math to estimate and measure the distance between the markers used in the dance.

๑ Create a story that describes an imaginary journey taken along the pathways of the dance.

๑ Integrate music by talking about and listening to different styles of music that will accompany the dance.

References

Alperstein, C., and R. Weyl. 1992. *Arts for everykid: A handbook for changes*. Trenton, NJ: New Jersey State Council of the Arts, Department of State and Alliance for Arts Education, New Jersey.

Anderson, A. 2002. Engaging student learning in physical education. *Journal of Physical Education, Recreation and Dance* 73 (7): 35-39.

Axelrod, A., and S. McGinley-Nally. 2001. *Pigs in the corner: Fun with math and dance*. New York: Simon & Schuster Books for Young Readers.

Benzwie, T. 1987. *A moving experience: Dance for lovers of children and the child within*. Tucson, AZ: Zephyr Press.

Blom, L., and L. Chaplin. 1986. *The intimate act of choreography*. Pittsburgh: University of Pittsburgh Press.

Bloom, B., M. Englehart, E. Furst, W. Hill, and D. Krathwohl. 1956. *Taxonomy of educational objectives: The classification of educational goals. Handbook I: Cognitive domain*. New York: Longmans Green.

Boynton, S. 1993. *Barnyard dance*. New York: Workman Publishing.

Brady, K., M. Forton, D. Porter, and C. Wood. 2003. *Rules in school*. Greenfield, MA: Northeast Foundation for Children.

Brookfield, S. 1995. *Becoming a critically reflective teacher*. San Francisco: Jossey-Bass.

Burleigh, R., and S. Johnson. 1997. *Hoops*. San Diego: Harcourt Brace.

Buschner, C. 1994. *Teaching children movement concepts and skills: Becoming a master teacher*. Champaign, IL: Human Kinetics.

Carle, E. 1996. *Little cloud*. New York: Philomel Books.

Chandra, D. 1993. *Balloons and other poems*. London: Sunburst Books.

Cleary, B., and J. Prosmitsky. 2001. *To root, to toot, to parachute: What is a verb?* Minneapolis: Carolrhoda Books.

Cone, S., and T. Cone. 2002. Using sport themes in creative dance. *Strategies* 16 (1): 9-12.

Cone, S., and T. Cone. 2003. Dancing, learning, creating, knowing. *Teaching Elementary Physical Education* 14 (5): 7-11.

Cone, T. 2000. Off the page: Responding to children's literature through dance. *Teaching Elementary Physical Education* 11 (5): 11-34.

Cone, T. 2002. *Off the page: Children's creative dance as a response to children's literature*. Unpublished doctoral dissertation, Temple University.

Cone, T., P. Werner, S. Cone, and A. Woods. 1998. *Interdisciplinary teaching through physical education*. Champaign, IL: Human Kinetics.

Cooper, E. 1998. *Ballpark*. New York: Greenwillow Books.

Council on Physical Education for Children. 1992. *Developmentally appropriate physical education practices for children*. Reston, VA: American Alliance for Health, Physical Education, Recreation and Dance/National Association for Sport and Physical Education.

de Mille, A. 1991 April 7. Measuring the steps of a giant. *New York Times*.

Donnelly, F. 2002. Make learning an electric experience! *Teaching Elementary Physical Education* 13 (2): 25-27.

Eisner, E. 1998. *The kind of schools we need: Personal essays*. Portsmouth, NH: Heinemann.

Endicott, J. 1988. *Listen to the rain*. New York: Henry Holt.

Fleming, D. 1993. *In the small, small pond*. New York: Henry Holt.

Fowler, C. 1994. *Music: Its role and importance in our lives*. New York: Glencoe.

Fraleigh, S. 1987. *Dance and the lived body: A descriptive aesthetics*. Pittsburgh: University of Pittsburgh Press.

Gardner, H. 1983. *Frames of mind: The theory of multiple intelligences*. New York: Basic Books.

Gilbert, A. 1977. *Teaching the three r's through movement experiences*. New York: Macmillan.

Gilbert, A. 1992. *Creative dance for all ages*. Reston, VA: American Alliance for Health, Physical Education, Recreation and Dance/National Dance Association.

Gillman, A. 1999. *Take me out to the ballgame*. New York: Simon & Schuster.

Goodrich, H. 1997. Understanding rubrics. *Educational Leadership* 54 (4): 14-17.

Graham, G. 2001. *Teaching children physical education: Becoming a master teacher*. 2nd ed. Champaign, IL: Human Kinetics.

Halsey, M. 2000. *Circus 1-2-3*. New York: Harper Collins.

Hanna, J. 1987. *To dance is human: A theory of nonverbal communication*. Chicago: University of Chicago Press.

Hawkins, A.M. 1988. *Creating through dance*. Hightstown, NJ: Princeton Book Company.

Holt/Hale, S. 1988. *On the move: Lesson plans to accompany children moving*. Mountain View, CA: Mayfield.

Jacobs, H. 1989. *Interdisciplinary curriculum: Design and implementation*. Alexandria, VA: Association for Supervision and Curriculum Development.

Johnson, I. 2002. Liven up those line dances. *Teaching Elementary Physical Education* 13 (1): 30-32.

Joyce, M. 1973. *First steps in creative dance*. Palo Alto, CA: National Press Books.

Joyce, M. 1984. *Dance technique for children*. Palo Alto, CA: Mayfield.

Kalan, R. 1981. *Jump, frog, jump*. New York: Scholastic.

Kane, K. 1998. *Move and learn: A kaleidoscope of creative movement activities for literacy development*. Grand Rapids, MI: Instructional Fair TS Denison.

Kaufmann, K. 2002. Adaptation techniques for modeling diversity in the dance class. *Journal of Physical Education, Recreation and Dance* 73 (7): 16-19.

Laban, R. 1976. *Modern educational dance*. 3rd ed. London: Macdonald & Evans.

Lazaroff, E. 2001. Performance and motivation in dance education. *Arts Education Policy Review* 103 (2): 23-29.

Martin, B., and J. Archambault. 1986. *Barn Dance*. New York: Henry Holt and Company.

McCollum, S. 2002. Reflection: A key for effective teaching. *Teaching Elementary Physical Education* 13 (6): 6-7.

McTighe, J. 1997. What happens between assessments? *Educational Leadership* 54 (4): 6-12.

Mosston, M. 1972. *Teaching from command to discovery*. Belmont, CA: Wadsworth.

Murray, R. 1963. *Dance in elementary education*. 2nd ed. New York: Harper & Row.

National Assembly of State Arts Agencies and the National Endowment for the Arts. 1994. *Design for accessibility: An arts administrator's guide*. Washington, DC: National Assembly of State Arts Agencies.

National Association for Sport and Physical Education/ American Alliance for Health, Physical Education, Recreation and Dance. 2004. *Moving into the future: National standards for physical education,* 2nd edition. Reston, VA: Author.

National Dance Association/American Alliance for Health, Physical Education, Recreation and Dance. 1994. *National standards for dance education*. Reston, VA: Author.

National Dance Association. 1995. *Opportunity-to-learn standards for dance instruction*. Reston, VA: Author.

New Jersey Literacy in the Arts Task Force. 1989. *Literacy in the arts: An imperative for New Jersey schools*. Trenton, NJ: Author.

Newnam, H. 2002. Overcoming your fears of teaching educational dance. *Teaching Elementary Physical Education* 13 (3): 10-12.

Pike, S. 2000. Hip-hop sport education. *Teaching Elementary Physical Education* 11 (5): 19-21.

Root-Bernstein, R., and M. Root-Bernstein. 2000. Learning to think with emotion. *Chronicle of Higher Education* 46: A 64.

Rovegno. 2003. Children's literature and dance. *Teaching Elementary Physical Education* 14 (4): 24-29.

Rovegno, I., and D. Bandhauer. 2000. Teaching elements of choreography. *Teaching Elementary Physical Education* 11 (5): 6-10.

Silverstein, S. 1974. *Where the sidewalk ends*. New York: Harper & Row.

Silverstein, S. 1981. *A light in the attic*. New York: Harper & Row.

Stinson, S. 1988. *Dance for young children: Finding the magic in movement*. Reston, VA: National Dance Association/American Alliance for Health, Physical Education, Recreation and Dance.

Stinson, S. 1998. Seeking a feminist pedagogy for children's dance. In *Dance, power, and difference: Critical and feminist perspectives on dance education*. Edited by S. Shapiro, 23-47. Champaign, IL: Human Kinetics.

The Square Dance Legislation Collection. 2004. Library of Congress American Folklife Center. www.loc.gov/folklife/guides/squaredance.html. Accessed June 23, 2004.

Tomlinson, C. 1999. *The differentiated classroom: Responding to the needs of all learners*. Alexandria, VA: Association for Supervision and Curriculum Development.

Townsend, J. S., and D. Mohr. 2002. Review and implications of peer teaching research. *Teaching Elementary Physical Education* 13 (6): 28-31.

Wall, J., and N. Murray. 1989. *Children and movement: Physical education in the elementary school*. Dubuque, IA: Brown.

Walsh, E. 1993. *Hop jump*. San Diego: Harcourt Brace.

Weeks, S., and D. Carter. 1996. *Noodles*. New York: Harper Collins.

Wiggins, G. 1998. *Educative assessment: Designing assessments to inform and improve performance*. San Francisco: Jossey-Bass.

Wiggins, G., and J. McTighe. 1998. *Understanding by design*. Alexandria, VA: Association for Supervision and Curriculum Development.

Wildsmith, B. 1970. *Circus*. New York: Franklin Watts.

Woods, A. 1997. Assessment of the cognitive domain. *Teaching Elementary Physical Education* 8 (3): 28-29.

Worrell, V., C. Evans-Fletcher, and S. Kovar. 2002. Assessing the cognitive and affective progress of children. *Journal of Physical Education, Recreation and Dance* 73 (7): 29-34.

Zakkai, J. 1997. *Dance as a way of knowing*. York, ME: Stenhouse.

Suggested Readings

Bennett, J., and P. Riemer. 1995. *Rhythmic activities and dance*. Champaign, IL: Human Kinetics.

Offers more than 190 activities applicable for an elementary dance program in addition to guidelines for developing social dance units and lessons.

Benzwie, T. 1987. *A moving experience: Dance for lovers of children and the child within*. Tucson, AZ: Zephyr Press.

A collection of ideas for designing dance activities. Ideas include props, space, sculpting, art, music with movement, communication, language, rhythm, name games, fantasy, range, and movement games and warm-ups. Lists suggestions for music selections to accompany activities.

Benzwie, T. 1995. *More moving experiences: Connecting arts, feelings, and imagination*. Tucson, AZ: Zephyr Press.

This book offers activities that integrate the arts and promote creativity. Ideas are applicable for students in the K–5 educational setting.

Docherty, D. 1975. *Education through the dance experience*. Bellingham, VA: Educational Designs and Consultants.

A description of the content and approach to teaching dance based on the work of Rudolf Laban. Includes many specific examples of lessons that can be easily adapted for teachers beginning to teach dance.

Fraser, D.L. 1991. *Playdancing*. Pennington, NJ: Princeton.

A discussion of the creative process and the important part it plays in education. Fraser provides activities that integrate movement with development of self-awareness, language, and interpersonal skills.

Gilbert, A.G. 1977. *Teaching the three r's through movement experiences*. New York: Macmillan.

Contains practical activities to integrate movement with other subject areas such as language arts, math, science, social studies, and visual arts. Includes a bibliography of books, films, and recordings that can be used as a resource for developing a movement experience.

Gilbert, A.G. 1992. *Creative dance for all ages*. Reston, VA: National Dance Association/American Alliance for Health, Physical Education, Recreation and Dance.

Provides a comprehensive resource of practical activities for teaching dance to students of all ages. The chapters focus on the elements of dance: space, time, force, the body, and movement. Includes information on assessment, integrating dance with other curricular areas, props, accompaniment for dance classes, and a music and video list.

Graham, G., S. Holt/Hale, and M. Parker. 2004. *Children moving: A reflective approach to teaching physical education*. 6th ed. New York: McGraw-Hill.

Includes content information on movement concepts with examples for practical application that are useful for teaching dance. Also included is a chapter on teaching creative dance, which presents content for a creative dance experience and a process for teachers and children to use on how to create dances.

Grant, J. 1995. *Shake, rattle, and learn*. Markham, Ontario: Pembroke.

This book supports movement-based learning as an essential component of a child's education. Each chapter focuses on a different theme that ranges from individual to whole-class activities. Themes integrate movement with language arts, science, drama, music, visual arts, social studies, and math. Activities are practical, fun, and appropriate for developing into dance lessons.

Hawkins, A.M. 1988. *Creating through dance*. Pennington, NJ: Princeton.

Focuses primarily on dance for secondary students and adults, although the book does discuss concepts universal to teaching dance at all levels. Defines the art of dance through creativity, aesthetics, performance, and evaluation. Provides examples for evaluation.

Humphrey, J. 1987. *Child development and learning through dance*. New York: AMS Press.

Presents an approach to teaching dance based on the stages of child development. Also suggests ways to integrate dance into teaching reading and math and to improve general learning ability through dance.

Joyce, M. 1973. *First steps in teaching dance*. Palo Alto, CA: National Press Books.

Contains practical information on the content and process of teaching dance. Author includes easy-to-follow lessons that are applicable for the elementary-school-aged child. Well-illustrated with photographs.

Joyce, M. 1984. *Teaching dance technique to children.* Palo Alto, CA: Mayfield.

Presents content that focuses on teaching the essential technical skills children need to become more proficient in creative movement to fully express their ideas. Provides descriptive experiences to help children understand how their body moves efficiently and expressively. Chapters cover basic locomotor movements, opposition, rhythm, alignment, and use of energy.

Kane, K. 1998. *Move and learn: A kaleidoscope of creative movement activities for literacy development.* Grand Rapids, MI: Instructional Fair TS Denison.

This book integrates children's literature with creative movement through offering practical activities applicable for the dance program. The author highlights 67 popular children's picture books and provides ideas for expressing the text and illustrations through movement in addition to visual arts, language arts, math, science, and social studies.

Kassing, G., and D. Jay. 2003. *Dance teaching methods and curriculum design.* Champaign, IL: Human Kinetics.

Includes an overview of the essential information needed to plan a dance program in the K-12 setting. In this book, educators can gain access to program models, dance education theory, and practical skills that emphasize effective teaching and program design.

Kogan, K. 1982. *Step by step: A complete movement education from preschool to sixth grade.* Byron, CA: Front Row Experience.

Provides practical experiences that can be used by teachers beginning to teach dance. Each experience is sequenced and offers specific language and directions for teaching.

Kooyackers, P. 1996. *101 dance games for children.* Alameda, CA: Hunter House.

Includes a variety of practical ideas for developing creative dance lessons for children. The book offers suggestions for choosing and organizing dance lessons based on available space, age of participants, amount of time, size of the group, and props required.

Kraus, R. 1962. *Folk dancing.* Toronto: Macmillan.

Describes fundamental positions, formations, skills, and steps for over 100 folk dances from the United States, Europe, Mexico, Russia, Israel, and the Scandinavian countries. Does not include African, Asian, Caribbean, Native American, and South Pacific dances.

Laban, R. 1976. *Modern educational dance.* 3rd ed. London: Macdonald & Evans.

Provides the theoretical background for movement education and educational dance. Describes 16 basic movement themes, 8 effort actions, and the use of the body and its movements in space. Laban is the pioneer in defining the movement principles used for dance.

Lane, C. 1995. *Christy Lane's complete book of line dancing.* Reston, VA: American Alliance for Health, Physical Education, Recreation and Dance.

Offers a comprehensive resource of line dances for a social dance unit. Includes easy-to-follow directions and diagrams.

Lloyd, M. 1998. *Adventures in creative movement activities: A guide for teaching.* 2nd ed. Dubuque, IA: Eddie Bowers.

Includes a practical approach to developing a creative movement lesson. The book is filled with helpful illustrations, sample lessons, and specific ideas to develop a meaningful experience for children.

Logsdon, B.J., M. Ammons, K.R. Barrett, M.R. Broer, L.E. Halverson, R. McGee, and M. Robertson. 1977. *Physical education for children: A focus on the teaching process.* Philadelphia: Lea & Febiger.

A comprehensive book on physical education that includes a chapter on educational dance. The chapter offers a clear description of each of Laban's 16 movement themes as the basic foundation for educational dance. Includes sample learning experiences illustrating the themes.

McGreevy-Nichols, S., and H. Scheff. 1995. *Building dances: A guide to putting movements together.* Champaign, IL: Human Kinetics.

Introduces educators to a clear, practical approach to creating dance lessons for elementary students. Includes strategies for observing dances and assessing dance learning along with over 200 easy-to-use cards that provide ideas for designing dance units and lessons.

McGreevy-Nichols, S., H. Scheff, and M. Sprague. 2001. *Building more dances: Blueprints for putting movements together.* Champaign, IL: Human Kinetics.

This book expands on *Building Dances* with over a hundred new ideas for creating dances and strategies for interdisciplinary connections.

Murray, R. 1953. *Dance in the elementary school: A program for boys and girls.* New York: Harper & Row.

One of the foundational texts used by many dance educators. The author provides a comprehensive description of the basic locomotor and nonlocomotor movements and the use of rhythm and music in dance. The process of creating new dances and learning dances is accompanied by many ideas and resources.

National Dance Association/American Alliance for Health, Physical Education, Recreation and Dance. 1988. *Dance curricula guidelines K-12.* Reston, VA: Author.

Describes what dance is, why dance should be taught, the content of dance, and the learning process in dance. Also includes practical examples of ways to address the elements and a list of dance curriculum resources.

National Dance Association/American Alliance for Health, Physical Education, Recreation and Dance. 1990. *Guide to creative dance for the young child.* Reston, VA: Author.

Presents practical information on the content and process of teaching dance for the early childhood level.

National Dance Association/American Alliance for Health, Physical Education, Recreation and Dance. 1991. *Dance education—What is it? Why is it important?* Reston, VA: Author.

Addresses dance education at all levels from early childhood to higher education. Includes information on dance for special populations and the role of private studios in dance education in addition to a list of references on arts education and resources available from the National Dance Association.

Nichols, B. 1994. *Moving and learning: The elementary school physical education experience.* 3rd ed. St. Louis: Mosby.

Includes two chapters that address dance. A chapter on creative dance provides a comprehensive chart of the movement content, specific tasks for exploring the content, and ideas for developing dance lessons. A chapter on singing games and American and international folk dance includes a resource list of dances and directions for teaching them.

Overby, L., ed. 1991. *Early childhood creative arts: Proceedings of the international early childhood creative arts conference 1990.* Reston, VA: American Alliance for Health, Physical Education, Recreation and Dance.

Several sections of the proceedings address dance for young children. Includes a resource for integrating dance with other art forms.

Parker, P., M. Fenton, J. Holme, A. Ireland-Echols, and G. Phillips. 1988. *Creative dance.* Ottawa, ON: Canadian Association for Health, Physical Education, Recreation and Dance.

Provides a detailed description of how to approach teaching creative dance. Clearly explains the selection of content, planning for a unit and lesson, and teaching strategies. Includes specific sample lessons.

Russell, J. 1975. *Creative movement and dance for children.* London: Macdonald & Evans.

Organizes dance content and lesson development in a sequence appropriate for the different ages of children. Includes many excellent photographs with descriptions to illustrate how children interpret the content.

Stinson, S. 1988. *Dance for young children: Finding the magic in movement.* Reston, VA: American Alliance for Health, Physical Education, Recreation and Dance.

Presents content and processes for teaching dance to young children. The author provides specific examples of experiences that teachers beginning to teach dance can use easily. Includes excellent appendix citing children's literature that can be a resource for developing experiences.

Wall, J., and N. Murray. 1990. *Children and movement: Physical education in the elementary school.* Dubuque, IA: Brown.

A general text on physical education based on Rudolf Laban's descriptive analysis of human movement. A section focuses on dance and includes the elements of dance, how to teach dance, and how to design specific learning experiences for singing games, folk dance, and creative dance. Examples are specific and helpful to teachers beginning to teach dance.

Willis, C. 2004. *Dance education tips from the trenches.* Champaign, IL: Human Kinetics.

Presents a practical approach to organizing, managing, and planning dance lessons and performances. The author includes helpful tips and suggestions for guiding students through the creative process from exploration to choreographing a dance.

Zakkai, J. 1997. *Dance as a way of knowing.* Portland, ME: Stenhouse.

The author addresses how dance is foundational to learning and offers a practical approach to including dance in the classroom and physical education curriculums. Specific information is included on how the elements of dance are developed into lessons that include learning, creating, and observing dance. Ideas for interdisciplinary connections are also included.

Zukowski, G., and A. Dickson. 1990. *On the move: A handbook for exploring creative movement with young children.* Carbondale: Southern Illinois University Press.

This book offers a practical guide for presenting creative movement in the classroom, physical education, and dance education curriculums. Included are movement games and activities appropriate for initiating dance lessons that integrate music, language arts, drama, literature, math, and science.

About the Authors

Theresa Purcell Cone, PhD, is a physical education and dance teacher at Brunswick Acres Elementary School in Kendall Park, New Jersey, where she also directs a children's dance company. She is also an adjunct professor at Rowan University in New Jersey and a teacher and choreographer at the Princeton Ballet School.

Dr. Cone is a past president of the National Dance Association and was named its first K-12 Dance Educator of the Year. She is also a member of the National Dance Education Organization, the Alliance for Arts Education/New Jersey, and numerous other professional organizations. Dr. Cone was coauthor of *Interdisciplinary Teaching Through Physical Education* (Human Kinetics, 1998).

In 2004, Dr. Cone was awarded a Presidential Citation by the American Alliance for Health, Physical Education, Recreation and Dance (AAHPERD). She also was awarded the Margie R. Hanson Distinguished Service Award by the National Association for Sport and Physical Education. Dr. Cone received her doctorate in dance from Temple University.

Stephen L. Cone, PhD, is a professor in the department of health and exercise science at Rowan University in New Jersey. Previously, he was chair of the physical education department at Keene State College in New Hampshire.

Dr. Cone is past president of the American Alliance for Health, Physical Education, Recreation and Dance and received their Honor Award in 2000. He is also a member of the New Jersey AHPERD, the Alliance for Arts Education/New Jersey, and numerous other professional organizations. He has written dozens of articles for physical education publications and was coauthor of *Interdisciplinary Teaching Through Physical Education* (Human Kinetics, 1998).

Dr. Cone was made a charter fellow in the North American Society for Health, Physical Education, Recreation, Sport and Dance Professionals in 2000. He also was named an American Council on Education fellow in 1993-94. He received a Presidential Citation from the National Dance Association in 1995. Dr. Cone earned his doctorate in motor learning and sport psychology from Texas A&M University.